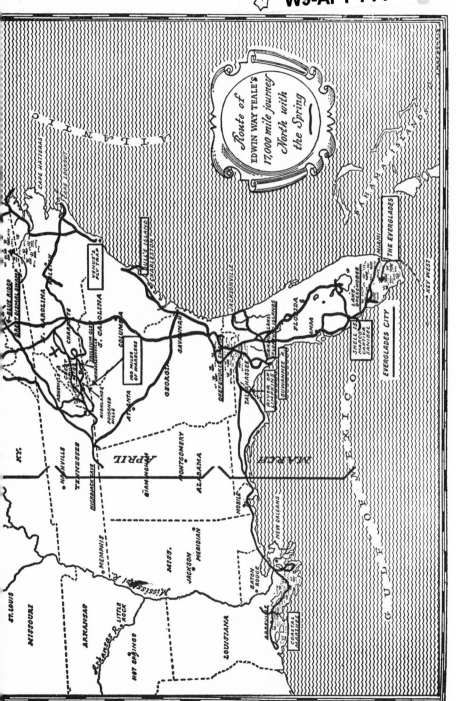

Route of
EDWIN WAY TEALE'S
17,000 mile journey
North with
the Spring

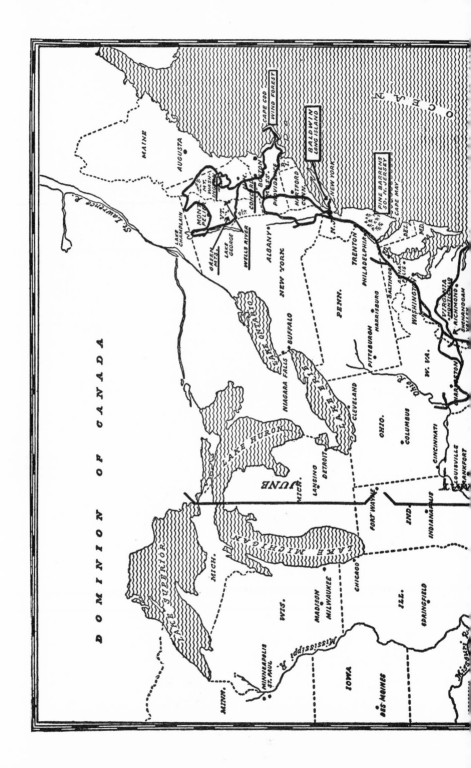

NORTH WITH THE SPRING

THE AMERICAN SEASONS

THE FIRST SEASON

NORTH WITH THE SPRING

THE SECOND SEASON

JOURNEY INTO SUMMER

THE THIRD SEASON

AUTUMN ACROSS AMERICA

THE FOURTH SEASON

WANDERING THROUGH WINTER

NORTH WITH THE SPRING

EDWIN WAY TEALE

A NATURALIST'S RECORD OF A 17,000-MILE JOURNEY

WITH THE NORTH AMERICAN SPRING.

PHOTOGRAPHS BY THE AUTHOR

DODD, MEAD & COMPANY · NEW YORK

1   2   3   4   5   6   7   8   9   10

A Dodd, Mead Quality Paperback
first published in 1981

Library of Congress Cataloging in Publication Data

Teale, Edwin Way, 1899–1981.
North with the spring.

(The American seasons ; 1st season)
Includes index.
1. Spring—United States.   2. Natural history—United
States.   3. Natural history—Outdoor books.   I. Title.
II. Series: Teale, Edwin Way, 1899–1981.   American seasons.
QH104.T355   1981, 1st season   508.73s   [508.73]   81-5470
ISBN 0-396-07956-3 (pbk.)   AACR2

Dedicated to
DAVID
Who Traveled with
Us in Our Hearts

ACKNOWLEDGMENTS

BEFORE, during and after our travels with the spring, so many people in so many places aided us in so many ways that it is not possible to acknowledge our indebtedness to each individually. Our appreciation of all these kindnesses, however, is deep.

For reading portions of the manuscript, aiding in problems of identification, providing the benefit of their specialized knowledge or assisting with personal help in the field, I am especially indebted to the following: Dr. and Mrs. Raymond Adams, John W. Aldrich, Ross Allen, Mrs. Cecil Appleberry, J. O. Artman, John H. Baker, William Baldwin, William Beebe, Charles M. Bogert, Mr. and Mrs. Arthur Brintnall, Carl Buchheister, Rachel L. Carson, Mont Cazier, William P. Comstock, Lee Crandall, Allan D. Cruickshank, Helen G. Cruickshank, W. H. Cummings, C. H. Curran, the late Clyde Fisher, John M. Fogg, Jr., James Forbes, George M. French, Johnny Gaspard, Willis J. Gertsch, Ludlow Griscom, Elizabeth C. Hall, Francis Harper, Henry B. Kane, Amy Loveman, Oliver P. Medsger, Charles Mohr, Harold M. Moldenke, Edmund Morgan, J. J. Murray, John T. Nichols, John Pallister, Isabel Paterson, George H. Peters, Roger Tory Peterson, Richard H. Pough, Herbert Prytherich, Marjorie Kinnan Rawlings, Benjamin T. Richards, Harold W. Rickett, H. Ravenel Sass, T. C. Schnierla, Herbert F. Schwarz, Frank A. Soraci, Arthur Stupka, Henry Svenson, R. Gordon Wasson, Richard L. Weaver and George E. Welch.

The chapter on the Ducktown Desert was originally published in *Natural History* and portions of the Floating Islands chapter appeared in *Nature Magazine*. I am indebted to the editors of these periodicals for permission to include the material in this volume. In the editing and production of the book, my debt is great to Edward H. Dodd, Jr., Raymond T. Bond, S. Phelps Platt, John Blair and Ruby Carr. One of the happy memories connected with this book of so many pleasant recollections is a week end in May spent in a rambling inn on the Jersey coast with Raymond T. Bond. Part of the day we worked on the first 25 chapters. The rest of the time we wandered along the sea-beach among migrating shorebirds. It was between Chapters 19 and 20 that we saw for the first time in our lives, in a sea-meadow near Beach Haven, the rare and elusive black rail.

August 1, 1951
Edwin Way Teale

CONTENTS

at play—Needle rushes—The bird locust—A solitary horse—The snake-hunter—Hush puppies and hominy—Battle of the catkins—Lowland lichens—Riddles of an island population—Lone star ticks—Wild gobblers on parade—Chuck-will's-widow—The deserted beach—Rainbows—Midnight on the barrier beach—The neon worm.

CONTENTS

ILLUSTRATIONS

ONE

WINTER

BARE trees imprinted the black lace of their twigs on a gray and somber sky. Dingy with soot, snowdrifts' had melted into slush and were freezing again. Behind us, as we drove south, city pallor was increasing. Tempers were growing short in the dead air of underventilated offices. That quiet desperation, which Thoreau says characterizes the mass of men, was taking on new intensity. February, at once the shortest and the longest month of the twelve, had outstayed its welcome. The year seemed stuck on the ridge of winter.

At such a time, when you look with dread upon the winter weeks that lie before you, have you ever dreamed—in office or kitchen or school—of leaving winter behind, of meeting spring under far-southern skies, of following its triumphal pilgrimage up the map with flowers all the way, with singing birds and soft air, green grass and trees new-clothed, of coming north with the spring? That is a dream of the winter-weary. And, for nearly a decade, it was, for Nellie and me, both a dream and a plan.

The seasons, like greater tides, ebb and flow across the continents. Spring advances up the United States at the average rate of about fifteen miles a day. It ascends mountainsides at the rate of about a hundred feet a day. It sweeps ahead like a flood of water, racing down the long valleys, creeping up hillsides in a rising tide. Most of us, like the man who lives on the bank of a river and watches the stream flow by, see only one phase of the movement of spring. Each year the season advances toward us out of the south, sweeps around us, goes flooding away into the north. We see all phases of a single phase, all variations of this one chapter in the Odyssey of Spring. My wife and I dreamed of knowing something of all phases, of reading all possible chapters, of seeing, firsthand, the long northward flow of the season.

Over and over again we laid out routes, calculated costs, made lists of things to take along. But obligations and responsibilities pushed the dream unrealized before us. Season followed season and year followed year. And while we waited, the world changed and our lives changed with it. The spring trip was something we looked forward to during the terrible years of World War II, during all the strain and grief of losing David, our only son, in battle.

When we talked over our plans with friends we discovered that our dream was a universal dream. They, too, had beguiled themselves, on days when winter seemed invincible, with thoughts of lifting anchor and, leaving everyday responsibilities behind, drifting north with the spring.

Our plan was to start where spring begins for the North American continent, somewhere south of Lake Okeechobee in that no man's land of the seasons, the Everglades. There, amid the sawgrass seas and hammocks, under the high, cloud-filled sky of southern Florida, spring gathers its forces. There, the first stirrings of the season become apparent. Working north, we would keep pace with its progress, zigzagging by car behind its advancing front. Above the peninsula of Florida we would swing wide along the Gulf to the Louisiana marshes, cut back to the Okefenokee Swamp, then trail the season through the Great Smokies, across the Piedmont Plateau, among the Jersey pine barrens, out to the tip of Cape Cod and through the mountains of New England to the green boundary of the Canadian line. I ruled off a map into zones, each zone representing roughly a week's advance in the northward movement of the season. This provided, in general, the timetable of our trip.

Ours would be no conventional tour. It would include wild and remote places the usual tourist avoids. We would see spring come to dunes and tarns and seashell islands, to caves and underground rivers, to estuaries and savannas. For 17,000 miles we would travel with a season. In 23 different states we would witness the defeat of winter, see the homecoming of the birds, watch the return of the wildflowers. This was the long spring. It would extend from February to June. The trip, for me, would have added pleasure because my companion, after years of married life, was the most congenial person still.

And so, on the 14th of February, we packed our black Buick, stuffed the glove compartment full of marked maps, stored away bird glasses, field guides, cameras and stoutly-bound record books. We eased ourselves into the front seat like a racing pilot squeezing into the cramped cockpit of a speedplane and waved goodby to our neighbors. I switched on the engine and we started south for our rendezvous with a season.

Long Island was hard with frost when we left. New York was a world of windows tight shut. Across New Jersey, the distant winter woods were smoky blue and, in Virginia, side roads cut away between brown hills, rutted and red. We saw the white sand of South Carolina pinelands replaced by the copper-colored soil of Georgia. We watched mistletoe give way to Spanish moss and Spanish moss give way to air plants in the cypress swamps of southern Florida. Our descent of the map ended south of the Tamiami Trail, at the little community of Everglades, near the Ten Thousand Islands of the wild Gulf coast. Here we reached the beginning of our travels with the spring.

TWO

WHERE SPRING BEGINS

———

WE first smelled smoke as we came creeping down a long green tunnel under overarching trees on a narrow road pockmarked with holes. Somewhere south of the Tamiami Trail we were driving north through a swampy stretch, picking our way with care. We felt uneasy. The air ahead became tinged with blue and the acrid smell of fire grew stronger. It stirred primitive emotions of alarm. But as yet there was no sight or sound of flames.

I looked at Nellie. She looked at the roadsides—muddy lowland on one hand, a brimming ditch on the other. The solid surface of the narrow roadbed offered no room to turn around. We could either back up or go ahead.

"Let's go ahead for a while longer," she suggested.

Close to the end of the tunnel I stopped the car. We listened. Somewhere ahead we could hear the faint rush and crackle of flames. Still we could see no fire. I nosed the car from beneath the trees. Under billows of blue-brown smoke, waves of flame were rolling toward us across the open country to the right. Red streamers flared from the higher grass tangles or roared skyward amid the dry fronds of the scattered palmettos. Already the fire had swept to the edge of the road ahead of us and was racing in our direction. But the flames ran down only one fringe of the roadbed and the vegetation was mainly high tangles of grass.

We decided to run the one-sided gantlet. Rolling up the car

windows we charged ahead as fast as the hole-riddled road would permit. Just as the main wave of fire came abreast of us, filling the car with sudden heat, the flames touched off the fifteen-foot torch of a dry palmetto, shaggy with fronds. In one leap, from base to crown, a sheet of flame rushed upward. The fronds exploded into blazing fragments, hurled aloft to descend like pieces of a fireworks fountain around us. Then the fire was racing away behind us and we were amid blackened, smoldering acres swept clean of life.

Everywhere we went, those February days in lower Florida, fires were raging across the Everglades. Once we counted nine great columns of smoke pouring into the sky around us. Another time, far down the Tamiami Trail, we rode toward a mile-long cumulus cloud, the only one in the sky. It was mushrooming upward at the top of a column of heated air rising from a widespread fire below. This man-made thunderhead was crowned with creamy white. But its undersides were tinted with tans and blues where smoke and vapor intermingled.

That $50,000,000 fiasco, the ill-advised drainage scheme of half a century ago, has lowered the water table of the Glades and left them a prey to endless fires. As far away as Key West visibility is sometimes reduced to 2 miles by haze and smoke from the Everglades.

In lower Florida winter is the dry season; spring the time of rainfall. During the final weeks of winter, before the spring rains begin, the water in the Everglades reaches its lowest point. Peat and grass are driest and conflagrations most frequent. Fires by night and pillars of smoke by day—these were the first and most spectacular indications we saw around us that winter's end was near and that spring was drawing close.

But there were other signs. A dozen miles or so east of Ochopee, one afternoon, we came upon clouds of tree swallows swirling over the sawgrass, thousands and thousands of the white-breasted birds skimming low, darting high, endlessly turning, feeding upon insects as they moved into the north. A black buzzard, with short tail and silver spots under its wing-tips, sailed by, its shadow crisscrossing the highway as it banked and circled. Speeding hundreds of feet above it, so high they were hardly larger than houseflies to the naked eye, were the topmost tree swallows. Through our glasses we could see, to right and left over the Everglades, other swallow clouds, immense flocks, loosely knit, rising, descending, turning, expanding, contracting, always in motion.

The day before, perhaps, many of these birds had been over the sea, coming from Cuba, or among the keys off the Florida mainland. Now the air around us was filled with their liquid calling. A little farther on, where the roadside ditch opened into a clear stretch of water free from the massed water hyacinths, thousands of the swallows were drinking on the wing. The birds pelted down like wind-blown raindrops to skim or strike the surface of the ditch and scoop up mouthfuls of water. Their snow-white underplumage caught the sun each time they rose and turned to dive again. Thus as long as we watched them the swallows climbed and swooped, rose and fell, revolving in a great wheel in the sky.

Driving south, at the beginning of our trip, we had encountered other concentrations of birds. The succession of homecoming migrants is as fixed as the sequence of blooming wildflowers. Each spring the birds come back in the same order. Pintail ducks are among the first waterfowl to fly north. Bluebirds and redwings lead the procession of the songbirds. Robins are early birds in both the day and the year. And so we met concentrations, waves, of the migrants in the order in which they would move north. They were the initial ripples of that vast tide of migration that soon would be running, full flood, up the continent.

All through South Carolina, overwintering bluebirds had been everywhere. Almost every dipping telephone wire held one of these gentle birds, sitting bolt upright, appearing a little round-shouldered at a distance, leaping aloft in a sudden rise and wingover as we rushed by. Then, near Waycross, Georgia, we encountered the redwings. A detour had shunted us down a side road. As we reached a stretch of swampy woodland, a storm of sound assailed our ears. All the trees were alive with blackbirds. Thousands swarmed among the branches, filled with the excitement of migration time. They were incessantly in motion, hopping, flying, alighting, combining their voices in a deafening clamor. A dozen miles beyond we ran through another concentration of overwintering redwings. Here the birds were scattered across a wide grainfield that recent rains had turned into a glistening sea of mud.

Just south of the Florida line we had met our initial wave of robins. All that day, as we drove through drenching rain down the western edge of the Florida peninsula, we saw robins flying, robins perching, robins running across lawns, robins swarming over fire-blackened open spaces among the palmettos. For miles on end we would see robins all about us. Then their numbers would thin away only to increase once more. Near the end of their winter stay along the Gulf the myriad redbreasts would soon take off on their flight to the north.

Passing thus from concentration to concentration we seemed moving down the line of march of a parade where different groups were assembled on side streets ready to take their places in the procession at the appointed time. All things affected by the spring have their times and seasons. The stars in their courses are hardly more dependable than the sequence of appearing life, bird, flower, batrachian. If you come north by train in midspring and have an ear for the swamp music of toads and frogs, you will become aware of something interesting. You seem to be running backward in time. As the spring becomes less and less advanced as you go north, you begin with the latest-appearing of the marsh-callers and progress backward to the earliest of the peepers, reversing the normal sequence.

Each morning, during these pre-spring days, we awoke while

it was still dark, to the steady throbbing of fishing boats moving out among the Ten Thousand Islands of the Gulf. With the earliest daylight came the strident alarm-clock of the red-bellied woodpecker amid the palms outside our cabin at Everglades. When we stepped outside, exciting new odors were all around us in the perfumed air of the dawn. The change from north to south, from winter to a subtropical climate, is reported most vividly of all by our sense of smell. In northern states winter is a kind of olfactory desert. The odors of spring arrive with dramatic contrast. Here amid the Everglades—where spring and autumn meet and intermingle and where winter is the lost season of the year—the perfumes of life and growth are never absent.

This intermingling of the seasons is one of the most striking features of the region. Fall flowers bloom in the spring and spring flowers bloom in the fall. The unrolling of the fruiting leaves of the cinnamon fern—an event familiar to every northern spring—occurs here in autumn. Flowers of summer and flowers of spring bloom side by side in December.

We saw along the road thistles and asters, flowers that brought to mind the dusty pasturelands of a northern fall. A whole field of higher ground, near Everglades, simmered with the early-autumn sound of innumerable crickets. We came upon beautifully shaded, purple-pink grass freshly gone to seed in February. Goldenrod, carrying us back a third of a year to the previous fall, bloomed by the Tamiami Trail. A few feet away, on the brown water of a drainage canal, water hyacinths opened the pale lavender of their earliest flowers of the new season. Here, near the southern rim of that vast, shallow, tilted bowl of oölitic limestone which holds the Everglades, we were in a land where the seasons were uncertain. Like the shore between the tides, it is an area where two zones overlap, where two forces meet in a competition that is endless and indecisive.

Nobody knows exactly where spring begins. The season has no starting point like a sprinter on a track. Somewhere south of Lake Okeechobee, in the watery wilderness of the Everglades, it comes into being, swells, gains momentum. Its arrival becomes more abrupt, more striking, its line of demarcation more evident as it progresses north. Here, in this southernmost part of the United States, there is no dramatic spring awakening as there is in some New England valley, suddenly rich with bloodroot and hepatica. Here, changes are gentle. The pendulum of the seasons moves slowly and the arc of its swing is restricted. Here we were, in a way, south of spring.

On the 22nd of February, we awoke to an unseasonable chill. Widespread blizzards had swept across northern states. Frost had descended into upper Florida. Even here, near the southern tip of the peninsula, the weather was uncomfortably cool. As we ate breakfast we talked of our pet cats and wondered how they were faring in the big snow. We had made nests for them in the garage and arranged with our next-door neighbors, the Veritys, to feed them. A few days later a letter from Alma Verity revealed our concern was unnecessary. The day after we left, she wrote, the cats had moved in with them. At the time of the blizzard they were comfortably draped over the radiators.

On that chill Washington's Birthday, we drove across the Everglades to the outskirts of Miami. Sawgrass and hammocks stretched away to the northern horizon. Nowhere else in the world can the sawgrass sea of the Everglades be duplicated. This sedge we call a grass, with its fierce cutting edges, was one of the early forms of plant life on our globe. The deep black muck of the Everglades is the product of its decomposition. No other plant known produces peat as rapidly as does sawgrass. Along the Tamiami Trail it crowded close, overhanging the ditches where gallinules flipped their little tails, anhingas swam with only their snaky necks exposed, and egrets fished above their white reflections in the dark brown water.

Later we wandered down the road that leads through Big Cypress Swamp toward Deep Lake and the town with a name that sounds like the call of a redwing, Immokalee. Here, the pale-green haze of new leaves enveloping the cypresses and the brilliant crimson tongues of the air plants are two of the earliest indications of the nearness of spring. The cypress is the only tree in the area that stands entirely bare in winter. So numerous are those aerial pineapples, the air plants—living as they do, at least partially, on atmospheric dust—that every cypress swamp we saw resembled a great rookery filled with nests. Each clump is a little bios, a world in itself, with a multitude of tiny inhabitants. The brilliant red tongues of *Tillandsia fasciculata* that appear in February are not, as is usually assumed, the flowers. They are bracts that protect the buds of the real flowers. Late in spring and in summer these buds unfold into slender, spiked blooms of purplish-blue.

These things—a green haze creeping over the cypress trees, swallows milling in clouds over the sawgrass, pillars of smoke around the horizon, crimson bracts lifting above the massed air plants of cypress swamps—these were the earliest indications of spring we saw on the edge of the Everglades.

Each evening we watched the strange flat land around us sink into the twilight and each night we watched the stars come out, bright and hanging low, studding the sky in a vast sweep that descended, uninterrupted by a silhouette, to the far rim of the horizon. To the green mist of the cypresses and the moving clouds of the swallows we could add the movement of the stars as a sign of the sure approach of the spring. With all its galaxies and planets and stars, the solar system was setting the stage. Daily the sun rode higher. Nightly the astronomy of spring drew closer. Far-off events were playing their part in the birth of a season.

COOT feeding among spatterdock, or yellow pond lily leaves massed on the surface of dark swamp water in the Everglades.

DARK water and moss-hung trees along the banks characterize
lowland streams that flow through lower Georgia and Florida.

RING-BILLED gulls flutter about the author on a Florida beach near the beginning of the northward journey with the spring.

HOVERING in mid-air, this gull was arrested in a split-second photograph as it settled to the sand of the Gulf Coast beach.

WATER LILY leaves form feeding platforms for a redwing and
a boat-tailed grackle along the edge of a lake in upper Florida.

ROUGHING it smoothly in jungle surroundings is possible at this manor house owned by the government on Bull's Island.

SPRING in the Great Smoky Mountains National Park is a time of white shadbushes and acres of woodland flowers in bloom.

COMMONEST of spring flowers in eastern America is the violet. More than half a hundred species grow east of the Rockies.

BABY cottontail rabbits begin life in the spring, one of a host of creatures born during the warm days at winter's end.

SEA meadows in the spring resound to the calling of the clapper rail. The bird nests in thick tangles of cord-grass.

RIPPLES extending across wide mud flats at low tide are a familiar feature of many places along the Atlantic seaboard.

UNFOLDING leaves of spring appear on twigs above a sphagnum swamp in the solitary pine barrens of southern New Jersey.

BLOODROOT in flower is a sign of the arrival of spring in rich open woodlands all the way from upper Florida to Canada.

RACCOONS inhabit all the area covered coming north with the spring. Their range is one of the widest among American mammals.

SWAMP streams in early spring in the North flow between massed skunk cabbage leaves and the fiddleheads of ferns.

FARTHEST north in spring's journey is represented by the top of Mt. Washington. Its spring is similar to that of Labrador.

SPRING IN THE SKY

IN the bottom drawer of my study desk lies a small envelope labeled "Star Dust." A gift from a friend, it contains powdered fragments from the spot where a meteor fell. Sometimes I let this dust run through my fingers, this memento of a celestial body that once rushed incandescent across the heavens. For a moment the streaming particles bring a sense of contact with all the remote and illimitable space that extends away in the night sky. As we watched the slow wheel of the constellations over the Everglades, that little packet of meteor dust came to mind.

Under those stars we felt a similar emotion of closeness to the world of outer space. We felt what we so rarely feel, a sense of comradeship for the distant suns and planets of the heavens. Usually the starry universe—that vastest of precision machines, that ultimate in the cold logic of physical forces—leaves us with imagination overawed. But here the movement of the stars took on an intense and personal interest. They were important actors in the drama of spring. For seasons begin in the sky.

At the end of its invisible tether, ninety-odd million miles long, the earth was curving through space on its yearly journey around the sun, spinning endlessly on its tilted axis. This axis holds the secret of our changing seasons. If, instead of leaning 23½ degrees to one side, the axis of the earth were straight up and down, the globe would always present the same aspect to the sun throughout the year. There would be no spring and summer, autumn and winter. Without change, the sun's rays would fall directly upon the equator. The earth would have varied climates but no varied seasons. At any given point on the globe, during all twelve months of the year, the season would remain the same.

Throughout its annual circuit of the sun, the tilt of the earth never changes. The direction of this slant remains constant. It is the continuously altering position of the planet in relation to the sun that produces the parade of the seasons. The upper, northern, end of the axis tilts toward the sun in summer, away from it in winter. And, during its curving progress from the tilted-away position to the tilted-toward position and back again, it passes progressively through the intermediate stages and we have those seasons of most dramatic change, autumn and spring.

There is a precise moment each year when the tick of a watch separates spring and winter. It is the moment—usually on the 21st of March—when the sun reaches the celestial equator, that imaginary line through the heavens above the Earth's equator. As the sun's center crosses this line, the season officially changes. This is the vernal equinox of the ancient astronomers. The rays of the sun fall vertically on the equator and everywhere on the surface of the globe day and night are of equal length. From then on, nights in the northern hemisphere grow shorter and days lengthen at both ends until the very last moment of spring, until the Summer Solstice, coming usually on the 21st of June.

At that time the sun is at the end of its northern swing. It rises and sets farthest north. During the twenty-four hours of that day it pours down one-fifth more heat on the North Pole than on the equator. For a time, just as spring becomes summer, the sun "stands still in the sky" before beginning its ponderous swing toward the south once more. Between these two astronomical events, the vernal equinox and the summer sol-

stice, our Northern Hemisphere undergoes the swift changes
of spring.

Although the official beginning of spring was still weeks
away we saw the coming season announced in the Everglades
sky. Orion rose earlier in the east. Twilight was lengthening.
The sun rode on a higher arc through the heavens. The angle
of its rays grew steadily less oblique and our noontime shadows
shortened. During the winter months, when our hemisphere
is tilted away from the sun, the rays strike it a glancing blow.
Now, and all through the spring, the angle of the rays would
become more direct. And the amount of heat imparted depends upon the directness with which the sun's rays strike the
surface of the globe. The more vertical the rays, the less heat-
absorbing atmosphere they must pass through.

This explains the paradoxical fact that we are coldest when
we are nearest the sun and hottest when we are farthest away
from the sun. The elliptical path of the earth about its solar
hub brings it within 91,500,000 miles of the sun in winter and
carries it 94,500,000 miles from the sun in summer. Although
we are 3,000,000 miles farther away from the source of our heat
in summer, the greater directness of the rays produces our
warmest weather. It is not the planet's nearness to the sun but
its position in relation to the angle of the rays that determines
the season.

Yet here is a second paradox. The sun is farthest north on
the last day of spring. It is moving south all during the summer
months. Then why does the greatest heat of the year come in
July and August rather than in June? The explanation lies in
the slowness of the earth to warm up after the long winter cold.
There is a lag in the heat of the season just as there is a lag in
the heat of a summer's day. On such a day the thermometer
reaches its peak not at noon, when the sun is highest, but about
two o'clock in the afternoon.

During the earliest days of our long spring adventure we
looked forward to the 21st of March as a kind of official starting

line. One minute it would be winter, the next minute it would be spring. The dividing line would be sharp and final. According to the mathematics of the astronomer, the notation in the almanac, the date on the calendar, such a hairline exists. But in nature all is fluid and divisions are blurred. Officially, spring begins the same moment in all parts of the country, east and west, north and south. Yet it finds conditions infinitely varied. In Florida and along the Gulf, spring is well advanced in early March. It arrives before the vernal equinox while ice and snow still hold sway in the North. It is a pre-spring spring.

The first day of spring and the first spring day it has been pointed out are not the same thing. The season is tardy one year, forward another. Each season, like each human being and each puppy, is an individual, unique. Our spring proved slow in starting. At first it appeared fully two weeks behind its normal schedule. But as it advanced up the map it gained momentum, running more and more nearly on time, until it reached the Canadian border with wild flowers opening on normal dates.

"Spring," says the Encylopedia Britannica, "is the season of the year which follows winter and ushers in summer." It is that—and infinitely more than that. It is the season of youth, of beginning again; the season of blank pages, of unhurried time, of belief and optimism. The farmer plants a new crop with high hopes. Life spreads before the new-born chick and calf and colt. The world's favorite season is the spring. All things seem possible in May.

Calendars to the contrary, nature's year begins with the spring. For Temperate Zone vegetation, spring is sunrise, summer is midday, autumn is sunset, and winter is night. Forty-four degrees Fahrenheit is the important thermometer reading for buds in spring. It is at that temperature that the first haze of green begins to envelop the twigs of trees as buds burst and leaves unfold. For robins, spring arrives with the 35-degree isotherm. At that average temperature, frosts are out of the ground and earthworms are coming to the surface. The birds move north in the wake of spring thaws as the average temperature reaches 35 degrees. On the west coast, as Ludlow Griscom points out in his *Modern Bird Study*, there is not any rise in temperature, as far as the robin is concerned, during the entire two months it takes to migrate from southern states to treeline in northwestern Alaska. The average temperature is always 35 degrees.

Spring peepers wait until the mercury has mounted another fifteen degrees before they begin their serenades in ponds and swamps. The average temperature is above 50 degrees before the batrachians begin to call. For honeybees, spring arrives with the first pollen; for swallows, it comes when flying insects return to the air; for woodchucks, it means consciousness after a winter of slumber; for second-year eels, it means the arrival at fresh water; for cows, it means lush new grass; for boys, marbles, kites, and baseballs; and for the ruby-throated hummingbird, it means the opening of nectar-filled flowers. Just as robins follow the advance of the 35-degree isotherm, so hummingbirds move up the continent in the wake of the unfolding flowers.

The changes of spring extend into every cranny of the hemisphere. Ocean tides reach their peak. In inland ponds the surface water gradually changes place with the water at the bottom. Babies born in the spring are, on the average, taller and heavier than those born at other times of the year. In spring growing children gain most rapidly in height. The increase is almost twice that of a similar period in fall. The very chemical composition of our blood alters slightly in spring; we sense the coming of the season in our lifestream.

Lengthening days of spring, adding to the hours of sunlight, set off the migratory urge in birds and stimulate many animals to mate. Everywhere, as the season advances, cells speed up their multiplication in plants and living organisms. Infusoria reproduce with incredible rapidity. In stagnant water, under the warm spring sun, a single one of these microscopic creatures may be the ancestor of a million by the end of a week.

All during our trip, in a hundred different places, we asked people what first came into their minds when they thought of spring. Their answers covered a vast range. At the top of the list stood the blooming of violets and dogwood, the return of the bluebirds, the songs of redwings and robins and the calling of the spring peepers. To some people spring meant strawberry shortcake; to others, muddy roads, plowed fields, and rivers rising. In other minds it was associated with skunk cabbage, white butterflies, the red of swamp maples and the peeping of baby chicks. In still others, it recalled jessamine flowers, jack-in-the-pulpit, circus billboards, straw hats, kite flying, kittens, calves, and housecleaning.

Spring is all things to all men. It is the bleating of lambs, the sound of the carpenter's hammer. It is the yellow of dandelion and the green of new grass. It is cumulus clouds and the smell of new-turned soil, brimming ditches and miles on miles of fruit trees in bloom. This time of shortening shadows, these months with music in them, form an event in everyone's life, an event in the life of every animal and tree and flowering plant in the northern hemisphere.

The astronomy of spring was bringing all this. Here, in this land of spring's beginning, the changing position of the Earth, reflected in the parade of the constellations over the Everglades, was ushering in the new season. The movement of that vast celestial clock that had ticked away, without haste, without pause, during so many aeons, was bringing spring to the sky, to the land, to the sea around us.

FOUR

SEASHELL ISLANDS

ON February 25, as we breakfasted on ham and eggs in a little restaurant in the town of Everglades—where two first-graders amused themselves in a corner with thirteen pencils, counting them, making a log cabin of them, laying them down to form railroad tracks, dropping them like bombs on a spot on the floor—four fishermen, sunburned and wearing long-visored angling caps, sat down at a nearby table. They ate scrambled eggs and drank coffee and talked about the red tide.

The mystery of the red tide, on that day, was being discussed all over Florida. For weeks fish had been dying in tinted off-shore waters along more than one hundred miles of the lower Gulf coast, all the way from Englewood to the Ten Thousand Islands. Reddish waves carried their lifeless bodies toward the beaches, where they piled up in windrows on the sand. Near Fort Myers bulldozers were scooping out mile-long trenches and plowing under the myriad decaying fish. In many places their stranded forms lay so thick that for every linear foot of beach there was 100 pounds of fish.

Other forms of sea life—shrimp, crabs, barnacles, oysters, turtles, even porpoises—succumbed. In the Fort Myers region, about 80 per cent of the edible oysters growing on piles died in the red tide. Residents along the shore were coughing and sneezing. Their throats burned. Their eyes became inflamed from mysterious fumes rising from sea and sand.

Rumor had it that the army had dumped Lewisite and mustard gas into the Gulf forty miles offshore and that currents were carrying it toward the land. Another theory explained the strange events as the product of noxious fumes liberated into the water by volcanic action beneath the sea. The real secret of the deadly tide was one of those sudden explosions of reproduction which occur at irregular intervals when the balance of nature is upset. Dinoflagellates, subvisible creatures of the sea that propagate by division like amoebas, had responded, perhaps, to some abnormal concentration of nutrient salts in the sea. Their number had increased beyond imagining. They swarmed in the surface water in such numbers that their microscopic reddish eyespots colored the waves.

Later that same day, and on the following day, on the beaches of Captiva and Sanibel islands, at Punta Rassa and elsewhere, we saw evidences of the potency of the poison they produced. Bloated fish, some a foot or more in length, lay along the high-tide line, rose and fell with the waves or littered the hot, dry sand of the upper beaches. At first it was assumed that the fish suffocated in the red tides, that the dinoflagellates consumed the oxygen in the water. But more recent researches have shown that the poison they give off apparently attacks the nervous system of fish and other marine forms of life.

Writing in the *Scientific Monthly* for February, 1949, Dr. Paul S. Galtsoff, of the U.S. Fish and Wildlife Service, reported that fishermen who had seen mullet entering areas of red water described their death as rather sudden. They came to the surface, whirled round and round, then turned on their sides or floated belly up. Experiments he has since conducted at the Woods Hole laboratories, on Cape Cod, have strengthened Dr. Galtsoff's belief that the poison of the red tide strikes at nervous centers controlling equilibrium and respiration.

One hundred thirteen years before the tinted waves appeared off the Florida coast, Charles Darwin, on the *Beagle*, dipped water from similarly colored swells near the coast of

Chile. Under his microscope he saw that every drop was swarming with active animalculae, each about 1/1000th of an inch long. He watched them "darting about and often exploding" in the water. His observations, included in the celebrated journal of his voyage around the world, form one of the earliest published accounts of the red tide. The phenomenon has been studied many times since in many parts of the world. Yet the poison produced by the rapid multiplication of the one-celled organisms has never been identified.

Although we heard reports of gulls and pelicans being killed by eating poisoned fish, we found no dead birds. Even where the fish lay most densely scattered on the shore we never saw a bird alight among them. However, those effective scavengers, the flesh flies, were everywhere. And the world's primal antiseptic, salt water, at each high tide flooded over the packed sand of the beaches.

The tide was at its farthest ebb that morning when we came out on the western shore of Marco Island. Our road from Royal Palm Hammock, south of Naples, had carried us past gumbo-limbo trees, coppery and gnarled, past Spanish bayonets and orange dodder vines that reached the crowns of twenty-foot trees and ran in tangled masses among their topmost branches. White-eyed towhees flicked in and out of dense thickets and, where the road ended at the shore, we found the beach edged with thick-leaved cocoa plums and sea grapes supporting glossy leaves so large that the Spanish explorers had used them for writing paper. Our feet crunched on shell fragments wherever we walked on that wide, flat beach. It seemed paved with lime. It curved away before us, white and shimmering under a cloudless sky. And all along its length, massed together or following the edges of the high-tide line, forming islands and windrows on the beach, were shells fresh from the sea. Each Gulf storm is a cornucopia that empties its multiform treasures on the shore.

If you mention Marco or Sanibel or Captiva anywhere in

the world where shell collectors congregate, the names will be familiar. Conchologists have crossed oceans to visit these famed seashell islands of the Gulf. Here the rare and beautiful Junonia sometimes is found on the wet sands after a storm. We wandered down the hard, white boulevard of this shell-island shore, the sunshine on our backs, the smell of salt spray around us, the tinkle of ripples running among the stranded shells and the crying of the terns in our ears. Before our eyes stretched thousands and thousands of shells, varied in color, diverse in form, some seeming hardly less delicate and fragile than the foam clinging to the wet sand.

Here were jingle shells, pen shells, scallops, lion's paws, cockle shells, tulip bands, and angel's wings. We became fascinated in turn with slipper limpets, apple murexes, turkey's wings, and lightning shells. For entranced miles we walked slowly, stopping, stooping, picking up, examining, throwing away, walking on, stopping, stooping, examining, saving. The beauty of shells like the beauty of butterflies, stirs the poetic sense and results in such names as star shells, moon shells, Florida bubbles, and zigzag periwinkles. So delicate, so beautiful, so fragile are these children of the sea that they, like snowflakes, seem to possess beauty for beauty's sake, beauty beyond the needs of utility.

The tide gradually edged up the beach as we walked on. Each wavelet now ran across a shoal of empty shells, advancing with a multitude of little tinklings. The seashell carillon was played by the advance and retreat of every ripple. Greater waves, in days past, had brought many things ashore. Scattered among the shells were sea urchins and sand dollars, nine-pointed starfish, whelk eggs like strings of costume jewelry, and sponges, brilliant red and orange-pink, branched and twisted like trees or candelabra or cacti.

We picked up one red sponge and discovered a tiny crab had backed into an opening where it fitted like hand in glove, red lines on its body camouflaging it effectively. Another sponge crab, *Dromia erythropus*, goes even further. It adds a trapdoor to its hiding place. Snipping out a piece of living sponge, it crawls into the opening and then uses the fragment it has cut away as a plug which fits tightly in place and conceals it completely. Closely related to this crab, incidentally, is another ingenious species, *Hypoconcha arcuata*. It uses two of its eight legs to hold a large clamshell on its back. Thus equipped, it moves about the beach like a miniature tank protected by the armor plating of the shell.

Since 1839, when the ill-starred Edgar Allan Poe attached his name to one of the first books on conchology published in America, the mollusks known to science have increased rapidly. In 1800 their number was about two thousand. Today it is about one hundred thousand. While most of them are small, less than half an inch in length, they all bring intimations of the strangeness of a sea-bottom world, a world where fighting conchs rasp with the thousands of teeth on file-tongues and where scallops follow a zigzag course, opening and closing their shells to force out water and drive themselves ahead by jet propulsion.

Scallop shells, wherever we went that day, lay thick upon the beach. These swimming clams are world wide in distribution. Their fluted shells have been seen and handled for a thousand years. Yet something that had never been noticed about them before was discovered, half a century ago, in a Long Island kitchen.

Dr. Frank E. Lutz, later head of the Department of Insects and Spiders at the American Museum of Natural History, was at the time earning his way at the Cold Spring Harbor biological station by waiting on table. As he carried empty scallop shells back to the kitchen, he began studying them. He found that he could determine the kind of surroundings in which the scallop had lived by looking at its shell. If it had lived in calm water, the flutings were shallow; if it had lived in rough water, they were deeply ribbed. Just by feeling the shells in the dark, without ever seeing them, this difference can be detected. The history of a scallop's life is written in a kind of Braille on its shell.

In fact, if our fingers were sensitive enough and our knowledge sufficient, we would discover nature's Braille embossed on every shell. The man who came nearest to this knowledge was probably the Cuban conchologist, Dr. Carlos de la Torre. Thomas Barbour, in A Naturalist at Large, tells of his feats of tactile identification. Holding a handful of small shells behind his back, he would amaze visitors by rolling them, one after the other, between his sensitive fingers and calling correctly the name of each.

Even among unlettered people there are a few who possess such extra awareness, whose association with nature has developed a keenness of perception unknown to their fellows. In the South Seas some native fishermen are able to guide themselves when approaching shore on black, moonless nights by listening for "the snapping of the shrimp." In shallows above coral reefs the shrimp produce a slight sizzling sound, like frying bacon. But that is enough for these seamen of the South Pacific. It is the sound of a natural bell buoy, a warning of reefs and shallows for all who can hear and comprehend. When Henry W. Bates, the English naturalist, was exploring the Amazon a century ago an Indian with whom he hunted was amazed that he could not tell what animals passed in the jungle night. He knew them all, identifying each by the sound of its running feet in the darkness.

As we rounded a stranded pine stump, plated in glistening white with the rosettes of innumerable barnacles, we came face to face with the wildest appearing pigs we ever saw. A black sow and a litter of six black piglets were nosing along the tide line in search of edible flotsam. For a quarter of a mile down the beach the lacework of their tracks, large and small, extended over the sand.

Nibbling at the seaward edge of this lacework, the mounting

ripples of the incoming tide advanced steadily. The highest tides of the year, the tides of spring, were approaching. Under this lifted high-tide level of the Gulf the change in the season would bring increased activity to the multitudinous forms of marine life. All these cold-blooded creatures are stimulated by warmth, made sluggish by chill. As the temperature rises, degree by degree, their lives speed up. Food increases. Microscopic forms of life multiply in the warmed and sunlit shallows.

Spring is spawning time, growth time in the sea. Many fish begin adding new and wider rings of growth to their scales. Just as the age of a tree can be determined by counting the annual growth rings in its trunk, so the age of cycloid and ctenoid fishes—those having round or comb-edged scales—can be determined by counting the rings, light and dark, on their scales. Narrow, dark ridges are added to the scales by winter growth; broader, lighter ridges by the more rapid development during warmer weather, beginning in the spring. Thus a history of the changing seasons is recorded on every scale. Sometimes, in village stores on Marco Island, I was told, huge fish scales, so large that they can be addressed and sent as postcards, are sold to visiting tourists. In the spring shellfish also start additions to their homes. The clam records its growth in ridges of lime as the fish does in additions to its scales.

Years ago, as a small boy in the Midwest, far from the sea, I listened a thousand times to the roaring of the surf that seemed captured within a large, pink-throated conch shell used as a doorstop in our home. I asked many people about this shell surf. One told me I was hearing the rushing of blood in my head. Another thought the sound was produced by drafts whirling within the spiral interior. It was, in truth, the product of that natural porcelain which mollusks begin to secrete more actively in the spring. This quick-setting form of carbonate of lime produces the hard, smooth interior which, in the conch, catches and magnifies those small, inaudible sounds that fill the air in all but soundproofed rooms.

Even in the interior of Marco, that day, we came upon shells, mounds of shells, many ancient and weathered and gleaming white against the white-gray sand. This northernmost of the Ten Thousand Islands was celebrated for its shellfish long before Columbus reached America. Indians feasted upon them for centuries, producing one of the most extensive kitchen middens in the country. Originally this pile of discarded shells is said to have been seventy feet high, taller than a five-story building. During the latter part of the nineteenth century the American archaeologist, Frank Hamilton Cushing, unearthed on Marco Island the remains of a prehistoric civilization. He found timbers, terraces, utensils, and ornaments carved from shells, and a great enclosure he called "The Court of the Pile Dwellers."

Talking of these forgotten people as we drove back from Marco—people who, like modern inhabitants, gathered their harvest from the sea—I recalled a long-abandoned scheme of mine, born of imprisonment within office walls. The plan was to spend successive vacations reliving the history of mankind— one summer living as a cave man, another as a lake dweller, and so on. That brought to mind the adventure-in-installments of a New York advertising man who walked to Toronto on weekends. Each Friday night he would take a train to the place where he had ended his previous walk and tramp ahead until Sunday evening, returning in time for work Monday morning. It was spring when he started; it was fall when he finally trudged into Toronto with a snow flurry around him.

Forty miles north of Marco, beyond Naples and Bonita Springs and Estero, two other famous shell islands of the Gulf lie off the mouth of the Caloosahatchee River. They are Sanibel and Captiva. These we planned to visit the following day.

Soon after dawn that morning, as we were walking along the waterfront at Everglades, we heard a rush and scrambling on a high veranda ahead of us. A black kitten came hurtling over the porch rail to crash into bushes below. Bewildered, it picked itself up and climbed the steps. At the top it was met by a sporting angler from the North, a squat, thickset man, his short legs covered by gray slacks, his baboon paunch and barrel chest encased in a striped T-sweater. Above the sweater, with almost no neck between, rose a head round and bald like an onion with little pig eyes glittering behind thick glasses. In a frenzy of superstitious rage this apparition rushed upon the black kitten, snatched it up, twisted it as though wringing a towel, hurled it over the rail once more. The injured animal struggled to its feet and limped away. Here was a winter of the spirit no spring could touch. The sight of that low lout adding to the sum total of the world's pain and injustice in the belief that it would protect his nonessential fishing from misfortune was the beginning of a day of frustration and mishap.

At Punta Rassa we missed the Sanibel ferry by a hundred yards and had to wait an hour for its return. We solaced ourselves by watching a bald eagle that sailed back and forth overhead in flight so steady that it seemed riding on rails and a grackle that took a bath and shook itself on a post until its boattail resembled a wildly wielded feather duster. At Sanibel we led the procession off the ferry and, with no one to guide us, took the wrong turn. Mile after mile we bounced and rattled over washboard roads, passing the Sanibel Community House, where the annual Seashell Fair is held in March, and eventually coming to Captiva. Then we discovered that the beach we were seeking was at the extreme other end of Sanibel. We rattled back, racked by the washboards, choking in white clouds of shell dust, sweltering in the heat when we closed the car windows. On the beach the sand shimmered and glared. Beautiful shells lay scattered all about us. But I was unable to appreciate them. My mind seemed dried out, hardened like putty left for years on a shelf. The midafternoon sunshine rested on us like a physical weight. It seemed to push us down-sun as a gust pushes us downwind. Victims of the mysterious poison of the red tide filled the heated air with the stench of decaying fish. We felt immeasurably depressed.

I remembered John Burroughs's winter entry in his *Journal*: "I long to be out of this accursed South." I remembered the speech of Shakespeare's Macbeth: "I 'gin to be aweary of the sun." I remembered the two fishermen we had heard at breakfast, vacationing in this land of sunshine and balmy breezes and talking with nostalgia in their voices of the delights of skiing amid sparkling snow and bracing air. How many times, on overcast winter days, had we looked at pictures of bathers toasting in the Florida sunshine and thought how happy, happy we would be if we were only there! And here we were, where we had dreamed of being, on our trip with the spring we had so long planned, in the very midst of days we would look back upon as long as we lived—and we were unhappy! I viewed myself with amazement. Yet still I wandered irritated and disconsolate along the Sanibel beach.

As our ferry wheezed homeward toward Punta Rassa we forgot our doldrums in watching the undulating sea serpent of half a dozen porpoises swimming, nose to tail, across the bay ahead of us. But no sooner had the ferry touched the weathered pier than we were on edge again. The ancient captain, waving his arms, began motioning for all the cars on one side to roll off first. The craft heeled over alarmingly. The drivers on the dipping side set up a shout. The captain, expectorating machine-gun bursts of tobacco juice, yelled:

"I never lost a car yet!"

The drivers shouted back:

"There's always a first time!"

Finally, with a flood of relief, we felt our wheels reach solid ground. We rolled away down a dusty road into Punta Rassa—once the northern terminus of the cable from Cuba and the first spot on United States soil to receive word of the sinking of the *Maine*—and headed south.

At our cabin we found the final disappointment of this ill-starred day. Arthur Eifler, Audubon warden, had planned to take us out among the Ten Thousand Islands, the greatest mangrove jungle on the face of the earth, on the following day. A note stuck under the door told us he had been called away. It would be three days before he would dock again. We decided we could not wait. That evening, as we were packing up to make an early start northward in the morning, we both broke out with hives. We tumbled into bed glad at the thought that we would wake up in a new and different day.

FIVE

OKEECHOBEE DUSK

ON the highway leading north from Everglades we passed cars and cars passed us. And all to the north of us and from ocean to ocean, on that day, the highway network of restless America was streaming with other cars—speeding corpuscles in the circulation system of a nation. There is an exhilaration in motion itself. Moreover, the eternal illusion of the traveler is the feeling that he is leaving his troubles behind. So, rebounding from the day before, our spirits soared as we sped northward.

Our travels during this day of sunshine carried us about two degrees of latitude up the map, some 120 miles northward, from Everglades to Wachula, inland from Sarasota. The season was advancing too. Blue lupines and golden coreopsis and white sticktights ran for miles along the highways. Flame vines were brilliant orange-red at Estero.

In groves along the way the harvest of oranges and tangerines was nearing its end—another sign of coming spring. At Wachula workers in the fields were picking strawberries—a sign we were to see repeated all the way to New England. Deriving its name from the Indian word for sandhill crane, Wachula is the home of extensive frog farms. That evening, as the batrachian chorus rose from swampy tracts, we drove down a side road leading to the west. We switched on our lights in the dusk and the beams picked out, in its staggering flight, our first bat of the trip. Twenty miles to the south that day we had seen our first black swallowtail butterfly drifting from flower to flower under trees festooned with Spanish moss.

When we looked at our map before going to bed we found we were in the midst of one of those meaningless coincidences that give us momentary pause because they reflect the mysterious workings of chance. Wachula is 77 miles north of Fort Myers; the town of Everglades is 77 miles south of Fort Myers. Moreover, Everglades, midway between the two ends of the Tamiami Trail, is 77 miles from Miami on the east and 77 miles from Fort Myers on the west. If you ask people to pick any number from one to ten, a magician once told me, the number most frequently chosen will be seven. To the Ancients, the number seven had special significance: "The Seventh Day," "The Seventh Wave," "The Seventh Son of a Seventh Son." For some little-understood reason, men through the ages have looked on seven as a number with magic in it.

Early the next morning we were running west toward the Gulf and Sarasota. Years before, a magazine editor had sent Nellie and me south in a trailer to get a series of feature articles on the life of a trailer nomad. At Sarasota we had spent a day with "Texas Jim" Mitchell, a likable, leather-lunged ex-circus barker who was just starting a reptile farm. He showed us how indigo snakes kill rattlers. He demonstrated how he de-fanged diamondbacks for use in sideshows. He entertained us with tales of his annual expedition with a Seminole chief into the Everglades for reptiles. The article that resulted attracted visitors and for years afterwards Texas Jim showed his appreciation by sending me baby alligators and similar ambassadors of good will.

We found him taking a party through his reptile farm, overflowing with animal spirits, putting on a show in which his serpents were only the background. After the party left, Mitchell and his wife cut a new cake in honor of our appearance and we sat in their parlor, where a sick baby monkey was being nursed back to health, and listened to stories of events at the zoo. A curiosity at the time was a screech owl living in the same cage with a dozen ringdoves. It had been hatched from an egg placed under a brooding dove and had grown up in the same cage with the smaller, gentle birds. It made no effort to harm them and appeared to consider itself one of their kind.

The following day we drove east, circling Lake Okeechobee, and arrived at dusk at the rambling Southland Hotel in Okeechobee City, three miles north of the lake. Cloud shadows raced ahead of us at forty miles an hour down long straight roads and, by the lake shore, we followed a highway wonderful with dragonflies. Thus we skimmed along until the last two hours of the trip. They brought strain and near disaster.

Shunted off the highway onto a road under construction, we crept behind graders, starting and stopping, attaining a five-mile-an-hour pace between stops. Our engine overheated. Radiator water boiled rapidly away. The temperature needle passed the danger mark and continued its swing. There was no way to turn out, no place to get water, no chance to stop. Thus we inched along until, almost too late, we escaped onto the open highway and found water for the car.

At the hotel a room was waiting. And that was lucky. For when I took a drink of water the glass wobbled in my hand. I felt hot. Nellie unpacked the thermometer. My temperature was 102. So with hot head and icy feet I went to bed while a great storm gathered outside the window.

Sometime in the night the tempest broke, a spring torrent of near cloudburst proportions. In ten hours nearly four inches of rainfall descended. And one inch of rainfall means that 65,000 tons, or more than 15,000,000 gallons of water, falls on each square mile. Wind and lightning came with the rain, the lightning followed by curious short claps of thunder that dissipated themselves quickly over this flat land with none of the cannonading reverberations of hilly country. The descending sheets drummed on the balcony roof outside our window.

Through this main watery roar I could hear other sounds—little dripping, simmering, sobbing noises, clamor of a different tempo, the ringing reverberations of a piece of loose tin struck by falling drops. During the hours of fever and sweating I diverted myself by noting all the different sounds produced by the descending rain. The next day, the first day of March, I remained in bed while the deluge, with its echoless thunder, slackened and increased, stopped and began again. A lid was on the sky, shutting us in all day long. After the storm of rain stopped, the storm of wind continued. But by the next morning the rain, the wind, and my fever were gone.

It was our great good fortune, while eating ham and eggs and hominy grits at breakfast, to recognize the back of a head at the far side of the Southland dining room. Richard H. Pough had come down to help Alexander Sprunt, Jr. lead Okeechobee field trips for the Audubon Society. The two had planned a side excursion of their own that afternoon to King's Bar, in Lake Okeechobee, and they invited us to go along. It was thus that we came to witness that stirring and beautiful sight, the homecoming of the glossy ibis at sunset.

Rod Chandler took us out in his shallow-draft boat, heading down the smooth, dark flow of the Kissimmee River to reach that expanse of shallow water which natives call "the Okeechobee Sea." The Kissimmee River, draining 5,000 square miles of prairie land, forms the main water supply of the lake. Its mud stains the surface two miles from shore. Only about six feet deep, Lake Okeechobee—the Seminole word for "big water"—has an area of more than seven hundred square miles. With the single exception of Lake Michigan, it is the largest body of fresh water wholly within the boundaries of the United States. Its shallow water is easily warmed by the sun so that the Okeechobee Sea provides a reservoir of warmth that prevents sudden changes in temperature; it is a balance wheel for the climate of the region.

Originally a depression in the bed of the Pamlico Sea of

Pleistocene times, the lake is roughly triangular and from 25 to 30 miles across. Before dikes and canals were constructed to control the lake, its southern edge was from 6 inches to 1½ feet above the level of the Everglades. In rainy seasons the water overflowed to the south. Lake Okeechobee was then called the "Wellspring of the Everglades."

On this afternoon of calm and sun, great slicks ran across the surface of the water, producing curious illusions where they met the horizon. Sky and water were of almost the same hue; their line of meeting was all but invisible; gulls and ducks, floating on the still surface of the lake, appeared riding at rest in the sky. A mud-bar, here called a "reef," projected like a pointing finger, seemingly above the level of the lake. As we passed one reef, fifty black skimmers—the "cut-waters" of old Mark Catesby—leaped into the air, barking like puppies. They flew low over the water, a few with long lacquer-red bills slicing the surface in their curious form of fishing. Before vegetation increased on this bar, gull-billed terns, birds with a call like a katydid's song, used to nest here.

Stopping occasionally to clear waterweeds from his propeller, Chandler worked us into shallower water. Sometimes he cut the engine and poled us down winding trails where the dark water was bordered with giant bulrushes, pickerelweed, cattails and southern cane. Every few hundred yards the "tossils" of the canes or a mass of bulrushes were knotted together—the lakeman's counterpart of the blazed tree on a forest trail. Wild celery, in coils that looked like bedsprings, rose from the bottom. Nutgrass, a favorite food of the coot, was scattered over the water. Occasionally we caught sight of one of these birds disappearing in the reeds, its head moving forward and backward in chickenlike motions as it swam. When we emerged into an open bay among the canebrakes a score of the birds rushed across the water, their feet sending up little geysers as they struggled to get into the air in heavy-bodied, tail-heavy flight.

Streaming back from the vegetation, clinging to our clothes, sailing almost invisible through the air, were silken threads of gossamer. Tiny spiderlets were ballooning in the spring sunshine just as they ride the autumn air in northern states. Spikes of arrowhead already bore their white flowers and the waves of climbing boneset were almost in bloom. Among thick stands of "wampee"—that favored food of the purple gallinule, the pickerelweed—we glimpsed snow-white masses clinging to the stems. A closer look revealed them to be the eggs of the snail *Pomacea caliginosa*. Each pearllike egg was about a quarter of an inch across. We found other masses of the eggs on cattails and on the broad leaves of the arrowhead. The snails that hatch from these eggs are hunted by the shy limpkin and the Everglade kite, that rare bird known here as the snail-hawk. Later we found some of the shells discarded by birds, roundish, dark, almost filling the hollow of a hand and with a bell-like, metallic ring when dropped on the bottom of the boat.

In one bay, surrounded by cattails, not far from Tin-Shack Cove, we slipped close to one of the most elusive birds of the region, a snail-hunting limpkin. Rod was poling silently along. Letting the boat drift, we froze at our field glasses. Nearly as large as an American bittern, with long, downcurving bill and gray plumage streaked with brown, it walked with a curious halting gait and flipped its tail in nervous jerks when at rest. Its feet were enormous, fitted for marsh walking. Watching us apprehensively with red eyes, it repeated a grating "Clock! Clock!" At one time limpkins were so abundant in the region that natives would kill a score or more on a short hunt before breakfast. They showed almost no fear of man. Now the few remaining birds are excessively shy, rarely seen and quickly disappearing. Our bird suddenly launched itself over the cattails and, flying low with strokes that had a quick flip on every upbeat, dropped out of sight. Later we caught fleeting glimpses of two other limpkins. Even at a distance the peculiar flight, with more rapid upward movement of the wings, distinguishes the bird.

Even more striking than its individual manner of flight is the call of the limpkin. Its local name the "crying bird" is well merited. Later, in the dusk, we heard it, a wild, catlike yowl that echoed over the darkening waters of the lake. Rod recalled one city fisherman who was unalterably convinced that he was hearing the howl of a Florida panther.

"When," he said, "you have bullfrogs and coots and limpkins all going at the same time you have got yourself a fuss!"

The sun was low when we swung around in open water to the west of King's Bar. The racket of the outboard motor ceased. Rod dropped the anchor and we rocked gently in the slow swells and waited for the ibis.

To the east of us lay an area of scattered bulrushes succeeded by a stand of cattails, then a belt of plume-topped canes beyond which we could see clusters of low willows. This was the home of the ibis. During the day, the birds scatter to hunt the crayfish, leeches, small snakes, grasshoppers, and other insects upon which they feed. But when evening comes they wing their way for many miles around back to the King's Bar willows. Our anchored boat lay in the main line of this homeward flight.

To natives of the region the glossy ibis, with its dark plumage and downcurving bill, is the "black curlew." This bird was familiar to Moses and the Pharaohs and all the dwellers in the valley of the lower Nile. Its breeding range extends around the world. It is found in Borneo and China and Australia and Persia and Greece and Spain. Yet, curiously enough, on the North American continent the glossy ibis is—like the great white heron of the Florida keys and the Kirtland's warbler of the Michigan pine barrens—a bird with a remarkably restricted range. When sunset comes, virtually every American glossy ibis—the *Plegadis falcinellus falcinellus* of ornithologists—in North America comes home to roost among the low willows of this one bar in Lake Okeechobee. A related species, the white-faced glossy ibis, is found farther west along the Texas coast.

Now the vanguard of the returning birds appeared out of the glowing pink of the sunset clouds—a long line of black dots approaching low over the water. The dots grew in size, took shape, became a skein of dark birds. They passed us silently, flowing over the obstruction of the cattails and canes as though each bird were a link in a pliant chain. The whole line of birds seemed a unit, an entity, rather than a group of separate individuals. Against the luminous sky each glossy ibis was imprinted sharply. Over the island they curved into a great wheel and poured downward in a spiral to alight in the willow trees.

Flock followed flock. Sometimes in loosely knit V's, sometimes in straggling clusters, sometimes in long lines or skeins that stretched for a mile or more above the water, the birds poured toward us. Sometimes they came in high in the air, sometimes low over the water—so low that their wingtips seemed to miss by only a hair the metallic-tinted swells of the surface. The smallest group contained about thirty birds, the largest more than five hundred.

"Man, oh Man! *Look* at that flock!" Sprunt shouted as the skein of half a thousand birds flowed toward us in a seemingly interminable procession. Like the other lines, it swung to one side to pass the boat at a safe distance. Natural shyness has stood the glossy ibis in good stead. Above the willows of their roost the flock wound up like a length of string as the birds descended. The wheel above the trees grew smaller as it revolved until it was gone and all the birds were down.

Through our field glasses, we could see the alighting ibises hopping awkwardly from branch to branch, working downward out of sight. As flock after flock descended, it seemed impossible for the willows to hold more. Still the birds came. Their formations continually altered like flocks of flying brant. Their undulating skeins ran like slow ripples across the sky—the birds black against the sunset-tinted clouds, their reflections black amid the tinted image-clouds mirrored on the smooth surface of the lake.

By now the frog chorus was in full swing in the shallows of the bar and, at intervals, the loud caterwauling "Me-YOW!" of a limpkin cut through it. All around us was the fresh smell of the lake. Once we heard the barking of a black skimmer behind us and several times we caught overhead the thin whistle of a baldpate passing by. Long after sunset a duck hawk scudded past and was gone before we had more than time to get it well focused in our glasses. Redwings and grackles, mostly boat-tails, came pouring into the cattail stands for the night. Numerous other birds besides ibis come home to King's Bar at evening. We watched snowy egrets and American egrets, their white plumage tinted pink by the sunset, come down to land with that awkward, falling-apart motion characteristic of herons. A great blue heron—a "Poor Joe," a "John Henry" of the South—sailed in followed by a Louisiana heron and an anhinga.

Shortly afterwards, another long line of glossy ibis arrived—all wings beating, all wings set in a glide, all wings beating again—while the final bird, like a white period at the end of a long black sentence, was a lone white ibis. It wheeled with the sooty birds that were its companions, was sucked down into the funnel of descending birds, and disappeared with them into the willows. Another time a single glossy ibis appeared flying fast and low above the water. All its fellows were in flocks; it alone arrived without companions.

Always for me these lonely birds, these avian individualists, these birds doing the unexpected, have a special interest. I remember an avocet, a western shorebird, that I used to see during most of one summer feeding among the flocks of greater yellowlegs on the Long Island shore. Roy Bedichek, in his *Adventures with a Texas Naturalist*, tells of a white egret that used to alight in a tree in a farmyard to spend the night with white pullets and roosters of a barnyard. One of the most celebrated of these lonely birds was the "king of the gannets," an albatross that appeared, in some mysterious manner, among the gannets of the Scottish coast, far from its normal range. For eighteen years it remained on the gannet cliffs, a familiar sight to the fishermen of the coast because of its greater size. Eventually it was collected for Lord Rothschild and its skin is now part of the collection of the American Museum of Natural History, in New York City.

In a Long Island park, a few years ago, a caracara was discovered feeding on crickets a thousand miles from its accustomed surroundings in Florida. Only this one bird of its kind, a lonely wanderer, a sort of Ulysses or Leif Ericson among caracaras, appeared in the North. When Olin Sewall Pettingill was searching for the nesting grounds of the whooping crane in 1948 he received the same report from various places along the upper Missouri River: a large white bird with black wingtips was seen flying with a flock of sandhill cranes, heading north on spring migration. Pettingill flew over the area and discovered the bird. It was a snow goose that had joined the cranes for some undiscovered reason and was moving north in their company.

The sun was well below the horizon, Orion was brightening, and a full moon was silvering the lake, but still the ibis kept coming. Each wave flowed over the barrier of rushes, now growing more black and solid in the fading light. Sprunt and Pough were keeping careful count. Their tally rose steadily. Four hundred, five hundred, a thousand, fifteen hundred, two thousand glossy ibises. They were still coming after the moon was well above the horizon. Now they were almost upon us before we could see them, the dark birds merging with the darkening western sky, then becoming distinct against the luminous, moonlit east. From over Tin-Shack Cove, a final snowy egret appeared, its form, silently stealing overhead, illuminated entirely by moonlight.

The chill of the evening, the night smells of the lake, rose around us while the wildness of the scene was augmented by the outlandish calling of the limpkins, yowling like hoarse tomcats in the distance.

The last flock arrived. Alex and Dick tallied up the score. We had seen 2,307 glossy ibises, virtually the entire population of the continent, wing their way to this island roosting place. This was in excess of the last previous count. It was heartening to discover that this rare bird, familiar to man from the cradle of civilization on the shores of the Mediterranean, was doing better than holding its own in eastern America. As we headed for home through the growing chill of the night, the line of moonlight across the water—the "moonglade" of the New Englanders—moved with us. We looked back for a final time. The reef lay black and silent in the moonlight. Within its darkness the dark birds, immobile now, rested secure for the night.

SIX

EAGLE TREE

———————————————

AS we looked from our window early next morning we saw
a Ford roadster charge past, pulling a narrow, two-wheeled
trailer, a stall-on-wheels, in which a black pony, saddled and
bridled, nonchalantly watched the buildings rush by. An Okeechobee cowboy, semimotorized, was starting for work on the
Kissimmee Prairie. Lake Okeechobee lies between two blank
spots on the map. The blank spot to the south is the Everglades; the blank spot to the north is the Kissimmee Prairie.
For half a hundred miles it spreads away, hardly interrupted
by road or village, a level grassland dotted with patches of
palmetto, cabbage palms, and, in small damp depressions, with
cypress. It is the chief cattle country of Florida.

It is also an ornithological island. Similar country attracts
similar birds. There is a geology and a geography of ornithology.
The prairie lands of the Kissimmee region reproduce conditions of the Far West. And here you find, isolated from their
species, separated by nearly a thousand miles from their main
breeding ground, two birds of the open lands of the West, the
burrowing owl and Audubon's caracara. Here also the Florida
sandhill crane is making its last stand. These three birds we
especially wanted to see: the bobbing little burrowing owl, the
heavy-billed, long-legged caracara, and the red-topped gray
crane.

At breakfast Dick Pough told us that in a couple of days
Charles L. Broley was driving over from Tampa to band eagles

on the prairie. Broley, a retired Canadian banker who took up the risky hobby of eagle banding when nearing sixty, is an almost legendary figure in modern ornithology. At sixty-seven he was then nearing his thousandth eagle. We decided to wait and join the expedition. And while we waited we roamed the prairie, looking for crane and owl and caracara and watching the first installments of spring arrive on this southernmost of the American plains.

Spring had been mostly fugitive—unless looked for, hardly noticed—in the tropical tip of the Florida peninsula. Here, north of Okeechobee, it was beginning to be a clear-cut season. Under a great wind, on that early March morning, we drove for miles over the wet prairie lands where the parade of the spring flowers had already begun. Pipeworts lifted white button flowers from pools of standing water and across acres of drenched plains, where the gray turrets of crayfish rose above the green of new grass, wild iris was massed, already beginning to blossom, soon to spread over the flatland in lakes of brilliant blue. Blooming demurely close by was that relative of the wild flag, the modest blue-eyed grass. Here, too, was the blue of violets—the first violets of our long trip. From the Kissimmee Prairie a tide of violets runs north. In later weeks we saw them everywhere, high in the mountains, along the coast, edging the dark northern forests. Fifty or more species bloom east of the Mississippi. More than any other wildflower, the violet is the emblem of the North American spring.

Everything that morning—violets, pipewort, blue-eyed grass, wild flags—dipped, waved, nodded, lashed about in the grip of the March wind. Where ripple patches raced across the standing puddles, sudden hard thrusts of the wind struck feeding grackles and swept their boattails around almost at right angles to their bodies. The spring chorus of the frogs reached our ears, swelling and diminishing with the violence of the gusts. Once, looking up, we saw a slender-winged, black-and-white bird sweep across the sky in a wind-blown rush, growing smaller instant by instant as we trained our glasses on it. The bird was that most graceful of American species, a swallow-tailed kite.

Somewhere up the old Bassenger Road, that afternoon, a living periscope, a small head on a long slender neck, lifted from behind a patch of palmetto. Our first Florida sandhill crane was looking at us from a distance of hardly more than two hundred feet. We slowed to a stop. The crane moved unhurriedly away, always putting palmetto clumps between it and us whenever possible, pausing behind each to lift its periscope and watch us anew. On a later day we saw nine of these magnificent birds flying over the prairie. With a wingspread of 80 inches, they flew with deliberate downstrokes and accelerated upstrokes, lifting their wings each time with a flip or jerk that recalled the flight of the limpkin. This characteristic movement of the wings identified the birds even when they had grown small on the horizon.

The Kissimmee cranes are specialists at finding the underground tubers of *Gyrotheca tinctoria*, the pinkroot, bloodroot, Indian root, or painroot of the prairie. Beneath the red-based, irislike leaves of this plant, rhizomes, ranging from a quarter of an inch in diameter to the thickness of a lead pencil, spread away just beneath the surface. On these rhizomes grow red succulent tubers, looking like radishes and frequently so numerous that they suggest red beads on a string. Using their long bills, the cranes deftly extricate these tubers from the ground. Hogs, I was told, are so inordinately fond of these tubers that they sometimes consume such quantities their whole bodies take on a pink or reddish cast.

On that day of wind we saw only one or two buzzards tossing about in the sky. The next day, hot and still, vultures were soaring all around the horizon—turkey vultures with uptilted wings and black vultures with short tails and quick butterfly flapping between glides. In all probability the vulture population of the Kissimmee region is greater today than it was when the Spaniards came to Florida, three hundred years ago. Just as Darwin noted a rise in the number of vultures as cattle increased on the Argentine pampas, so the spread of cattle raising on the Kissimmee Prairie has provided food for a greater number of buzzards. In similar fashion, James E. DeKay, in his *Zoology of New York*, published in 1844, reports that vultures increased along the main highway between New York and Philadelphia in the days just before the first railroad linked the two cities. Rivalry between stagecoach proprietors reached its peak and horses were lashed on until they collapsed. Their carcases, abandoned beside the highway, attracted an increasing congregation of turkey buzzards.

On several occasions far across the prairie we saw wheels or funnels of soaring vultures. Most of the time such a wheel marked the spot where some rich feast had brought the carrion feeders together. But not always. Once or twice we noticed the circling birds rising steadily higher. They had found an escalator in the sky. Warmed lower air occasionally breaks through the overlying layer of cold air and rushes upward. At such times vultures soar from all directions to ride the ascending air far into the sky. In California condors have been observed using such updrafts to aid them in transporting heavy prey back to the nest. Instead of carrying the food directly home, such birds have been seen flying in the opposite direction to reach a more or less permanent column of ascending air. In it they rise effortlessly to a great height and then soar like a sled coasting downhill toward their nest.

Whenever a fire runs across the prairie buzzards jockey about it in the turbulent air. There, too, are birds of prey. Marsh hawks and sparrow hawks coast or hover overhead to take their toll of rodents fleeing the flames. Swallows dart close to the advancing front of the fire to scoop up small insects. Prairie flames provide a harvest for birds of many kinds.

At one point our road led us past blackened prairie land, still smoldering. Clusters of cabbage palms rose in little oases in this black desert. In each at least a thousand robins congregated. The uproar of their calling filled the air with excitement like the excitement of an apiary at swarming time. Flocks that would spread out over orchards and lanes and fields, over hundreds of square miles of northern countryside, were assembling for the long flight home.

Beyond one oasis we came suddenly upon three large birds, about the size of ospreys but long legged like turkeys. They were tearing at some animal killed by the fire a hundred yards or so from the road. We recognized them at once as Audubon's caracaras. These birds, feeding on living animals as well as carrion, are remarkably fearless. A few years ago a pair nested within the city limits of Okeechobee. As our car slowed to a stop, the three birds merely ceased their feeding to watch us. Not until we climbed out, after observing them for some time through our glasses, did the caracaras spread their wings, conspicuously marked with lighter patches toward the tips, and flap into the air.

In the aristocracy of carrion feeders, the caracara ranks first. It justifies its local name of king buzzard. Just as in many a northern feeding station, the starling gives way before the blue jay and the English sparrow before the starling, so here, on the Kissimmee Prairie, black buzzards and turkey buzzards move back to let a caracara feed when it alights beside a dead animal. The turkey buzzard, apparently, stands lowest in the scale. Once we came upon a sight, a literal description of which ran jingling through our heads the rest of the day: five black buzzards on a dead red cow. The black buzzards were tearing the body of the animal while three turkey buzzards obtained what they could around the edges. Usually the turkey buzzards will hang back until the black vultures have satisfied their hunger. This dominance is reflected in the territory of the two birds in the Southeast. Black vultures oftenest are found along the coast and in the teeming lowlands, where food is plentiful, while turkey vultures range over hill country and farther inland. The effortless, soaring flight of the turkey vultures enables them to search for food over wide areas with a minimum expenditure of energy.

We had now seen two of the three birds we had especially hoped to find on the prairie. We had also seen, fifty feet up in a dead pine tree, a brown eaglet exercising its wings on the great stick nest Broley was coming to visit. However, only the handiwork of our third bird was visible that day—white mounds of sand marking the tunnels of burrowing owls. We were on the high hurricane dike at the northern end of Lake Okeechobee the next morning, near a stretch of great tussocks of grass, when this third bird first appeared in our glasses. An osprey had just passed over, struggling with an alligator gar, a fish so long and so slender that at first we thought it was a snake. As we lowered our glasses we focused them on a small splotch of white on the side of the dike. There in the doorway of its burrow stood a long-legged little owl, about the size of a screech owl, turning its head to one side, then to the other, then staring straight ahead for minutes at a time. We were looking at the burrowing owl, the billy owl of the Florida prairies.

Its head began bobbing in little jerks as we drew near. It had the appearance of some polite Oriental bidding us welcome. I slipped a telephoto lens, with a 15-inch focal length, on my Speed-Graphic and, with the camera on a tripod, edged toward the bowing little owl. When I remained motionless, it would regard me steadily with its yellow eyes, then turn abruptly to stare to the right, then snap its head back to watch me closely again, then suddenly rotate its neck to peer to the left, then fix its gaze on me once more. Its head nodded in quick bobs whenever it faced me.

Each time the owl looked away I would edge my camera one step ahead, freezing in position before it turned my way again. Thus I advanced closer and closer while the image on the ground glass increased in size. After I had photographed the owl half a dozen times I began to notice an interesting thing. Each time I would watch the image grow until it reached a certain size. Each time I would think if I could make one additional step I would be able to record the plumage in greater detail. But never once was I able to gain even half a step.

Whenever I advanced beyond that point, the owl was off the instant it turned my way. Its eyes measured distance with remarkable accuracy. I became so engrossed in this game, stalking the bird over and over again, that I forgot to take pictures. The image on the ground glass is an accurate yardstick. It always records the same objects the same size at the same distance. Thus, my camera was determining exactly the flight distance of the burrowing owl.

Each wild creature has its flight distance, the closest it will permit a human being to approach. Some, like fleet animals of the western plains, are alarmed at the approach of a man miles away; others, like the camouflaged woodcock, will remain without moving until they are almost stepped upon. Along the highways of the South we noticed that if we sounded our horn black vultures flapped up from the roadside at a greater distance than if we approached silently. From their association with automobiles they had developed a second flight distance, based on sound.

The fearlessness of the burrowing owl makes it an easy prey for gunners. Although it is a beneficial bird in its feeding habits, destroying innumerable insects, it is widely shot by cattlemen— the same Florida cattlemen who a few years ago slaughtered wild deer and dined on venison out of season for months before scientific tests could prove that their contention that deer were spreading a cattle disease was without foundation.

Once, when the owl was away, I measured the entrance of the burrow. It was almost four inches high and five inches wide. How far it descended into the side of the dike I could only guess. Some tunnels are as much as eight feet long. Alexander Sprunt, who has watched billy owls at work, told us they begin by scratching like chickens. As they descend deeper into the sand, a steady stream of excavated material comes flying from the entrance. In at least one case a pair began digging their burrow in the hardened rut of a country road. At the end of the tunnel the birds dig out a circular cavity. They line it with hair, grass—in one instance with shredded newspapers—and with dried horse or cow dung. Here, sometime between the middle of March and the end of May, the female lays from three to seven eggs. The hatching of baby burrowing owls is a feature of every Kissimmee spring.

While I was bending over the entrance to the owl tunnel, an airy rustling increased in volume above me. I looked up. In uneven skeins, like overlapping wave marks on a beach, more than two hundred white ibis were passing overhead. The sun shining behind them made each bird glowing and luminous against the blue of the cloudless sky. Hardly breathing, we watched this radiant spectacle move across the heavens and grow small in the distance.

We were brought back to the dikeside by the shrill "b-e-e-e-p!" of a loggerhead shrike. This bird had been flying from post to post along a barbed-wire fence that ran down the slope not far from the burrow of the owl. Several times the owl had landed beneath the fence. The shrike paid no attention. But this time the owl had curved upward and alighted on a fence post. In an instant the smaller black, white and gray bird was rushing to the attack. It uttered a series of harsh, buzzing "b-e-e-e-ps." It swooped, hovered over the owl, ceased its attack only to renew it again. The attitude of the shrike, apparently, was that the fence was its province, the ground under the fence was the owl's territory. It was attacking the intruder as birds often attack interlopers of their own species after they have staked out nesting territories in the spring.

All during the spring days of our trip we saw birds of many species defending their territories. Springtime, nesting time, is the period of the year when the territory sense of birds is keenest. Once we saw a meadowlark pursue another meadowlark across a fence between two pastures. The fence apparently was a boundary line for meadowlarks as well as for farmers. In its own field the spirit of the fleeing bird revived and it turned on its pursuer.

Where territories join, two birds will sometimes engage in a kind of pendulum chase that swings back and forth from one area to the other for hours at a time. The belligerency of the fleeing bird grows as it nears the center of its own area; the combativeness of the pursuing bird lessens as it penetrates its rival's territory. W. C. Allee tells of an instance in which a male bird defended a larger area in the morning than in the afternoon, probably because its energy and stamina were greater during the early part of the day. In the case of the burrowing owl and the loggerhead shrike, although the shrike swooped without touching and the larger bird merely ducked its head at the passes of the smaller, the owl soon took wing and landed once more near its burrow.

Outside the Southland Hotel, the next morning, we met the Broleys. They had driven over from Tampa the evening before. Both the eagle bander and his writer-wife were people we liked at once. Five feet, nine and a half inches tall, 150 pounds in weight, with a sense of humor as keen as his blue eyes, with his hair cropped so short that he has been referred to as the "bald-headed eagle bander," this retired banker was one of the most remarkable men we met on our travels. Although he was nearing seventy, he was ascending cypress trees 115 feet high and climbing trunks so rickety that they swayed with his weight and went down in the next heavy storm.

"Don't you ever have nightmares about falling out of trees?" I asked him.

"No, but I do have nightmares about rattlesnakes."

Once near Bradenton after he had descended a tree, wearing rubber-soled climbing sneakers, he stepped back to look up at the nest. He felt something like a rubber hose move under his foot. At the same instant, there was a thrashing rattle behind him. He leaped away. He had stepped on a diamondback. Fortunately, his foot had descended on the forepart of its body, pinning the venomous head to the ground. Diamondbacks, he has come to believe, are especially numerous around eagle trees. Perhaps the scraps of food that fall from the nest attract small animals upon which the reptiles prey.

We started west and north toward the dead pine where we had seen the eaglet exercising two days before. Along the way an American egret lifted from a roadside ditch and flapped in steady parallel flight. Keeping pace with it, we clocked its speed at 18 miles an hour. A few minutes later the shadow of a turkey buzzard swept down the road ahead of us. Again we kept pace. The shadow-of-a-bird was traveling exactly 20 miles an hour.

When we reached the farthest point the cars would go, nearly three-quarters of a mile of palmetto-studded pasture separated us from the pine tree. The land had been burned over and the reddish rosettes of sundew stood out amid the thin green blades of the new grass. Broley spread out coils of rope, three rope ladders, lead sinkers, stout fishline, a broom handle with a teaspoon taped to one end, a slingshot, a pair of rubber-soled shoes, and other odds and ends. With this equipment checked and shouldered, we started out—Dick Pough, Alex Sprunt, Mr. and Mrs. Broley, Nellie and I. Behind us three huge white humped Brahma bulls of uncertain temperament snuffed the air with outstretched necks.

Under the eagle tree our eyes ran upward along more than half a hundred feet of trunk to an immense nest of sticks massed against the sky. Bald eagles keep adding sticks to their nests year after year. Sometimes the weight of the accumulated material will exceed a ton. Broley's largest nest, perhaps the largest in America, is lodged in the top of a Florida pine near St. Petersburg. His measurements show it is 20 feet deep and 9½ feet wide. Among the sticks of another nest he once found about three-quarters of the handle of a heavy ash oar.

A deep soft mattress of Spanish moss covers the sticks in most bald eagle nests in Florida. Two years before, in a tree near Punta Gorda, Broley had come upon an eagle nest with streamers of colored paper hanging down the sides. Instead of Spanish moss, the birds had used shredded colored paper, such as is employed in packing dishes, for lining the nest. Piles of this paper, evidently washed ashore, lay several feet deep on the sand flats nearby.

From the Gulf coast beaches of Florida, bald eagles, especially the males, bring home to the nest a surprising variety of oddments. Broley showed us a boxful of objects he had found in eagle nests. They included a gunny sack, a rubber shoe, a corncob, an electric light bulb, a handkerchief, a Clorox bottle, a clothespin, a loaf of bread, a candle, a sugar bag, and seashells of various kinds. In one instance Broley found a female brooding a white rubber ball a month and a half after her own egg had hatched. Many nests contain epiphytes, or air plants. Once, at the end of his climb, Broley found an *American Weekly* Sunday supplement in an eagle nest. He sat on the edge of the nest, with an eaglet on either side of him, and read an article about his native Canada.

Fish lures—one with 70 feet of line attached—have been discovered in a number of nests. Perhaps they arrived attached to fish or their bright colors may have caught the eye of the eagle. At any rate, they present a hazard to the young birds. On one occasion Broley extracted a hook that had become embedded in the leg of an eaglet and unless removed would have left it a cripple. Another eaglet that owes its life to his hobby had the sting of a ray thrust through its cheek and almost into its throat when Broley found it.

He never knows, in ascending a tree, what will lie at the top of his climb. Moreover, each tree presents a fresh set of problems. The dead pine under which we stood rose for more than twenty feet before the first stub of a limb jutted out. One cypress Broley climbed had its first limb seventy feet from the ground. And, in Canada, he once reached a nest at the top of an 80-foot basswood tree which had lost all its lower limbs. In this case he threw a weighted fishline directly over the nest itself, by means of his slingshot, and with this pulled up his rope ladders. For less lofty throws he uses the broom handle with the teaspoon at the end. We watched him place a lead sinker, attached to a stout fishline, in the spoon and flip it over the stub of a limb with a deft sweep of the wooden handle that was a tribute to his years as a lacrosse player. To the fishline he attached a rope, pulling it over the limb and attaching it, in turn, to a 40-foot length of rope ladder with wooden steps. When this was fastened securely in place and he had changed into rubber-soled sneakers he was ready to begin the climb.

We could see the brown eaglet perched on the edge of the nest. It was almost ready to fly, about three months old. During the first three weeks of its life it had been shielded from the sun by the body or wings of the adults. At eight weeks it had begun waving its wings, strengthening the muscles for flight. For several days before it launched itself on the air it would rise in vertical, helicopterlike flights, ascending a foot or several feet above the nest, keeping its eyes fixed upon it and settling back on the mass of sticks. Whenever possible, Broley tries to band eaglets before these final days to reduce the chances of their leaving the nest too soon. In every case where a young bird takes wing and, unable to mount, descends on a long slant to the ground, Broley carefully hunts it up and returns it to the nest. For eagles, like herons, never feed a fledgling on the ground.

The two adults, with snow-white heads and tails, circled overhead. They uttered curious, creaking, cricketlike calls. They did not scream. They made no attempt to dive on the man climbing toward their nest. Never once has Broley been attacked by eagles. Occasionally they fly low over him but most often they keep their distance; frequently they land in nearby trees and sometimes they disappear entirely.

Standing on the first limb, Broley threw sinker and fishline over the highest limb and repeated the process of pulling up rope and ladder. This enabled him to reach the edge of the nest. Now came the ticklish job of getting over the side. The last few feet are the most important in his climb.

Once, near Port Ritchie, Florida, Broley lifted his head above the rim of the nest just as one of the parent eagles was landing with a red-breasted merganser in its talons. Which was more surprised, eagle or eagle bander, is not known. The bird braked its descent so fast that it nearly somersaulted backward off the nest. Another time, in Canada, just as he put his weight on the nest, a supporting branch cracked. The great mass of sticks tilted downward at a steep angle. Broley and the eaglet barely missed being catapulted into space. The next day, worried about the fate of the young eagle on the tilting nest, he returned with workmen and tackle and hauled the nest back into position and braced it with timbers. He often wonders what hunters think when, after leaves have fallen from the trees, they come upon this eagle's nest equipped with two-by-fours.

Dieting to keep his weight down, Broley told us, he loses as much as fifteen pounds during the banding season. Tampa, his winter home, was for years the center of the greatest concentration of eagle nests he knows. Until 1950 when a building boom along the lower Gulf shore destroyed many of the nests, there were 140 in a 165-mile stretch of coast. For long distances there was an eagle nest every mile. Apparently this is as close as the nests are built. Bald eagles, like shrikes and meadowlarks and robins, have their territories. They normally want at least half a mile of open space, unoccupied by any other eagle, on all sides of the nesting tree.

The same tree is used by the same eagles season after season. The highest nest Broley has visited is 125 feet above the ground in the top of a giant cypress. In contrast, when the pines were cut on Bocagrande Island, north of Captiva, eagles began nesting in the black mangroves, only 15 feet from the ground. Once Broley found an eagle nest actually built on the ground. It contained an egg and a newly hatched eaglet. As long as possible, in spite of changes, the birds return to their accustomed nesting places. On Gadsden's Point, near Tampa, in 1942 a pair of bald eagles continued to nest in a tree in spite of the fact that every other tree around it was felled, that bulldozers churned over the ground underneath, that army planes roared past all day long, and that bombs continued to explode on a target close by. One of the few things, Broley has found, that will dislodge an eagle from its nest is a great horned owl. Yet in one remarkable instance near Englewood, Florida, he discovered a great horned owl and an eagle occupying the same nest, raising their young only three or four feet apart, neither molesting the other.

As Broley pulled himself up and onto the nest above us— first his head and shoulders disappearing, then his legs projecting out into space and shortening until they were gone— patches of loose bark sloughed away from the upper trunk and fell to the ground. For ten minutes he was hidden behind the wall of sticks. But we could visualize events on the nest high overhead. Before making the ascent he had demonstrated the steps required in banding an eagle.

Waving a pair of shiny pliers in his left hand, he holds the attention of the eaglet. Although he has nothing to fear from the adult, he takes no chances with the fledgling. In this instance it was already almost as big as its parents and, just before it left the nest, it would be actually bigger. One of the paradoxes of eagle life is the fact that, because there is a slight contraction of the bones in later life, the eaglet is larger than the eagle, is bigger on the day of its first flight than it is at maturity.

While the glinting pliers holds the attention of the eaglet,

Broley reaches quickly with his right hand from the back and pulls one leg up behind the wing, obtaining a kind of half-nelson grip on the bird that prevents it from turning and using its other talon while he attaches the numbered metal band on the leg in his hand. The great curving hooks of an eagle have a spread of 7½ inches. The narrowest escape Broley ever had taught him how dangerous those needle-sharp claws can be.

During his early days of banding, as he reached for the leg of an eaglet, the bird clamped one talon on his hand. In intense pain, he bent down, struggling to wrench free the embedded hooks. As he did so, the eagle fell on its back and darted out its other foot, clutching Broley's face, one hook on his jaw, the others on top of his forehead. Blood poured down, blinding him. In a moment of panic he thought his eyes had been destroyed. Somehow—he has never been able to determine exactly how—he loosened the talons and got free. But ever since he has approached an eaglet on a nest with redoubled caution.

When his legs appeared over the edge of the mass of sticks and he came down the tree, loosening ropes and letting down ladders in his wake, he had banded his 932d eagle. Since then he has passed the 1,200-mark. He has banded more eagles—a dozen times more—than all other birdmen put together.

For many years this hobby of his will continue to bear fruit, enriching our knowledge of eagle life. Already his bands have revealed hitherto unknown facts. We now know that bald eagles born in southern Florida may summer along the Maine coast and that young eagles migrate north ahead of the adults. The very first band returned came from Columbiaville, New York, 1,100 miles north of St. Petersburg, Florida, where the bird had been banded in a nest only four months before. Eagles are strong and steady fliers although not especially fast. Broley timed one in straightaway flight. He found it was traveling 35 miles an hour.

It is during the nuptial flights of the mating season that

bald eagles show their greatest speed and airmanship. We all envied Broley the moment when he saw a pair of bald eagles grasp talons in mid-air and come cartwheeling down through the sky, turning over and over in a wild plunge that carried them earthward for hundreds of feet.

He recalled this moment, and others, that evening when we all dined on some of the thickest and tenderest steaks east of the Mississippi at John and Sarah's Restaurant, under the ridge of the Okeechobee dike, three miles south of town. Our meal was a kind of farewell dinner. The next day the Broleys were driving back to Tampa. And we were leaving for Ocala in the morning.

SEVEN

THE BIG SCRUB

AT two o'clock in the afternoon, on the 8th of March, 20 miles south of Ocala, we collided head on with summer. Heavy-headed heat engulfed us. The highway wavered and shimmered before us. The mercury hung at the 90-degree mark. Here, so near the place where spring begins, the season is shortest of all. With little of the slow transition of a northern spring, it breaks through violently into the full heat and glare of summertime. We breathed slowly. Our eyelids felt weighted with lead. The languor of extreme spring fever gripped us.

The medical profession, apparently, is in something of a quandary about this lassitude which had overtaken us. One authority ascribes it to a lack of vitamins. Another says spring fever is caused by insufficient calcium in the blood stream. A third maintains that it does not exist at all, that it is merely a state of mind. A fourth explains that it is a mild attack of scurvy. Rather, I should think, it is a temporary attack of anemia.

With a sudden rise in outside temperature, as Dr. H. C. Bazett, Professor of Physiology at the University of Pennsylvania, has pointed out, the body works harder to eliminate its internal heat. Arteries and capillaries of the skin dilate. They bring more blood to the surface where heat is dissipated by radiation. To meet this sudden increase in the capacity of the blood channels, the body has to manufacture about a quart of new blood—something like 20 per cent of the fluid in the lifestream at that time. Plasma forms more quickly than corpuscles. Thus the blood is suddenly diluted. This temporary reduction in the richness of the blood stream, it seems logical to conclude, is the chief factor in producing that languor which we call spring fever. A feature of the coming of every spring is this increase in the amount of blood within our bodies. The high spring tides of the ocean have their small counterpart in the high tides of our blood streams.

Near Ocala, on the road to Silver Springs, we found a cabin and in the cabin we found a morning paper and in the paper we found spring memorialized by a local poet: "I know the season must be spring. The reason? Cats are kittening." That, plus a cool shower, proved the medicine we needed to revive us.

Our drive that hot day had carried us up another third of the Florida peninsula. We had left the wide expanses of prairie and Everglade behind. We were in a land of groves and farms and small towns and innumerable lakes. Our road had carried us past Lake Wales and Florida's modest Matterhorn, Iron Mountain, the highest point in the state, 324 feet above sea level. We had mounted the central ridge of Ocala limestone that forms the backbone of the peninsula and divides the rivers of the east from the rivers of the west.

The next morning at the General Delivery window of the post office we found a letter marked: *Hold Until Called For.* It was from Marjorie Kinnan Rawlings, author of *The Yearling,* who has made the big scrub of northern Florida her special literary province. "Suppose," she wrote, inviting us to Cross Creek, "we made a definite date for Tuesday. If it is a nice day and the idea pleases you, you might enjoy our taking a picnic lunch and going to 'The Yearling' country, where the dogwood should be in full bloom in the sinkhole."

About nine that Tuesday morning we drew up at the low rambling white house at Cross Creek. There is no name on the mailbox; no telephone wires lead to the house. Orange trees heavy with ripened fruit extended away to the rear and not far down the road the banks of Cross Creek were overhung by limbs shaggy and gray with Spanish moss.

Mrs. Rawlings had been working late the night before and pages of interlined manuscript, weighted down with a box of Keeboard Redemption Bond, were strewn about a low table near the fireplace at one end of the living room. Open bookcases extended along the wall under an original Audubon print. A few weeks before, Mrs. Rawlings had discovered that termites were tunneling through two of her most prized volumes, Peter Scott's *Dawn Chorus* and a rare first edition of William Bartram's *Travels*. During his wanderings on the Florida peninsula before the American Revolution, Bartram had crossed Orange Lake and forded the River Styx only a mile or two from the spot where, more than one and a half centuries later, we examined the termite-riddled copy of his book.

Responding to our concern over her leaving her work, Mrs. Rawlings assured us:

"I always welcome a chance to get back to the scrub."

She lived on this extensive sandy plateau east of Ocala when she first came to Florida. "Cab" Long and his wife, with whom she stayed, farmed one of the small "islands" of higher, richer soil. Then known as Pat's Island, this area is now part of the Ocala National Forest. It has been renamed Baxter's Island in honor of the leading characters in *The Yearling*.

When we started for the scrub that morning a wicker hamper rode with us. It was crammed with fried chicken, boiled eggs, potato salad, layer cake and oranges fresh from the Cross Creek trees. That was our picnic lunch. In the evening, back at Cross Creek, we dined on broiled halves of grapefruits, scrapple, string beans, baking powder biscuits, mangoes and a special food for the gods, the white heart of a cabbage palm. Its smooth-textured, chestnutty-flavored slices melted gradually away in our mouths. Later during our trip we ate crayfish bisque in Louisiana, conch stew in South Carolina, chicken shortcake in New Hampshire, salmon chowder along the Canadian line. All were luscious foods. But nowhere else in our travels did we meet so many culinary stars on a single table as at Cross Creek. And nowhere else did we find anyone more generous or directly sincere that Mrs. Rawlings. She made the hours of that day ones we will long remember.

It is 45 miles from Cross Creek to the big scrub. All along the way the signs of spring were multiplying. We saw the white of wild plums, the yellow of jessamine. Sparkleberry bushes had put forth new oval leaves that shone as though varnished. A few weeks more and the bushes would be covered with small white bell-shaped blooms.

When we turned into the sand roads of the big scrub 20 miles east of Ocala we rode over the poorest and driest soil in Florida. Lying between two rivers, the St. Johns and the Oklawaha, the arid plateau has a length of about 40 miles, a width of about 30. It is formed of coarse, porous sand underlaid by hardpan. Rain sinks into this soil almost as fast as it falls. Laboratory tests have shown that the white sand of the scrub has a water-holding capacity of only 20.01 per cent—more than 6 per cent less than that of the yellow sand of the high pinelands.

Because of the nature of this soil, the scrub has a special character of its own. Here, 50 miles from the coast, sea myrtle grows. Here, in stands of straight tall trees, is found the world's largest concentration of the sand pine, *Pinus clausa*. Here grow silk bay and dog fennel and staggerbush and beargrass that resembles a century plant and used to provide country people with leaves long enough and strong enough to use for ropes in hanging bacon and hams. Florida is the land of the woolly-bucket tree, the buckwheat tree, the fishfuddle tree and the pondapple tree and here, in the scrub, we came upon a monkey fooler or toothache tree—our first prickly ash with its silvery bark and thornlike projections.

"Along about here," Mrs. Rawlings said after we had driven

a mile or so into the scrub, "we ought to see Florida jays."

Hardly a minute went by before we saw two birds with blue wings and tails and buffy shields on their backs fly from a bush to the top of a small tree beside the sand road. We stopped and swung our glasses on the jays. Their colors were subdued. Their plumage had a satiny sheen. They lacked the white spotting and the metallic blue of the common jay. They were without crests. But in the manner of all jays they set up a raucous screaming as soon as the car rolled to a stop. Like the burrowing owls of the Kissimmee Prairie, these Florida or scrub jays underscore the geology of ornithology. Nowhere in the world except in peninsular Florida are they found. And nowhere else in Florida do they live except on the dry sandy plateau east of Ocala and in a few smaller areas of scrub where conditions are the same.

Within half a mile we saw seven of these colorful birds. Two were romping among the branches of a tree at the edge of the sinkhole when we slowed to a stop. Here, as Mrs. Rawlings had predicted, the dogwood was in full bloom. All around the curve of the amphitheater-like depression in the earth, it rose in clouds of white above the dark green of magnolia and loblolly bay—the first dogwood of our trip. Later we saw it all the way from Florida to New England. The white of its flowers preceded us up the map. In the East the dogwood is like the violet, a common denominator of the North American spring.

We descended a trail that dropped steeply down the side of the sinkhole. Ages before, the limestone had fallen in to a depth of twenty feet or more. At the bottom of this wide depression slanting rays of sunlight among the trees glinted on the pulsing flutter of sandgrains and water where little springs danced without ceasing. Their water slid away in the shallow and transparent beginnings of a stream. This was the spot Marjorie Kinnan Rawlings had in mind when she described the Silver Glen, that "secret and lovely place" where Jody built his fluttermill in the opening chapter of The Yearling.

Other springs, some no larger than a silver dollar, fountained upward beneath a live oak that lifted limbs feathery with ferns not far from the place where we ate our picnic lunch. It was in this shaded stretch of moister, richer ground—where we watched the boil of three small springs adding their flow to the headwaters of Juniper Creek—that we caught sight of a flower associated with the spring season in the north, a jack-in-the-pulpit. It shone out like a face from home. It provided a link with all the springs we had known in the past.

Another scene, a scene of delicate, almost eerie beauty, always comes to mind when we remember that day in the Florida scrub. We were at the northern end, somewhere near Lake Kerr, when a turn in the dirt road carried us beneath twisted trees sheeted with long pendants of Spanish moss. The low beams of the afternoon sun filled the shaggy branches with glowing light. In a variable wind all the trees came to life with wagging beards and fluttering robes. We moved in a realm as strange as though we had suddenly been transformed into fish and were swimming in a dim shadowy world of waving waterweeds.

In this place and along the River Styx, near Cross Creek, we saw Spanish moss at the peak of its abundance and beauty. Not a moss but a flowering plant with pale green blooms that produce parachuted seeds, *Tillandsia* draws no nourishment from the tree that supports it. It is not a parasite. It does not kill the tree on which it grows. It is an airplant manufacturing its own food. Its roots are chiefly organs of anchorage. It grows as well on a telephone wire as on a live oak limb. The winged seeds that develop from the green flowers of April and May are not liberated on the air until late the following spring. Contrary to Linnaeus's opinion, Spanish moss thrives best in moist surroundings. The Swedish scientist was so convinced that this airplant disliked moisture that he named it after Elias Tillands, a student with such an aversion to water that he once walked more than 1,000 miles around the head of the Gulf of Bothnia rather than make the relatively short crossing from shore to shore.

Late in the afternoon Mrs. Rawlings turned toward Cross Creek. We left the scrub and crossed the Oklawaha River where the red of swamp maples ran for miles down either bank. And as we rode along Charles Darwin's lament came to mind. "It is the fate of most voyagers," Darwin wrote during his naturalist's journey around the world on the *Beagle*, "no sooner to discover what is most interesting in any locality than they are hurried from it." On our trip with a season we longed for a separate spring in a hundred different places. But we had only one spring, a season that was always flooding ahead of us, and we must hurry on. Our regret for this shortness of time was often keen. But nowhere was it more acute than at the close of this swiftly-passing day in the Florida scrub.

EIGHT

DIAMONDBACKS

ACROSS the road from our cabin at Ocala a multi-hued village on wheels extended away under the trees of a trailer camp. An Ohio family, Reginald G. Thorpe, his wife, and two small children, David and Holly, lived in one of the trailers. We came to know them well. Thorpe was in his mid-thirties, a mild-mannered man whose days were spent in hair-raising adventure. He was a diamondback hunter for Ross Allen's Reptile Institute at Silver Springs.

Half a dozen times on back roads, in lonely, out-of-the-way places, we had seen signs nailed to fence posts or tacked to rickety porches. They read: "Snakes Bought Here For Ross Allen." Every few weeks a light truck makes a 500-mile circuit of these collecting stations to pick up a new load of reptiles. More than 150,000 diamondbacks, as well as several hundred thousand cottonmouths, coral snakes, and other serpents, have been collected for Allen by natives and by a few professional hunters like Reg Thorpe.

In the mind of the average man a professional rattlesnake catcher is pictured as some ignorant, unshaved, uneducated native driven by extreme and desperate want to risk his life recklessly. Reg Thorpe was none of these things. He was a cultured, thoughtful. well-educated man. During the war he had been head of a plant near Cleveland, Ohio, where military machines were weatherproofed. At the war's end he was able to retire for a time and do what he wanted to do—hunt Florida diamondbacks. He had always been interested in natural history, especially reptiles. He had studied snakes scientifically. He had studied their ways, their temperaments, the effects of weather and surroundings on them. His dangerous business was for him a game of calculated risks.

"Some of the best rattlesnake country in Florida," he told us one evening, "is around Cross City above the mouth of the Suwannee. I'm driving up tomorrow. How would you like to come along and watch me catch a diamondback?"

We started early. Thorpe is a collector who has collectors collecting for him. So along the way we stopped to pick up snakes and turtles and lizards that were duly stored in bags and jars in the trunk of the car. A minister at Horseshoe is one of his spare-time snake catchers, adding to his meager salary by hunting diamondbacks on the side. A major in World War I is another. And when we pulled off the dirt road beyond the River Styx and stopped near a low cabin set in a clearing amid palmettos and moss-hung pines, a swarm of children poured forth to greet Thorpe as an all-year-round Santa Claus.

While he exchanged nickels and dimes and quarters for box turtles, scaly-backed lizards, and green grass snakes, the children raced about the clearing, hunting up creatures they had captured on previous days. Chickens flew. Pigs scattered. Kittens scampered. One black-and-white kitten attracted our attention in the midst of this melee. It possessed superabundant energy. It pounced on a box turtle. It rolled over and over as it tackled a black piglet larger than itself. It seemed devoid of fear. And near the conclusion of our visit we almost saw the end of its venturesome little life.

A 5-foot diamondback had been left for Thorpe in a metal drum near the cabin. He fished it out at the end of his snake stick. The children screeched and scattered. Estimating its length, Thorpe placed the angry rattler momentarily on the ground. The black-and-white kitten was fascinated. It pranced toward the buzzing reptile. Its world was a world of play, and playfully it crouched to spring on the ugly lance-head moving toward it on the ground. Its life was saved by a kick from the bare foot of the oldest boy. It sailed footballwise through the air and somersaulted unharmed onto a pile of Spanish moss. No instinctive warning had made the kitten pause. Its unsuspecting approach revealed that it had inherited no appreciation of the menace of poison fangs. The fear of venomous serpents, for it, was acquired wisdom rather than inborn knowledge.

In Cross City Thorpe had rented a vacant store opposite the post office as a storage depot and collecting center. We climbed from the car and walked across a sidewalk littered with peanut shells. They had been dropped there the night before when patrons of the local theater, a few doors away, had stopped to peer through the windows at caged snakes within. A thin man with a knotted gunny sack at his feet leaned against the door. The sack contained two large land tortoises, one of which promptly bit Thorpe on the thumb. Asked about snakes, the native drawled:

"There's jest two kind of snakes I don't like."

"What ones are they?"

"Big snakes and little snakes!"

As for Thorpe, snakes do not bother him except late at night in an automobile. Sometimes he has nightmares about being in a smashup with a load of diamondbacks. At least once that nightmare came close to becoming a reality. Speeding down a narrow side road after a long and wearying day, with more than a dozen diamondbacks tied in bags in the back of the car, he dozed off. When he snapped awake his right wheels were riding the lip of a deep roadside ditch. In a smashup, if the snakes didn't bite him, he is sure nobody would come to his rescue with a dozen diamondbacks crawling about the car.

One of Ross Allen's other collectors told me an experience almost as hair-raising. After a day of climbing over rocky ledges in the mountains of a northern state he found himself at night far from his car and with several bags of rattlesnakes on his hands. He decided to sleep in a cave. Carefully placing the bags at the far side of the cavern he lay down, and was soon fast asleep, at the other side. He had not noticed, however, that the floor of the cave slanted slightly downward. As he moved about in his sleep he gradually worked down the incline until he awoke in the morning snuggled up among the bags of venomous serpents.

As we drove west from Cross City, following wheel tracks into wild pine and palmetto country, Thorpe recalled several small snakes that had got loose in his car. Once he discovered a young hog-nosed snake twined about the clutch pedal. Another time, as he was driving home late at night, he felt a tickling along his right leg. In the dim light of the instrument panel he made out the tail of a slender snake disappearing into his trouser leg. It looked like the coral snake he had caught that day. Drop for drop, the neurotoxic venom of a coral snake is more deadly than that of any other North American serpent. It bites and chews like a cobra rather than striking like a diamondback. Consequently, it has to secure a hold on some small surface like a finger or toe. Relying on this fact, Thorpe took a chance. He shook the reptile out of his pants leg. To his great relief he saw it was a harmless chicken snake.

When he first came to Florida, Thorpe had long arguments with natives who maintained that garter snakes are poisonous. Then he discovered that in this region—where turtles are called "gophers" and gophers are called "salamanders" and lizards are called "scorpions" and scorpions are called "stinging lizards" and the peeping of the oak toad is known as the "call of the blacksnake"—the coral snake is known as the "garter snake."

The coral snake is justly feared. But it is the diamondback that is supreme. To the Seminoles the diamondback was the Great King. To Texans it is the Lord of the Night. To scientists it is the biggest rattlesnake on earth, the world's most powerful pit viper. It exceeds both in body-bulk and poison-gland capacity the famed bushmaster of the tropics. While the bushmaster is longer, sometimes exceeding ten feet, it lacks the thick-bodied solidity of the Florida rattler. The biggest diamondback on record measured 8 feet 9 inches. However, few exceed seven feet. For years Ross Allen, who pays collectors a dollar a foot for live diamondbacks, has had a standing offer of $100 for an 8-foot rattlesnake. None of the 150,000 he has received has come up to this mark.

When Thorpe stopped his car we were in a wild region, blank on any map of Florida. Around us stretched blackened ground. A fire had swept across a wide stretch of palmetto and pine stumps. Dotting this blackened earth with spots of white were a score or more mounds of sand. Each marked the entrance to a "gopher" hole. Fully 50 per cent of Thorpe's rattlers are found in the abandoned tunnels of these land tortoises. Dry sinkholes and caverns under decaying stumps are other favorite homes of diamondbacks. The tunnels most favored are those in open fields near the edges of woods. Here the reptiles lie in hiding during the day, sliding forth to hunt at night. After a fire Thorpe examines every gopher hole for diamondbacks.

We helped him unload his collecting equipment from the back of the car. First came a cloth bag and a length of wire, then a long-handled net, suggesting a butterfly net with the bag made of stout canvas, and finally a snake stick, resembling a long broom handle ending in a steel crook that looked like a letter "U" laid on its side. These were the tools of his dangerous trade. One other piece of equipment, probably the most important of all, was already in place. This was a pair of thick, $44 snakeproof boots that encased Thorpe's feet and lower legs. Formed of specially tanned moosehide, extra thick, extra tough, extending almost to his knees, they were impervious to the fangs of the biggest diamondback. A compact snakebite kit, ready for emergency use, bulged out one of his hip pockets.

Searching the ground and stepping with care, we followed Thorpe across the "burn" from gopher hole to gopher hole.

Our watchful progress brought to mind our old friend, William T. Davis, the Staten Island naturalist, and one of his sayings: "No doubt rattlesnakes have benefited men by making them more observing. While on the lookout for snakes, they may see some of the other wonders of the world." Here, however, there were few wonders to see, only charred palmetto stems and the black ashes of grass. By the same token, there was no lurking place for a serpent in the open. The greatest danger in this area comes in summer, when diamondbacks are in the habit of sunning themselves in palmetto thickets, stretched out two and a half or three feet from the ground. Pushing his way through thick palmetto at this time of year, the man who comes suddenly upon one of these elevated serpents is likely to be struck in the side where tourniquets are impossible and where the poison reaches vital organs almost immediately.

At each white mound of sand Thorpe stopped to look for the telltale track of a serpent leading into the tunnel. When one was found beside a weathered pine stump, he stopped up the mouth of the hole with rags and continued his search. There are several ways of getting diamondbacks out of gopher holes. One is digging them out. As the holes are deep, this is the most laborious of all. Another is drowning them out. As it often takes 200 gallons to flush out a diamondback, this procedure is almost as laborious as digging. A third method of routing out a rattler is by lowering a smoke bomb at the end of a 20-foot cable. Far simpler than any of these, and just as effective, is the method Thorpe employs most often. This is simply stuffing a wad of cloth into the opening of the tunnel. Diamondbacks seem to suffer from claustrophobia. They dislike being shut up. They move close to the blocked-up entrance and later, when the plug is removed, the snakes soon crawl out into the open.

This happened at the hole by the pine stump. Hardly eight minutes went by after the rags were cautiously removed before the flat head, the lidless eyes, the flickering tongue of a pit viper appeared at the opening. It was followed by five and a half feet of black and yellow-brown body ending in the gray of the horny rattle. Thorpe, snake stick ready, stepped toward it. The rattler coiled. It stood its ground. Its tail blurred in a buzz of menace. Thorpe took another step. The scaly body tightened into steel-spring tautness. Another step. The forebody arched upward. The triangular head lifted. It turned toward Thorpe, remained taut, unmoving, aimed like a poised lance.

The shark in the sea, the tiger on the land, the vampire bat in the night, all these are creatures of menace and dread. But the lifted head of a large diamondback is death in its most visible form. The lidless eye of the pit viper, to most people, is a personification of malevolence and evil. Deliberately, step by step, Thorpe moved in. His right hand extended the snake stick. His left gripped the handle of the net, holding its open mouth toward the reptile. Thus man and snake faced each other. This was an old story for Thorpe but it had the palms of our hands wet with nervous perspiration.

The strident buzzing of the coiled serpent rose to a higher pitch. Travelers' stories of these snakes "with bells on their tails" were received with incredulity when they first reached Europe. William Bartram was greatly impressed by the "fair warning" of the diamondback. To him it was a gentleman serpent, "the magnanimous rattle-snake." Modern studies have tempered that judgment. They show that not infrequently a diamondback lashes out without previous warning. These snakes, incidentally, cannot hear whether they rattle or not. For diamondbacks are deaf.

A yard from the coiled serpent, just out of striking range, Thorpe stopped. The metal crook of his snake stick began sliding toward the rattler. The pit viper drew back its head, cocking its venom gun, setting it on a hair trigger. Its body lifted in a higher arc. The stick continued its advance. There was a lash of black and yellow-brown as the rattler struck. It pulled itself back and reared again. The metal U was sliding under its coils. The white net was moving in from the left. It drove the lance point of its head at the advancing canvas and trickles of orange-yellow venom ran down the cloth. One of Thorpe's booted feet moved closer. The diamondback slashed in its direction. On each strike it gaped its mouth wide, tilted its head far back, thrust its fangs straight ahead, twin hypodermic needles charged with haemotoxic venom. The fangs sank into the leather of the boot but failed to pierce it. The snake slithered backward to coil once more.

But now Thorpe had the crook of his stick under its body. He began to lift it from the ground. Its tail became a blurred fan in its frenzy of buzzing. Its head swung from side to side. Its forked tongue flickered in and out, searching for its mysterious enemy. And thus it reached the edge of the collecting net. As it slid in tail first, its weight tipped down the rim of the net. Before Thorpe could twist the handle and fold over the top of the canvas bag, the flat, menacing head of the rattlesnake slipped swiftly outward. The snake's body lengthened over the edge, flowing with a terrifying glide that made the hairs tingle across my scalp.

Holding the net away from his body, Thorpe slid the metal crook of his snake stick forward, seeking to draw back the escaping serpent. The rattler glided effortlessly through the U of metal. When almost half its length was extended straight out in mid-air, it stopped. Afraid of falling, it balanced itself on the crook, swinging from side to side, still seeking its mysterious foe. But the struggle was running against it. Slowly, carefully, Thorpe worked it back until most of its weight was over the open mouth of the net. Then he lowered the snake stick suddenly. The rattler slid backward, disappearing into the canvas bag. Thorpe gave a quick twist to the net handle. The top of the bag overlapped itself and the diamondback was imprisoned within. Nellie and I let out a long breath.

"It really isn't hard," Thorpe said. "And there isn't much danger connected with it." We started to join him in a laugh at this understatement. Then we saw he really meant it.

One sign of spring in Florida diamondback country, he told us, is an increase in the number of trails crossing sand roads. The snakes begin roaming about more in the spring. They are cold-blooded creatures, active when warmed, sluggish when chilled. During cold spells in Florida the diamondbacks remain dormant for days at a time. But they do not hibernate and they never den up, collecting in masses in caves and rocky crevices, as do rattlers in the North.

This habit of northern snakes, together with the paralyzing effect of cold, was made use of in a curious way on Cape Ann, in Massachusetts, a century or so ago. In the 1840's a man by the name of James Hildreth won renown by ridding the community of Manchester of rattlesnakes. In winter he would build huge fires around the rocks where the rattlers had denned up in the fall. Stimulated by the increasing warmth, the reptiles would awaken from their torpor and crawl to the mouth of the den. As each appeared, Hildreth flipped it with a stick onto a neighboring snowbank where it quickly chilled into rigid helplessness.

Within its canvas bag our diamondback had quieted down. We could see the cloth molded over its stout body as it lay passive. It was tired from its struggle. It had expended much of its venom on the net, the snake stick, and Thorpe's moosehide boots. The calculated risks of catching it were now reduced. I was just thinking of this when Thorpe asked:

"Why don't I let it go and you catch it?"

Common sense had a ready answer for that one.

But it was not common sense that spoke. It was the voice of none other than myself and to my amazement the voice was saying quite calmly:

"All right. I'd like to."

Thorpe tumbled the diamondback out onto the ground. It

whirred and pulled itself into a tight coil. Then it became silent and watchful. The snake stick and net were in my hands. I noticed that the wood of their handles was impregnated with a curious, penetrating, snaky odor. I could smell it on my fingers for days afterwards.

Keeping well out of range, with the net as a shield between me and the coiled rattler, I cautiously advanced the snake stick. The metal U touched one of the coils. The snake came to life in an explosion of black and yellow-brown. It had both fight and venom left. Again and again I slipped the crook of the snake stick beneath its tensed body, lifting it toward the net. Each time it dodged or slipped from the metal U. Five minutes went by before the top of the bag twisted shut, imprisoning the rattler within.

Paradoxically, those five minutes came as an unprepared-for anticlimax. Perhaps it was because, like an artilleryman in battle, I was concentrating to the exclusion of everything else on the work at hand. Or it may have been because my emotions had tired, as muscles tire, and I was less capable of responding to thrills. At any rate, diamondback catching experienced first-hand seemed less exciting, less dangerous than the feat had appeared when Thorpe was in action. The rattler struck half a dozen times. It lashed ahead. It jabbed to the side. But my confidence grew as the minutes passed. The outcome was sure. I even felt nonchalant as I steered the rattlesnake closer to the net. That is the way I felt inside. But that is not the way I looked outside. The snapshot Nellie took at the time shows the world's most worried-looking snake catcher in action.

Half a century ago a Florida guide became celebrated for picking up, barehanded, coiled rattlesnakes in the palmetto scrub. With widespread feet well out of striking range, he would lean over the diamondback. Holding its attention by fluttering a bandanna handkerchief at the end of his extended left arm, he would slowly lower his right hand directly above the coils until he was able to seize the serpent just behind the head. A rattler can strike ahead. It can strike to the side. But it rarely strikes upward. Because of this fact, deer and horses are able to trample or cut to ribbons a coiled diamondhead with impunity, simply by rearing up and bringing their forelegs straight down on the head and body of the serpent.

Before Thorpe finally transferred the rattlesnake to the carrying bag, wired the top tightly shut, and loaded it into the trunk of the car for the trip back to Cross City, he demonstrated this reluctance of a diamondback to drive its fangs upward. Lowering his right hand slowly above the coiled serpent, he extended a forefinger and scratched the top of its head.

"Do you want to try that?" he asked me.

Both common sense and I answered at once.

And our answers were the same.

NINE

LAKE OF THE FLOATING ISLANDS

FLOATING islands—like geysers, volcanoes, underground rivers, and disappearing lakes—are natural phenomena that verge on the miraculous. So it was with special interest that we turned down a side road the next morning, a dozen miles south of Gainesville, and drove east to Orange Lake. This crooked, 16-mile-long body of water, curving from north to east like an irregular quarter-moon, is celebrated for islands that float on the surface of the water and drift about with the wind. Each unanchored raft of land is like a continent in miniature. It is freighted with various forms of animal life, with plants and bushes and even trees. It moves about supporting a fauna and flora of its own.

In brilliant morning sunshine we stopped in front of a weathered building covered with a kind of thatching of Spanish moss. This building, on the west shore of Orange Lake, is the makeshift headquarters of a remarkable one-man nature center. More than a decade before, Don McKay, a slender naturalist in his late thirties, had obtained a toe hold of land at the spot. Born on a ranch a hundred miles west of Oklahoma City, McKay had first heard of floating islands while in the navy. They had attracted him to Orange Lake. Here he was making a career of showing them, and the wildlife around them, to visitors.

Gradually his toe hold had been widened. When we visited him he owned 400 feet of frontage at one of the few landing places along the shore. Solar heaters of his own invention had financed his project. In spare time he had built and sold some two hundred devices of the kind for using the sun's rays to heat water for Florida homes. Sun-power heaters had also provided money for building a singular naturalist's boat in which McKay carries parties to visit the drifting islands of the lake.

This craft is flat bottomed and scow shaped, 26 feet long and 9 wide. With 25 passengers aboard it can navigate in water hardly more than two feet deep. Each square-cut end terminates in steps. These permit passengers to descend to floating islands or to examine at close range the vegetation along their edges. A solid platform extends over the boat to provide an upper deck where nature photographers can work unhampered. The craft is provided with a tunnel stern that aids in navigating among the shallows. McKay designed and built the boat himself. When a shipyard asked $3,500 for constructing the craft, McKay read books on boatbuilding and, in a year and a half and at a cost of less than $1,000, produced it on the edge of Orange Lake.

We mounted the steps of this curious passenger craft and McKay started the Gray motor. Guiding the craft with a home-made tiller formed of 1-inch steel piping fitted together with plumber's joints, he steered away from the moss-hung cypress trees along the shore and followed a lane through water hyacinths and spatterdock out into the open water.

As soon as the motor went into action, ring-billed gulls and boat-tailed grackles came flying from all directions. On every trip, McKay throws pieces of stale bread overboard, training the birds to follow him. He has noticed that shy birds will let the boat come much closer when it is surrounded by an escort of gulls. At one point for instance we nosed up to within a dozen feet of an American bittern on the edge of an island. For miles the birds followed us, as many as thirty ring-billed gulls at a time milling about the boat. Among them was a single Bonaparte's, smaller, white-winged, marked with black spots on either side of the head. At first a dozen boat-tailed grackles and four or five coot competed with the gulls for the bread. One of these grackles had the appearance of a spindle with wings. It had lost, for the time being—in some accident— the long-keeled boattail that normally extends so far to the rear. It was able to fly and balance itself in the air but it had lost its ability to stop or turn suddenly. Again and again it would overshoot its mark and, speeding in a wide turn, see some other bird dart down, turn, stop, and snatch the food from the water.

We soon left behind the grackles, all except one. It followed us for miles, hovering, calling, alighting to rest on little floating buoys of water hyacinths, walking over lily pads, competing with the gulls for food, actually alighting on the water and fluttering up again in its eagerness to snatch the bread McKay tossed from the boat. Once, as we neared an island, it out-raced three pursuing gulls and reached safety with a crust in its bill.

Orange Lake has an estimated breeding population of about 1,500 boat-tailed grackles. It represents a center of population for them. Wherever we went among the larger, stationary islands, spring was apparent in the behavior of these birds. Male grackles were riding on the giant bulrushes, seesawing up and down, facing each other, swelling their breasts, drooping their tails, lifting their bills skyward and uttering a series of squeaks and squawks and chattering noises whenever a female appeared. Among these grackles the females outnumber the males and are the ones that do the selecting of mates. Springtime mating, with all its curious manifestations, was occurring among the grackles of Orange Lake that day. The males postured in groups, competing for the eye of the passing female. Sometimes they all rushed with laboring wings into the air to pursue a female that had swept close. In all the instances we observed the females outdistanced the males and the latter returned to their posturing again. If one of her pursuers is found attractive, the female swoops down beside him. Immediately all the other males give up the chase. Once mating is over, the paired birds part. The female alone builds the nest and rears the young.

On several occasions McKay worked the boat so close to a group of males striking their statuesque poses among the bulrushes that we were able to see through our glasses the golden or brownish color of their eyes as contrasted with the whitish eye of the boattails of the eastern coast. Just after one group had rushed in pursuit of a female and then had wheeled back to settle again, a wood ibis flew over us, scratching its head with an awkward foot as it sailed by. Among the low trees of one of the larger stationary islands we saw the masses of sticks that formed the nests of ibis and anhingas. These latter birds, with long necks and widespread tails, hurried this way and that over the trees, alternately flapping and sailing. Among them, as among the redwings of the neighboring cattails and the purple gallinules feeding on arum seeds, the season was spring, a time of activity stepped up, the exciting start of a whole new cycle of life.

The floating islands, in their own individual way, also reflected the coming of spring. They were riding higher, becoming more buoyant. During winter months some had even sunk below the water with only their bushes visible above the surface. Production of the gases of decomposition that keep these land rafts afloat is stimulated by the increasing warmth of the advancing spring.

Floating islands have been reported from many parts of the world. In Chile, in 1834, Charles Darwin visited the celebrated mountain lake, Tagua-Tagua, where unmoored islands, usually circular in shape and from 4 to 6 feet thick, were formed of the stalks of dead plants intertwined, on the upper surface of which seeds had sprouted and plants developed. Ferried by the wind, these islands drifted from one side of the lake to the other.

Some were so large they transported cattle and horses from shore to shore.

More than 2,300 years ago, the first written record of a floating island was set down by the Greek historian Herodotus. Next came Pliny the Elder with a chapter devoted to "Floating and Swimming Islands" in his *Natural History*. It is Pliny who reports a battle in Asia Minor in which soldiers escaped on a floating island by poling themselves across a small lake to the opposite shore.

When Henry Thoreau and his brother, John, were rowing up the Merrimack River, in 1839, they stopped at the mouth of Salmon Brook to rest. There they met a talkative haymaker whose mind was stocked with tales of bottomless ponds and floating islands. Always nomad islands have appealed to the imagination and frequently they have been viewed with superstitious reverence. In Greek mythology, the birthplace of Apollo and Artemis was the drifting island of Delos. Seminole Indians, in the early days, believed that the souls of the dead buried on the floating islands of Orange Lake went to the "Land of the Sure" when the islands sank.

Both Henry W. Bates, in his *The Naturalist on the Amazons*, and H. M. Tomlinson, in *The Sea and the Jungle*, tell of observing islands of vegetation drifting from the interior down the Amazon toward the ocean. Similar land rafts descend the Congo and the Nile and the Ganges. Some represent a fragment of the jungle. They are covered with trees and bushes and even carry wild animals for long distances. In a single night, during pioneer times in Montevideo, Uruguay, drifting islands that had descended the flooded Paraná River landed four South American tigers in the vicinity of the town. Occasionally these river-borne islands ride the waves far out to sea. Charles Lyell, in his famed *Principles of Geology*, tells of derelict islands being sighted from fifty to a hundred miles out from the mouth of the Ganges.

The most dramatic instance of a seagoing island occurred in 1893. In the spring of that year a ship sighted a land mass drifting in the Gulf Stream off the coast of Florida. Almost two acres in extent, with trees rising as high as 30 feet, it was visible from a distance of 7 miles. Its subsequent wanderings are preserved in government records. Traveling slowly northward in the Gulf Stream, it reached the latitude of Wilmington, Delaware, by the latter part of July. A month later ships sighted it on a line with Cape Cod. It slowly veered toward the Grand Banks and then followed the steamer lanes toward Europe. By September it was in mid-ocean and, when last sighted, this island Ulysses had wandered to a position northwest of the Azores. Whether it eventually reached the coast of Europe or broke up in the October gales no one knows.

This was an unusually large and strongly knit-together island. Most unanchored isles are small. And, although old records tell of instances in which they have lasted for more than a century, most are short lived. They come into being in a number of ways. In small mountain tarns of the north, sphagnum moss occasionally forms such dense, thick mats that they will support the weight of a man. Along the steeply sloping sides of northern ponds, a shelf of sphagnum occasionally is reinforced with cattails, Labrador tea and pitcher plants. Such water-loving shrubs as sweet gale, cassandra, high blueberry, sheep laurel, and wild rosemary help bind together the spongy mass of the sphagnum. A sudden rise in water level breaks off the mass and sets it adrift on the pond. In some instances, when such a shelf extends from shore all around a small circular pond, high water loosens it all at the same time so that a ring or doughnut or atoll of vegetable matter is set afloat.

Sudden changes in water level are almost always needed for the production of floating islands. During the building of the Panama Canal the construction of Gatun Dam flooded the swampy area of the Chagres River and caused loose vegetable matter, small trees, logs, and branches to drift about in Gatun

Lake. On these tangled masses grass and plants began to grow. Eventually these derelict islands formed a menace to navigation in the canal and had to be dynamited and destroyed by government engineers. The most extensive collection of this kind was probably the great raft of driftwood that clogged the Atchafalaya, an arm of the lower Mississippi, about the time of the American Revolution.

For a distance of 10 miles, the massed timbers formed a solid roof, 8 feet thick, over the 600-foot-wide river. Pioneers used it for forty years as a natural bridge in crossing from side to side. Although this decaying mass supported a luxurious vegetation and even trees that reached a height of 60 feet, it rose and fell with movements of the water beneath it. In the early eighteen hundreds, when the great raft was destroyed in order to restore navigation on the river, the work required four years.

In lower Louisiana and in the great Okefenokee Swamp of the Georgia-Florida line the quaking bogs of the North have their counterpart on a vaster scale. Water underlies the spongy land, affecting its stability. Okefenokee means the "Land of the Trembling Earth" and the Creole swampers in Louisiana named certain sections of their region *prairies tremblantes*. Suddenly raise the water level in such an area and floating islands are born.

This happened in spectacular fashion in the spring of 1903, when a break in the west-bank levee, 37 miles above New Orleans, poured a flood of Mississippi water into the great Des Allemands Swamp which stretches, with its network of lakes and bayous, 150 miles to the Gulf of Mexico. The *prairies tremblantes*, built up of logs, branches, leaves, and vegetable mold over the centuries, tore free in irregular sections to form hundreds of floating islands. The spongy soil, filled with the gases of decay, had a depth of six or eight feet. It was held together by interlacing roots. These islands, many bearing large trees, drifted with the flooding water toward the Gulf.

In the lakes of the swamp their shifting about altered the landscape from hour to hour. Many descended the Bayou des Allemands, endangering the bridge of the Southern Pacific. For weeks a large force of men was kept busy dynamiting the islands into fragments before they reached the bridge. When the land rafts entered smaller bayous they dammed them up, flooding the surrounding country.

In keeping floating islands buoyant, a leading role is played by minute bacteria, working in and between the cells of decaying vegetable matter. They produce CH_4, methane, the swamp gas that is thought to provide, by spontaneous combustion, the eerie glow of the will-o'-the-wisp. This gas increases with the increased activity of the bacteria in the spring. It reaches its maximum in summer, sinks to its minimum in winter. Moreover, the gas expands with heat, contracts with cold. In consequence a few islands are periodic. They appear and disappear according to the activity of the bacteria; rise above the surface with an increase in their gas content, sink out of sight when it is reduced. In some rare instances floating islands have been so delicately balanced that they appeared during the day and disappeared at night. Experiments have indicated that the bacteria begin manufacturing methane when the water temperature rises to 60 degrees F. Because spring is a time of both rising water and rising temperature, it is the season when most floating islands come into being. Lambs and colts and baby chicks—and floating islands—are born in the spring.

But this does not necessarily hold true at Orange Lake. The buoyant islands of this shallow body of water, McKay told us, are produced in a different manner from any of those previously considered. He swung the boat into a patch of lily pads, one of many such patches we encountered on the lake. Each is a potential floating island. The great, spongy, gas-filled roots of the spatterdock crisscross in the mud of the bottom to form an interlacing mat. Later we examined some of these roots. More than a foot in circumference and extending, sometimes, for more than twenty feet, they suggested large pipes or water mains running beneath the mud of the lake bottom. During severe storms the pounding of the water in the shallow lake will sometimes break loose one of these mats of spatterdock roots. Rising to the surface, it brings with it a great raft of black, humus-laden mud, rich soil that is quickly crowned with vegetation. As this vegetation decays, it in turn produces gas that adds to the buoyancy of the island.

McKay once saw half a dozen floating islands pop up to the surface almost at the same instant. He was clearing a channel near the mouth of Cross Creek, at the northern end of Orange Lake. A stick of dynamite, detonated on the lake bottom, jarred loose rafts of spatterdock roots over a considerable area. One burst to the surface just ahead of McKay's boat. He reversed the engine and looked back in time to see another pop up just behind him. Bream and speckled perch were attracted to the spot by dislodged particles of food. For hours the fish concentrated in the area.

Fish and floating islands seem to go together. Perhaps the land rafts provide a place of shelter as well as a place of food. Half a century ago, in Sadawga Lake, near Whitingham, Vermont, an unanchored island was a favorite spot for local anglers. They cut holes in the island and dropped down their lines to enjoy the summer counterpart of fishing through the ice. Sometimes, at Orange Lake, anglers will become so engrossed in fishing in some bay of an island that they will not notice the approach of a drifting islet until it has bottled them up, turning the bay into a lake temporarily surrounded by land.

To meet emergencies of this kind, McKay carries a long crosscut saw on board. Twice he has had to saw through a small island to release his boat. The thickness of the land rafts ranges from two to five feet. Black and peaty, the wet mud stings like fire when it touches the skin in summertime. This is probably the result of acids produced by decomposition. Once a helper of McKay's stepped on a thin place on a floating island and plunged into five feet of water, emerging black with mud from head to foot.

The wind was blowing from the east on one of the days we visited Orange Lake and all the floating islands were drifting west. On a subsequent stop there the wind was from the west and the fleet of unmoored islands was moving toward the east. A few weeks before, an itinerant island had remained for several days near McKay's landing. Then winds from the north and west had begun to drift it away and now it had disappeared entirely. On several occasions McKay has tried anchoring down small land rafts with cables and concrete blocks. The result is always the same. In the first storm the cables tear away. Once he carried the steel cable over the whole top of the island and anchored it on either side. As soon as the waves began rocking the land raft the cable sawed it in two, slicing downward with the ease of a wire cutting through cheese. About a mile from shore we passed one floating island that had the appearance of an atoll. Its center had sunk and the depression was filled with water; it was a floating island with a floating lake in the middle of it.

Here and there on the surface of the lake we encountered 5- and 6-foot sections of spatterdock roots floating like life preservers or buoys. McKay fished one out. Scars, showing points of cleavage where stems had broken away, gave the root the appearance of being braided like a rawhide whiplash. McKay pulled up one of the stems as we passed through a stretch of water strewn with the immense green hearts of the floating water-lily leaves. It looked like a smooth green hose and measured eight feet long. The longest stem McKay has encountered had a length of 12 feet. A few of the water-lily buds, giants in comparison with those of northern plants, were already showing the waxy buttercup yellow of the unfolding petals. The height of the blooming season for the spatterdock of Orange Lake is April.

With the motor eased down, McKay swung the squared-off

nose of the boat up on the edge of one of the drifting islands. Years ago, when he first came to Orange Lake, he pulled up beside a similar island in a small boat and, assuming without thinking about it that it—like other islands—had a shelving beach, jumped off into the water over his head. The scow-like prow of our boat pushed through the outer fringes of water hyacinths, water lettuce, arum, cattails, smartweed, and saw-grass up onto solid ground. We climbed out to walk about on a floating island.

The sensation was a little like advancing across a circus acrobat's net. The ground gave slightly beneath us at every step. It seemed to rise and fall as we advanced. Here was a Land of the Trembling Earth in miniature. Each footfall set the plants quivering. The strength of the mat of interlacing roots seemed to determine the firmness of our footing. Once McKay's left foot found a soft spot and his leg shot downward into soft mud up to his knee.

Everywhere around us familiar plants appeared in giant form. The stalks of last year's goldenrod rose almost as high as Nellie's head. Bulrushes lifted the curving green needles of their stems eight feet in the air. The summer before, brown-eyed Susans had nodded at the top of stems six feet high. On both the stationary and floating islands of Orange Lake rich soil and plentiful moisture combine to stimulate rapid plant growth. We stopped beside a last year's pigweed. It rose like a bushy tree. Its tip was fully 10 feet in the air and its bulging base was so great that my two hands reached less than half around it. Boat-tailed grackles alighted on this pigweed, as on the branches of a tree, to perform their mating antics. Nearby we came upon the moldering remains of an alligator nest, one of the few McKay had seen recently. Air-driven boats, carrying hunters everywhere, have led to the virtual extirpation of the saurians at Orange Lake.

Getting out his one-handed cross cut saw, McKay sliced into the island. Near the site of the pigweed the land raft had a thickness of about three and a half feet. Later in the year it would support masses of blooming loosestrife and spider lilies. One mass of lily plants formed an unbroken carpet almost thirty feet across. When the white flowers of such massed plants are blooming, their heavy scent carries far over the water; the perfumed islands drifting through the darkness can be detected a long way off.

Sometimes, McKay told us, swamp rabbits elude pursuing dogs or wildcats by swimming out to floating islands. There they often find dangerous sanctuary. For during the summer cottonmouth moccasins are active and lying in wait. Floating islands are also a basking place for turtles. Clambering out of the water, they lie for hours at a time motionless in the sunshine. Of all the creatures, big and little, that are associated with the roving islands of Orange Lake none have more unusual adventures than birds that place their nests in bushes or trees that alter their position from day to day. Like the tree swallows that, some years ago, built their nest on a ferryboat crossing the St. Lawrence at Ogdensburg, New York, or like the female robin that, near my home, was nesting in a tree in a nursery when the tree was dug up and transported 20 miles with the robin still sitting on the eggs, the females of the Orange Lake birds raise their fledglings in a nest that doesn't stay put. They are able to keep track of it because the islands drift slowly, changing position gradually, and because the period of nest building, egg laying, brooding, and caring for the nestlings is relatively short.

Buttonball and elderberry bushes were crowded together in clumps on some of the islands. Once, toward sunset on our last day at the lake, we skirted a sunken island, 100 feet across, riding a couple of feet below the surface with only the upper part of the bushes visible. It had dropped lower and lower during the winter months; with warmer weather it would gain in buoyancy again. Here and there among the islands the season was reflected in new leaves expanding, turning the twigtips green on elderberry bushes and sapling willows. Everywhere the record of spring was being written in green ink—the green of chlorophyll.

Many of the elderberry bushes rose to a height of seven or eight feet. A young willow, rooted to one floating island, stood head and shoulders above the highest shrubs. McKay has seen a cypress 12 feet tall on one island, and a solidly rooted water maple 18 feet tall on another. In certain rare instances a tree may become too large for the island to support. A water maple reached a diameter of more than a foot. Then suddenly the ground gave way beneath it. It plunged downward a dozen feet to the bottom of the lake, tearing a hole from the center of the island, its top rising from the opening like a twig thrust through the hole of a floating doughnut.

Usually a different fate overtakes the tree and the island. A leafy tree is like a spread sail. Rising above a small island, it is sometimes caught by gusts during wind storms and the whole island is capsized like a boat. We ran beside a floating island which had one side curled up as though a giant plow had turned a furrow there. All the trees and bushes along that edge lay flat, pointing inland. They had gone down in a sudden gust and the strength of their roots had wrenched the edge of the land raft up and over in their wake.

During our days at Orange Lake, days we wished might have been weeks, the wind was light, ruffling the water and drifting the islands at an almost imperceptible rate. As we turned west toward the landing, on that last day, we were moving in the same direction as the land rafts. And in that movement history was repeating itself after a hundred years.

In *Letters From the Frontiers*, an account of army life in the South in pioneer days, Major General George A. McCall recounts his first impression of this lake of moving islands, seen about the middle of the last century. Ending the story of a march through northern Florida, he writes:

"We reached the shore of Orange Lake, that fairyland of

gorgeous vegetation. What a charming view was presented to my eyes! As the sun was past the meridian, I lingered only a few minutes to look at a green island which at a distance of half a mile raised its head above the bright waters. The following morning, I looked out upon the lake when, to my no little surprise, the island I had observed the previous day had disappeared and, on further examination, the water of the lake seemed to have receded from the shore nearly a hundred yards. It was not until I walked down to the lake that I discovered that the island I had noticed the day before had drifted with the wind against the shore where I stood. These floating islands, as I afterwards learned, are found in many parts of Orange Lake."

The spot where General McCall and his soldiers encamped apparently was not far from the landing, under moss-hung cypress trees, where McKay's "floating-island boat" nosed up on the shore. The wind that day, as on the day of the general's visit, was bringing the nomad islands in its direction.

As we jumped ashore we heard a sound that carried us worlds away from the cypress trees and the Spanish moss around us. In one swift rush we were transported far to the north, to mountain lakes and lonely forest ponds in Maine. The sound was the call of a northern loon. The migrating bird, so strangely out of place, had been found slightly injured beside the highway. During our absence someone had left it near the landing, confined within a circle of corrugated tin.

We crowded around. Even as we looked, and it stared back with glowing ruby eyes, the bird lifted its head slightly and, hardly opening its bill, uttered a long, low, sad, flutelike call, a kind of whisper song that ended in a dying cadence. It caught at the heart. How many times have we thought of it since, that cry of imprisoned wildness! And the memory of its strangeness has become blended with memories of the strangeness of a lake which, with its independent, unanchored islands, represents in its own way a spirit wild and untamed too.

TEN

LIMPKIN RIVER

THE hands of my watch pointed in opposite directions—
the minute hand straight up, the hour hand straight down.
We watched the minute hand. It crept to 1, plodded to 2,
passed the third minute mark beyond. At that instant, at thirteen minutes and twenty-two seconds past six o'clock in the
morning on the 21st of March, the sun's center was directly
above the equator. The vernal equinox had arrived. Night and
day were of equal length. It was spring, officially spring, all over
the North American continent.

It was spring where snow lay drifted under balsams in northern Maine. It was spring where crows settled on black and
frozen bottom land in Illinois. It was spring where eucalyptus
trees lifted shaggy trunks in sunshine, beside the Pacific. In
all these places, and in tens of thousands more, people felt a
lift of the spirit. Newspapers carried editorials on the coming
of the favorite season of their readers. In skyscraper elevators,
in country stores, in buses, on street corners, people discussed
the same subject—the arrival of spring.

For us the official beginning of spring came in the panhandle
of Florida, south of Tallahassee. It came on the banks of a
strange wide river, born of a single spring—the Wakulla. For
weeks in peninsular Florida, in a world of lost winters, we had
been watching the beginnings of a season. We had lived in
a pre-spring spring. These weeks had been surplus, velvet, bonus
weeks. We still had all the spring on the calendar, the whole

official season of the year, before us. On this day we had crossed a boundary line, a psychological equator. Now spring seemed really spring.

Woven through all our memories of that first day of spring is the crying of the limpkins. Wherever we walked on trails along the river the wild, far-carrying wailing of these snail hunters re-echoed through the woods. Wakulla Springs is the only place I know where these rare, shy birds can be seen in numbers close at hand.

Between the call of the loon at Orange Lake and the crying of the limpkins along the Wakulla there had intervened days of wandering. We had swung east and followed the St. Johns River. We had skirted the coast where masses of wiry, wind-shorn shrubs were alive with catbirds, brown thrashers, and towhees. We had rolled through pine flats where mile after mile the trees were slashed and bleeding in a spring harvest of turpentine. Not far from Jacksonville we had run through a concentration of phoebes with a flycatcher tipping its tail on almost every fence post. We had seen a puzzled Negro orange picker walking down the road, his picking sack over his shoulder, a long piece of paper—an income tax blank—in his hand. Somewhere south of Starke we had passed a farmer's wife hanging her wash on a barbed-wire fence, primly placing men's clothing on one side of a gate, women's clothing on the other. And near Florida's famous disappearing lake, Iomonia, north of Tallahassee, we had halted to delight in a cascade of blue, a flood of spring violets running down a slope amid the rusting tin cans of an abandoned dump.

Along the way cypress swamps now mirrored in their dark waters the yellow flowers of the floating bladderworts. Beneath each upright spike and bloom the leaves radiated out spokewise from the central stalk, supported by small carnivorous bladders. With the approach of spring the plants had risen to the surface for their period of blooming. We passed one swamp where the wheels of the bladderworts were so thick that the brown water seemed a vast machine filled with innumerable intermeshing cogs. Not far beyond we came to a wooden bridge. It spanned a transparent stream in which we could see each darting fish, each waving strand of eelgrass, each swirl of current-sculptured sand. Night and day half a million gallons of water a minute flowed in a wide river under this bridge. Yet less than half a mile upstream there was no river at all.

Instead, there was a great orifice, a drowned circular chasm of greenish-white limestone dropping away for 185 feet straight down into the earth. This was Wakulla Springs, the "Water of Mystery" of the aborigines, the largest and deepest spring on the face of the earth. Although the orifice descends more than 170 feet below the level of the sea, the water is untainted by salt. It pours forth, pure, transparent, its temperature remaining the same—between 70 and 72 degrees F.—winter and summer. At the rate of three or four miles an hour, the flood of 800,000,000 gallons a day flows down the 18-mile bed of the Wakulla River, descending 13 feet on its way to join the St. Marks and pour into the Gulf of Mexico. Watching a river appear before your eyes, seeing it pulled from nature's magic hat, so to speak, is a sight so prodigious that you gaze at it hour after hour with undiminished interest.

Above the spring, looking straight down from a drifting boat, we seemed floating in a balloon over gorges and mountains. Ripple rainbows run down the water-smoothed limestone. Far below, at the bottom of the chasm, a kind of white, underwater dust drifts with the current. Little knots of bream and bass and gar and blue-hued catfish float at different depths, some darting among tree trunks that turned to stone ages ago. Mastodon and mammoth skeletons, encrusted with lime, have been taken from the walls of the spring. The wondering eyes of Ponce de León's men, no doubt, beheld them when they paddled up the Wakulla River in the sixteenth century in search of the Fountain of Eternal Youth. For De León, paradoxically, Wakulla was the Fountain of Death. It was on the river not far from the spring that he was felled by the arrow that ended his life. The Wakulla is a stream rich in history. It is unique in a number of ways. But above all, in our memory, it stands out as the River of the Limpkins.

Hardly had we stopped at the wooden bridge before we heard the wailing of the "crying bird" up and down the river. That evening the dusk was filled with its "kur-r-ee-OW!" or "me-YOW!" rising to a caterwauling crescendo on the last syllable. We heard it when we awoke, during that last night of winter, in the Wakulla Springs Lodge. We heard it at dawn and we heard it above the ticking of my watch as the hands moved toward the birth moment of a new season. It followed us down trails where the sand of tiny anthills was as white as table salt and where redbud petals lay on the brown of woodland mold, on the gray-green of strands of fallen Spanish moss, on the tan carpet of live-oak leaves. It was part of the morning crescendo when cardinals whistled, blue jays screamed, and the woods rang with the "chur-r-r!" of the red-bellied woodpeckers. Sometimes the limpkins lifted their voices singly. At other times half a dozen yowled at once.

Thus, with the crying of the limpkins around us, we spent the earliest hours of the spring.

Half a century ago these birds were common in Florida. They were relatively tame. Their natures were unsuspicious. So their slaughter was easy. In the 1920's, noting the scarcity of limpkins on a trip down the Kissimmee River to Lake Okeechobee, T. Gilbert Pearson wrote: "The bird is so easily killed, so highly esteemed as food, and is found in a state where so little attention is paid to the enforcement of the bird and game laws, that the prospects for its long survival are not at all encouraging." Under the continual pressure of persecution the limpkin, or courlan, became wary and retiring. It is now one of the shyest of southern swamp birds. The limpkins we saw at Lake Okeechobee slipped away like rails among the reeds or, with upflipping wings, scaled quickly out of sight over the rushes and cattails. Here at Wakulla, however, where the birds have been afforded years of protection, they have regained the fearlessness of their original dispositions.

No more than a hundred feet from the rail of a wooden bridge on which we leaned, one of these spotted, brownish, bittern-sized birds probed the river bottom for snails. These snails, of the genus *Ampullaria*, grow in abundance along the edges of the Wakulla River. Again and again the limpkin thrust its slightly downcurving bill, open, under the water. Minutes of searching went by. Then the probing bill located a snail. The limpkin tugged. It twisted. It dragged to the surface its prize, a large, dark snail shell to which clung fragments of waterweed. With its long neck outstretched, its slender legs hanging down, and the shell clutched in its bill, the bird flapped 10 or 15 feet to the base of a cypress tree.

Here it dropped the snail and clucked loudly. Upstream, behind us, a hidden limpkin yowled in reply. The bird with the snail moved the shell with its bill into a crevice between the cypress roots. With one of its long-toed feet it held it solidly in place. Then, hidden from our view, the tip of its bill began working away at the shell. Just behind the tip the two halves of a limpkin's bill are separated by a slight aperture. This provides a tweezerlike tip that aids in extracting snails from their shells. In some instances the bills of these snail eaters are bent slightly to one side or the other at the end. This apparently is the result of forcing them into the curving opening of the spiral shell in extracting the snail.

When the limpkin lifted its head it had succeeded in wrenching away the operculum, or "door," of the snail shell and the soft slug-body of the extracted animal was in its bill. A backward toss of the head and the snail was swallowed. Then the bird returned to its hunting. This time it teetered along a fallen branch, pushing its bill down into the shallows on either side. Hardly a minute went by before it located a second snail.

Again it clucked and again, from upstream, came the answering wail of another limpkin.

We wondered if the unseen bird was the hunter's mate, brooding the eggs. For at that time a number of Wakulla limpkins were nesting. Normally the nests of these birds are hidden in vine tangles and thick marsh vegetation. One we observed from a distance of 40 feet, however, was constructed in the crotch of a sapling cypress nine feet above the water at the edge of a small island. Above the Spanish moss that draped the sides of this nest we could see the head and long bill of the brooding bird. From the blotched eggs, being warmed beneath her body, would hatch fluffy, cinnamon-brown baby limpkins. They would be able to swim, or follow their mother about like baby chicks, almost as soon as they stepped from the shell. And they would grow into adults that could clamber about in treetops, stride across lily pads, swim in open water, or, in spite of the halting gait that has given the limpkin its name, run swiftly enough to elude dogs in a maze of marshland paths.

The next morning, I returned to the bridge with my camera and telephoto lens to record the snail hunting of the limpkin. I focused on the cypress roots littered with empty shells. The morning light was perfect. The limpkin appeared. But so did a truck filled with shouting road menders. At that particular hour of that particular morning the powers-that-be had decided the planks of the bridge should be replaced. Sledges clanged. Dust filled the air. My camera quivered on its tripod. Old planks were ripped out. New planks were hammered into place. In the clanging and confusion the limpkin departed and the Speed-Graphic, with film unexposed, went back into its case.

We comforted ourselves by watching the first yellow palm warbler of our trip, darting, alighting, wagging its tail among the branch-tip twigs of a live oak. We talked of some of our other "firsts," enjoying them in retrospect: our first firefly lifting its greenish light from a weed clump near Lake Okeechobee; our first bat reeling through the dusk above the road to Sarasota; our first violets on the Kissimmee Prairie; our first conehead grasshopper shrilling in the dark near Jacksonville; our first jack-in-the-pulpit rising beside the boil of a little spring in the Florida scrub.

Later, when we packed up and headed away for a scythelike swing along the Gulf—west to the Mississippi and beyond— we stopped by the wooden bridge once more. The road menders were gone. The limpkins were snail hunting among the eelgrass of the shallow borders. The river rang with the wildness of their calls. Theirs was a voice that spoke for an older time, a long-ago time when primitive men believed that tiny folk, four inches tall, danced in the waters of Wakulla. It was the voice of the dark, the swamp, the vast wilderness of ancient times. It links us—as it will link men and women of an even more urbanized, regimented, crowded tomorrow— with days of a lost wildness.

ELEVEN

WINGS OVER THE DELTA

SOPCHOPPY passed on our left, Panacea dropped to the rear, Wakulla lay 20 miles behind. The road lifted us, on a long causeway, over the estuary of the Ochlockonee. We curved west, skirted the Gulf, ran on mile after mile down a lonely highway cutting through sand barrens shimmering in the sun. This empty, westward-leading road, with the blue of the Gulf flickering past whenever the trees thinned into openings, is one we remember well. It was the road of the butterfly parade.

We were crossing the Ochlockonee when we first caught sight of the black and orange of a monarch butterfly. It was beating its way upstream, flying north into the wind. A few miles beyond, where the gravestones of an isolated cemetery rose above bare sand, two other monarchs fluttered past us. That was the beginning. All that day and the next, as we followed the windings of the Gulf road on our way to the Mississippi, we encountered milkweed butterflies. They were the remnants of that vast army of migrants which had streamed south during the previous autumn.

We saw them among the dunes along the coast, near Money Bayou and Crooked River, at Bay St. Louis and Pass Christian. They were over the rust-colored water of the Apalachicola and flying where coastal paper mills poured forth the sickish-sweet fumes of their enveloping smoke. The monarchs were scattered, most of them flying singly. Nearly all were tarnished.

Only at rare intervals did we see one that had the brilliance of a butterfly fresh from the chrysalis. During our trip we were to see other monarchs, drifting aimlessly or flying north. We saw them among the live oaks of western Louisiana, along the Suwannee River, and at the edge of the Okefenokee Swamp, among the barrier islands of the South Carolina coast, over Newfound Gap in the Great Smokies, at the edge of Lake Drummond in the Dismal Swamp, amid the pitch pines of the New Jersey barrens, and along New England rivers. But nowhere did we see large numbers together, nowhere any mass movement to the north.

The spectacular butterfly concentrations of fall are not duplicated in the spring. Like migrating hawks, the monarchs move south in numbers and work their way north again in the spring singly, scattered over a wide area, in a migration that is hardly noticed. Dingy winged and travel worn, they are inconspicuous. Dr. Austin H. Clark, of the U.S. National Museum in Washington, D.C., reports that most of the monarchs coming north in spring are females while the southbound butterflies of autumn are about half and half males and females. Each male carries on his hind wings two packets of hollow scent scales which emit a faint perfume that, it has been suggested, may play a part in attracting a mate. That these minute scent scales may have another function in the life of the monarch seems indicated by an event my wife and I once observed near the seacoast on Long Island.

At sunset on a September evening we were walking down a lane about an eighth of a mile from a grove of white oak and tupelo trees. The breeze was blowing from the grove toward us. Each year monarchs settle among these trees, sometimes in thousands, when night overtakes them during migration. We noticed one butterfly drifting along parallel to the lane. As it came opposite the grove it turned, almost at right angles, and headed directly for the trees. A few minutes later a second butterfly appeared, flying in the opposite direction. It, too, made a sudden turn and followed upwind to the grove. Farther out over the open fields a third monarch straggled past. Like the others, as soon as it reached a point opposite the grove it turned abruptly and headed in that direction.

At the time thousands of monarchs had settled for the night, clinging in brown masses to the twigs. A roadway of perfume apparently was being carried downwind by the breeze from the scent pockets of innumerable males. Latecomers followed this invisible trail to the grove where the butterflies were congregating for the night. Honeybees use a similar method of attracting stragglers to the cluster at swarming time. The insects in the cluster open glands and, fanning their wings, send scent trails through the air which are followed by bees that are still on the wing. Moths fly through the dark, along trails of scent, to find the females. In a curious way scent trails played a part during the early days of the war in the Pacific. Australian troops employed an insecticide with a peculiar odor. Later it was discovered that the Japanese were able to detect concentrations of men as much as 15 miles away by this unfamiliar scent carried on the wind.

When the male monarchs are most numerous—during the southward flight in autumn—the insects tend to congregate and to fly in flocks or in straggling masses. When the males are extremely rare—during the spring flight north—such concentrations are unknown. While many factors are involved, it may well be that the scent pockets of the males are an important factor in holding together the great flocks of the monarchs during their southward movement. At Pacific Grove in California, where tens of thousands of monarch butterflies congregate on cypress trees in winter, visitors remark upon the unusual perfume that is apparent even to human noses in the vicinity of the trees.

Year after year, during the southward migration of autumn, monarchs tend to congregate for the night on the same trees. None of the insects has ever made the trip before. What guides these successive generations of butterflies to the same identical trees? In a recent letter concerning a chapter on "Insect Mystery Stories" in my *Near Horizons*, J. A. Simes, a Fellow of the Royal Entomological Society of England, suggests the scent glands of the male monarch as the solution of the mystery.

"The monarch," he writes, "belongs to the Danaidae family of butterflies, a group notorious for its scent-producing organs. Insects that have been dead for years have been known to exhale scent and in many species the process has gone so far that they have brushes on the anal segments which they can dip into the scent pockets on the hind wings and then shake out to diffuse the odor. Such insects could hardly roost in a tree without leaving strong scents behind and when the roosting is done by tens of thousands night after night the tree must get so strongly impregnated that the odor would last for months or years. I suggest that it is this residual odor which attracts the butterflies like a magnet to the same tree year after year."

The long treks of these frail insect voyagers always attract wide attention. In many parts of the world mass migrations of various species of butterflies are an annual occurrence. Spectacular numbers flutter across land and water at irregular intervals. Thomas Moufett records great flights in the years 1104 and 1543 and another just before the death of Maurice of Saxony, in 1553. The painted lady, *Vanessa cardui*, each year spans the Mediterranean during its north-and-south migration. While on its long flight this insect undergoes a curious reversal of instinct. Normally a diurnal creature, like other butterflies, it suddenly adopts the nocturnal flying habits of the moths and flutters through darkness on its journey across the Mediterranean Sea.

Cutting as we did along the Gulf through four states we observed a significant repetition of events in connection with the spring movement of the monarchs. In the open country, between rivers, we often saw the monarchs working their way along the coast. But where each river—the Escambia, the Perdido, the Pascagoula, the Mobile, the Pearl, the Mississippi—emptied into the Gulf the butterflies would be turning north, heading upstream along the banks or over the water. They seemed to be following the river valleys northward from the coast.

All the rivers were rising during those March days. Spring rains inland were adding to their burden of silt. Acres of fertile topsoil flowed past us to stain the blue of the Gulf with brown or rusty-red. Streams are literally heavier in the springtime. During that rainy season, when the fields are bare, the runoff water furrows the hillsides and adds the greatest silt burden of the year to the flow of rivers.

It was late on a Saturday afternoon when we reached New Orleans. A quarter of a century before, I had started in a rowboat at Louisville, Kentucky, to follow the Ohio and the Mississippi to New Orleans and had gone as far as Cairo, Illinois. Two and a half decades later, by a widely roundabout route, I had reached the goal. Cairo had been dominated by the Mississippi. New Orleans was not. The brown tide of the river rolled smoothly along, confined within its artificial banks. Somewhere, not far from where we stood on the levee, Lincoln had come ashore from his flatboat, in 1828, and John James Audubon, two years earlier, had boarded the *Delos*, with his bird paintings carefully packed for his voyage to Europe and fame.

Over the river and the city lay a blanket of humid heat. Weary and sweltering, we drove from tourist court to tourist court. Each bore the same sign in front: No Vacancies. We had almost reached the bridge across the Mississippi before we found a run-down cabin on a courtyard paved with clam shells behind a nightclub-roadhouse. There we tossed until three o'clock in the morning while a band blared, dancers stamped, tosspots sang, drunks brawled, and roadhouse-Bedlam-on-Saturday-night continued. Cars rolled over the clamshells with a crunching roar that reverberated in the court. About two o'clock one reveler tried to attract the attention of another inside by nineteen blaring blasts of his auto horn. An hour later, just as we were dozing off a final homegoing carouser flooded his engine and ground his starter over and over again, the battery getting weaker and weaker until it went dead. We were laboring with the laboring starter when we went to sleep.

Next morning, as Samuel Pepys used to confide to his diary, we lay late abed. Then we shifted our quarters to a quieter place, a court beside a railroad switchyard. The sultry air was close to the saturation point when we drove to Audubon Park that afternoon to visit the zoo. English sparrows were stealing straws from the lion cage to add to immense nests in nearby trees, nests that resembled those seen in pictures of Africa and revealed the relationship of the sparrows to the weaver finches of that continent. But it was a far rarer bird than an English sparrow that we had come to see, one of the rarest of all American species—a whooping crane.

Some years before, a muskrat hunter had found it caught in one of his traps in the Louisiana marshes. We looked at the stately white bird, larger than a great blue heron, as it stalked about its enclosure, turning its red face toward us from time to time. We looked at it with an emotion akin to that which must have been experienced by those who gazed at the last passenger pigeon on earth before its death at the Cincinnati zoo in 1914. The great bird before us was probably the last whooping crane to be confined in a zoological park.

Its subsequent history has given this bird a special niche in the Whooping Crane Hall of Fame. Not long after we saw it it was released, with another crane, at the Aransas National Wild Life Refuge of western Texas in a pioneer breeding experiment conducted by the U.S. Fish and Wildlife Service. At the time there were less than forty whooping cranes in the world. The bird was named Joe and was believed to be a male, although among these cranes males and females are indistinguishable. Even experts are fooled—and they were in this case. The name Joe had to be changed to Jo when the crane mated, laid an egg, and became celebrated as the mother of the first whooping crane ever hatched in captivity.

On our way back from the zoo we were caught in a good imitation of a cloudburst. The saturated sky seemed to let go of its moisture all at once. In spite of the windshield wipers a sheet of streaming water obscured the road ahead. This rain swept the humidity out of the atmosphere. It also altered our plans. We had expected to drive south on Monday along the west bank of the Mississippi to Venice, at the end of the road on the delta, and there go by boat to the ever-changing region at the very mouth of the river. A low-lying land of somber names—Dead Man Bayou, Death Pond, Dead Women Bend— it is cut by endlessly altering passes, dotted by transient ponds, made impassable in places by jungles of roseau cane and alligator weed, and characterized at its outer edge by the mudlump islands, those strange, transitory masses of clay that are forced up through the silt from time to time, that are born, live, and disappear in the course of a few years. The downpour left stretches of the Venice road a quagmire. Our only chance to view the wild, river-built delta country to the south was as it is seen by the heron and the gull—from the air.

A shell road led us, on Monday, to the Callendar Airport, downriver and west of the Mississippi. Don Maurice, a young pilot for the Intercoastal Airways, had a Piper Cub ready on the runway. Across the field, where the rain had left shallow puddles here and there, plover were feeding. Maurice told me they were called locally "poppabodies"—apparently a corruption of the French word for upland plover, "peppabotte." The Cub had but a single passenger seat so Nellie watched the poppabodies while Maurice and I taxied down the field. Facing a pounding wind from the south, we were up like a helicopter. The turbulence of the ground gusts dropped away. With the airport almost standing still beneath us, we lifted up and up as soaring birds sometimes do. We were at 3,000 feet before we leveled off and began nosing south.

Below us the brown serpent of the river crawled into the haze toward the sea. Duplicating each sweeping curve along its western side was the white thread of a shell road. A cargo steamer, red and rusty, crept downstream. The shadow of our plane slid along the water, overtook and passed the ship, slipped silently inland over the small squared fields of plantations huddling close to the levees, over a postage-stamp-sized cemetery with red gravestones. Ahead of us and to the west spread away the russet-green flatness of the delta marshes, cut by winding inlets.

All this land before us was formed from the rich soil of Iowa and Missouri and Ohio and Illinois, from silt borne downstream by the river day and night, winter and summer, spring and fall. In the course of a single year the Mississippi transports more than 400,000,000 tons of soil and rock stuff to the Gulf. The Father of Waters is also the Father of Lands. The mountain of sediment it has dropped into the sea at its mouth is calculated to be 30,000 feet—almost six miles—thick. Placed beside Mount Whitney, in California, it would tower more than twice the height of this tallest mountain in the United States. Sediment has actually lifted the river bed and the banks on either side above the level of the delta around it. Thus the Mississippi is flowing on a plane above the surrounding country. It has made its channel as it pushed the land farther and farther into the Gulf. Each year, geologists compute, the delta front advances an average of 340 feet farther into the sea. The Mississippi created all the land beneath our wings. The season was spring; upriver floods had darkened the chocolate of its waters; delta building was at its yearly peak.

The rich soil, the plentiful water, the heat of the sun, all make the delta of the Mississippi—as they make the delta of the Nile—a vast spawning ground for wildlife. Everywhere I looked below birds were flying. Great blue herons were wing-ing their way in stately flapping flight over the marsh. Louisiana herons, with faster wingbeat, started into the air while, gleaming white, the snowy egrets and American egrets, in the air and on the ground, caught the eye from afar. One snowy zigzagged wildly below us as though escaping a hawk and once near the river, when our shadow trailed across a flock of crows, the birds hastily landed. We were a greater bird above the birds of the delta.

In the Everglades, at Lake Okeechobee, among the floating islands, I had seen the white-breasted tree swallows moving north. Now I saw them again from an unusual vantage point. Large numbers were migrating over the delta. At one side, and lower down, hundreds of the birds appeared and disappeared, now steel-blue and almost invisible against the marsh, now gleaming white, as they turned and twisted, hawking for insects as they worked northward. Near the river we came abreast of a high-flying gull soaring only a hundred feet or so below us. Its snowy wings with black tips stood out in the brilliance of the cloudless sunshine and it was so close I could see the dark ring around its bill. Flocks of redwings and boat-tailed grackles labored low over the wind-whipped vegetation and here and there a marsh hawk, its white rump patch visible at a great distance, hung tossing in the air, sliding sidewise with the wind.

Nowhere in all that vast extent of the delta marshes did I observe a human being. Canals, like straight strokes of a brush dipped in brown paint, cut for miles across the tarnished green of the morass. Beside one of these waterways a cluster of weathered cabins, connected with catwalks, perched on piles. From the air they suggested the village of some modern tribe of lake dwellers. They were the seasonal homes of muskrat trappers. Fine brown lines, like taut threads, stretched away from the canals as straight as roads on the Kansas prairie. These were boat trails of the rat trappers. In this land of eternal water and grasses, the poled boats of generations of trappers had kept the trails open through the dense vegetation below us.

These were things I noticed on the delta marshes on that day in spring. But most of all, dominating the scene below, strange in infinite numbers, was the multitude of muskrat houses, miles on miles of them, extending as far as I could see like a million yellow anthills speckling a russet-green meadow. Some years, Maurice shouted above the roar of the engine, the water rats "almost eat up the earth." He slid back the throttle and the roar diminished. We swept in a great curving spiral down to less than a thousand feet. Now I could see that each yellow anthill was surrounded by a circle of brown, the water visible where the muskrat had cut away vegetation in building its house.

In each of these tens of thousands of conical houses the first litter of the year was already growing to maturity. Three out of every four muskrat pelts taken in North America came from Louisiana. In some years rat trapping here is a $10,000,000 industry. As many as 20,000 trappers work in the coastal marshes. In spite of an annual take of several million pelts, muskrats swarm in this flooded land. They also hold their own in spite of natural enemies—raccoons, cottonmouth moccasins, and ants. Curiously enough, the ant ranks high as a menace to muskrat life. These insects breed in astronomical numbers on the delta marshes. They oftentimes nest in the vegetable masses of the muskrat houses and the skeletons of young rats have been found picked clean by the swarming insects.

Hurricanes come to the rescue of the water rats. They sweep away the infested houses and the decaying logs where the ants are breeding. Otherwise the insects would multiply almost unrestrained; they would overwhelm nests and muskrat houses alike; fledgling birds and baby rats would have little chance to survive. In his classic *Ants, Their Structure, Development and Behavior*, William Morton Wheeler reports a stratagem developed by colonies of the fire ant, *Solenopsis geminata,* in the Louisiana lowlands: "When a nest of these ants is flooded, they agglomerate to form a ball, 16–25 cm. in diameter, which encloses the brood in the center. This ball is borne along on the surface of the water while its living units keep shifting their position to avoid too prolonged immersion, till the shore or some projecting rock or tree-trunk is reached, when the colony scrambles out of the uncongenial element."

The hurricane, in another way, is a friend of the muskrat. It drives great waves of salt water into the coastal marshes. These areas are a natural battleground where warfare between fresh and salt water, between water and land, has been raging for thousands of years. It is a region of endless change, a place of continual building up and tearing down, the meeting point of opposing forces. And the fate of the vegetation in any particular spot depends upon the outcome of the battle. If it were not for the salt baths brought by hurricanes, the marshes would more and more become fresh-water areas. Sawgrass, useless as a food for muskrats, would spread in the fresh-water habitat. The best food plants for both the rats and for overwintering waterfowl demand brackish water. This is provided with the help of the hurricane. It is a benefit of disaster.

Changes left in the wake of destructive wind storms also sometimes aid other species of wildlife. Where they level climax forests of beech and maple and let a new succession of forest trees begin, they provide a varied habitat for nesting birds. Fully 100 species of North American birds cannot live under climax-forest conditions. Moreover, the cloudburst rains that accompany hurricane storms in Florida give the Kissimmee Prairie the added water it needs to support the vegetation that covers it.

In a curious way, some years ago, a hurricane helped solve a scientific dispute. Along the South Carolina coast a bird of the sea marshes is the Worthington's long-billed marsh wren, *Telmatodytes palustris griseus*. Its range is limited and it is a year-around inhabitant. At one time this latter point was questioned. Some ornithologists believed that the bird migrated; others contended that it did not. The hurricane that settled the point struck the Carolina coast late in the season after migration time had passed. It virtually wiped out the wrens in the area. They were extremely scarce for years afterwards. If the birds had left the area on migration they would have been unaffected by the storm and would have returned in usual numbers in the spring.

Natural calamities serve the ends of varied forms of life in other ways. In the pine barrens of north-central Michigan, the Kirtland's warbler depends upon forest fires to produce its nesting sites. And, according to John Muir, one of the pines of the California mountains, *Pinus tuberculata*, reproduces with the aid of fire. It never drops its cones and its seeds are discharged only after the tree dies. In this species life comes only with death. The pine grows along fire-swept ridges. In the wake of a forest fire, when the trees are killed and the ground swept bare, the cones open and shower down their seeds. Thus this phoenix among trees rises from the ashes. Wherever there is a stand of these mountain pines the trees are almost always about the same size. Their beginning dates back to the same disaster.

Through the haze that hung over the Gulf I could see the far mouth of the Mississippi dividing and redividing, forming a maze of channels that, from the air, had the appearance of some anatomical chart showing lungs or circulation systems reproduced in brown ink. And all the time, even as we watched, speck by speck the submerged mountain of sediment was growing beneath the waters of the Gulf. During the short hour we were in the air, between 40,000 and 50,000 tons of silt were added to the pile.

Our shadow swung over the marshes and raced ahead of us as we turned in a wide arc toward home, altering our position in relation to the sun. The wind was with us now. Our shadow skimmed swiftly over the brackish pools, the hurricane-stranded stumps, past patches of open mud where runoff and evaporation had left long streaks of white, past a turkey buzzard soaring in the same place, circling and circling. It overtook a string of barges being inched upstream by a laboring tug. It flicked across the straight chalk mark of the shell road by the levee. To the southwest a succession of lakes and pools burst into sheen as they were struck by the sun. Out there was hurricane country. Everything was low, nothing offered obstruction in that plain of grass and water.

As our wheels touched the airport in a slow into-the-wind descent, the poppabodies darted into the air in wild plover flight. They circled twice and landed to feed again. I closed my eyes for a moment. I wanted to recapture that last glimpse of the delta marshes, stretching westward to the hazy horizon, that gull's-eye view I had had just before we coasted down to a landing. It was a view that stimulated my desire to see close at hand the life of the marsh. A hundred miles to the west, a few days later, that desire was satisfied. A craft more unusual than an airplane made it possible, a craft that, in its way, flies on mud as an airplane flies on air.

TWELVE

MUDBOAT

———

IN the space of a mile or two, as we drove west from New Orleans, we came upon two mourning doves, two logger-head shrikes, two martins, two sparrow hawks, each pair sitting close together, side by side, on telephone wires. As in the days of Noah's ark, the animals appear two by two in the spring.

All across the black loam of the Louisiana lowlands, during those late-March days, buds were opening, flowers unfolding. In gardens peas bloomed, cabbage heads were beginning to set, patches of mustard greens were topped with yellow flow-ers. Spider lilies, white and fragrant, bloomed beside the high-way. And across the black levels of immense fields sugar cane pushed up like sprouting corn.

Our destination this morning was Abbeville, 165 miles west of New Orleans, 80 miles this side of the Texas border, on the edge of those great coastal marshes I had seen stretching away to the western horizon. The road, lifting slightly, carried us along the Teche River, over lazy bayous, into the Evangeline country of western Louisiana. Immense live oaks, trees as beau-tiful and impressive, in their way, as the western sequoias, trees like cathedrals, extended great limbs, shaggy with "long moss," over the highway. This was Cajun country. Farm wagons were painted red and blue and men in the fields wore bright-colored shirts.

Chimney swifts, our first chimney swifts of the spring, were crackling through the air above the courthouse at Abbeville.

We carried our bags to a top-floor room in the stucco-covered hotel across the street. Then a curiously unreal half hour began. We seemed in some Coney Island House of Fun. I started to lift an armchair nearer to a window and the arms came off in my hands. I shut the closet door and the knob fell to the floor, leaving our clothes locked inside. Nellie turned on the water in the bathtub. It poured from the faucet tinted purple-blue. She adjusted the hot water. The wooden handle fell off and floated, bobbing about, on the water. We looked at each other.

"What next?" we asked.

That night we found out. About 2:00 A.M. we started out of a deep sleep at the sound of a long wail followed by a sudden "flap! flap! flap!" suggesting great bat wings in the dark. The sounds came from the closet which we had managed to work open during the afternoon. A gaping hole had been broken through the end wall at some previous time to reach the plumbing and a piece of window shade, glued along the top, hid the opening. Whenever the wind blew from a certain direction, we discovered, a mournful, long drawn-out moan would be produced by the draft in the catacombs of the inner wall spaces, followed by the flapping of the piece of window shade.

In spite of its peculiarities, that room is one we remember with special affection. It was clean and spacious. Everyone at the hotel was friendly and obliging. Once, when we returned from a trip to Avery Island and found new draperies hanging at the windows, they all inquired—from bellboy to manager—how we liked the drapes. Here, less than a hundred miles from the Texas border, we dined on the thickest and tenderest of T-bone steaks when we were not trying rice with onion sauce or sampling the delights of villainous-looking shrimp-and-oyster gumbo.

Laid out like a village in Provence, with narrow, tree-lined streets, Abbeville is only 20 feet above the level of the sea. It lies on the northern edge of the great prairie marshes. In Vermilion Parish alone there are 826 square miles of open marsh.

For thousands of years before the Spanish explorers threaded their way west from Florida this land of drowned rivers and water prairies was the ancestral feeding ground of overwintering waterfowl. It was formed at a time when the Mississippi meandered far west of its present course. This was the unfenced wilderness I had seen from the air. Then it had been spread out and remote; now it was close at hand. A few days later, through the kind arrangements of George E. Welch, of Abbeville, I traveled into the very heart of the marshes over mudboat trails on the vast Stanolind Oil Company tract south of Gueydan, 20 miles west of Abbeville.

The day was the last Thursday in March. The barometer was falling, the wind rising. Storm warnings had been posted all the way from Brownsville to New Orleans. Animals along the way to Gueydan seemed restless and excited. On such wild days of wind and threatening storm, when the barometer is falling, hogs tend to fight, horses to bolt, and normally docile cows to become unruly. Men and women also respond to a rapidly falling barometer. At such times, the records show, they are more quarrelsome, have more nightmares, leave more parcels on streetcars and buses, and are involved in more traffic and industrial accidents.

At Gueydan I turned south to the Florence locks, relic of the old rice-plantation days. Here Jules Beloir, a hearty Cajun of about sixty, waited with the *Mallard*, a stubby brown sea sled powered with a Ford V-8 engine. We headed south down the canal, the flat bottom of the boat slapping and pounding on waves tossed up by the wind. Thunderheads boiled up along the western horizon. Booming gusts ripped at the canalside bushes. In the southwest the sky was swollen and black. Once we had passed the Intercoastal Canal, where a seagoing freighter was moving slowly westward, we were butting into the full weight of the wind sweeping unhindered over half a hundred miles of open marsh.

For nearly ten miles we fought our way out into the lonely,

level expanse. The flat marsh around us stretched to the horizon in all directions. Then a small cluster of green buildings perched on piles appeared before us. This was the camp of Johnny Gaspard, the Stanolind caretaker. A handsome outdoorsman in his mid-thirties, Gaspard was standing in hip boots on one of the catwalks. He was studying the western sky, debating whether to take his family inland. In the hurricane of 1940 they all had come close to losing their lives. The waves had smashed at windows and doors and the water had risen above the level of the floor.

"One more big blow," he told us, "and we all would have been drowned in the ocean."

As we watched, little by little the sullenness of the sky grew less. The wind still buffeted the marsh as before but gradually the menace of the storm dissipated. Gaspard took down a 9-foot push-pole ending in a curious paddle shaped like the feathered end of an arrow. With it he worked a flat-bottomed, rectangular craft, 22 feet long and 5 feet wide, out of the boat shed. We climbed down beside him. We sat in a kind of cockpit near the rear of the craft, looking ahead through a slanting windshield of glass. Beneath our feet the bottom of the boat was formed of solid, 1-inch oak. Once it had gained momentum, this mudboat can shoot across shallows where its propeller is spinning partly in silt: It is an airplane of the marsh, a glider that glides on mud and water. And, like an airplane, it is controlled by a vertical stick. Gaspard pulls back the control stick to swing to the right, pushes it ahead to swerve to the left.

"When I've got her wide open," he declared, "she goes like the devil beating tanbark."

Ahead of us a 200-horsepower, 12-cylinder engine roared. Behind us a 3-bladed, semiwheel propeller churned up the mud and water. We gained momentum and the craft slid into a narrow water trail leading away into the windy marsh. A hundred miles of these mudboat trails wind through the Stanolind tract. In cutting new ones, Gaspard substitutes a special 2-

bladed, full-wheel propeller that does not foul up with grass and waterweeds. At times the trail ahead of us narrowed until it was almost closed. Yet, wherever there was enough room for the propeller to whirl, the craft shot ahead with undiminished speed.

All around us were breakers in the sea of wind-lashed vegetation. Muskrat houses appeared and disappeared. Redwing nests flashed past among the cattails. Dark water, strewn with the reddish-green disks of new water-lily leaves, rushed toward us and streamed away to the rear. And once, far out in this windy wilderness of marshland, I caught a momentary glimpse of a lone monarch butterfly being whirled away over the pounding surf of the cattails.

Birds were lying low on this abnormal day. Our rushing advance frightened individuals up from time to time, black ducks shooting into the air with the silver of their underwing feathers shining against the still-stormy sky, Louisiana herons and little blue "cranes" and American bitterns flapping out of the vegetation to go whirling away like oversized gale-blown leaves. From time to time redwings and grackles rose in little clouds, their clamor reaching us above the noise of the engine.

In an attempt to get high-speed photographs of marsh birds rising in the wind, I clambered ahead, beyond the protection of the windshield, into a little cubbyhole with a plank seat at the bow of the boat. Clinging there, struggling to get my breath in the smashing drive of the wind, I watched the marsh rush toward me. A great blue heron, looking as big as the fabled roc, shot upward and was carried backward by the wind. An American egret appeared in a sudden white apparition over the bow. Once a Louisiana heron rose almost too late. It barely missed striking me in the face as the wind hurled it back over the scudding boat.

To anyone looking on from a distance the course of the hidden mudboat probably would have been apparent from the rising of alarmed birds in its path. Yet it is just as probable that if the boat had made hourly circuits of the course the fear of the birds would soon have subsided. For wild birds exhibit a surprising capacity for becoming accustomed to abnormal sounds and situations.

During the early years of World War II, a colony of black skimmers nested on the eastern end of Fire Island, off the Long Island coast. They remained even after the Army Air Force established a strafing practice range for pilots across the barren sand close to their nesting site. Each day airmen would dive and pour into this strip bullets from their machine guns. Day after day, with lead plowing up the sand close by, the skimmers continued to nest and rear their young. Another instance of the kind is related by Ted S. Pettit in his *Birds in Your Back Yard*. At a Boy Scout camp in the East, a few years ago, thousands of 22-caliber bullets were fired each day at targets placed against a backstop formed of 12-by-12-inch logs. In knotholes between the targets three pairs of house wrens built their nests. In spite of the fact that rifle practice continued all summer, the birds successfully raised their young and two of the three pairs produced two broods during the season.

Rising above the other vegetation, dominating the marsh like groves on a prairie, were a few islands of sawgrass. As we rushed toward one, the water trail seemed a dead-end road. A high wall of dry grass rose before me. At the last moment, when I felt sure we were plunging headlong at 40 miles an hour into the ripping leaves of the sawgrass, Gaspard shoved the control stick ahead. The mudboat banked like a turning plane, wheeled to the left in almost a right-angle turn and, with the sawgrass wall streaming past us, went charging down another narrow lane of water.

Lacking the food value of many other marsh plants, sawgrass is eaten by neither waterfowl nor muskrats. But recently a newcomer to the coastal marshes has added it to its bill of fare. This is the coypu. Several pairs of these South American rodents, which sometimes reach a length of three feet and a weight of twenty pounds, were kept in cages on Avery Island. About 1940 a few escaped. They established themselves in the surrounding marshes and since have multiplied until they now range from the Mississippi to the Texas line. The muskrats and the coypu seem to eat different things and no immediate conflict between the two was noted. So far the main mischief laid at the door of the newcomer is tunneling into levees and thus weakening them. In the course of a single season Louisiana trappers now take as many as 50,000 coypu, or nutria, pelts. As each one brings about three times as much as the best muskrat skin, the spread of the water rodents from South America has proved an important new source of revenue.

From time to time we would slow down in little openings, wild water gardens in the marsh, brilliant with the spiked blooms of the golden club. In masses these "bog torches" lifted above the dark water. Submerged by our passing, their "never-wet" leaves rose to the surface shedding the water like drops of quicksilver. As is the case with its relatives, the skunk cabbage and the jack-in-the-pulpit, the golden club generates heat, runs a kind of botanical fever, when it blooms in the spring.

As we ran south, the mudboat burst more frequently into open stretches of brown water. Each time the wind hit us broadside; the boat yawed, slowed down, swerved back on the course; then the engine roared and we were off again. In the unstable world of the marshes, a change in the direction of the wind affects the level of the water. On this day of strong winds from the southwest the water was higher than usual.

And everywhere we went, no matter in what direction we turned, the water of the marsh was strewn with fragments of roots and waterweeds—scraps left from the banquet of the waterfowl. All winter the delta marshes had teemed with ducks and geese. Then, led by the pintails, the spring parade up the Mississippi flyway had begun. Among the last to leave were the blue geese. Virtually all the blue geese of the continent winter in Louisiana. Spring comes late to their far-northern breeding grounds—Baffin Island, Southampton Island, and the upper part of Hudson Bay—and they delay their start until resident waterfowl in the delta marshes have already mated and are preparing to nest. Less than a week before, the blue geese had started north. I had missed them by only a few days. Departing, these last of the waterfowl hosts had left the marshes like some vast deserted banquet hall behind them.

Gaspard pushed the control stick ahead again. The mudboat heeled over in a wide curve to the left. With the wind behind us we raced down a long serpentine trail toward home, the boat tilting into the turns, the thunder of the engine rising above the roar of the wind, walls of grass passing in a dizzying blur. At the cluster of green buildings beside the canal Jules Beloir and I climbed back into the khaki-colored *Mallard* and started north.

Before we left, Gaspard swept his arm in a wide gesture toward a meadowlike portion of the marsh across the canal.

"Over there," he said, "my wife and I used to see as many as fifteen whooping cranes playing like turkeys."

That was before the 1940 hurricane. In that year nearly all the cranes disappeared, probably driven by high tides out of the marshes into the interior where they were killed for food. A single pair lived in the vicinity as late as 1946. In the fall of that year a farmer hunting ducks saw the two birds fly north in the morning over a clump of willows on the bank of the Intercoastal Canal. That evening he saw only one come back. The lone bird remained for a time and then it, too, disappeared— the last whooping crane seen in the marshes of Louisiana. On the way out I took a picture of the willow clump. Like the boy who reported that his grandfather's cow had swallowed a grindstone and if anyone did not believe him he could show him the grindstone, I could always show a picture, not of whooping cranes, but of trees over which whooping cranes had flown.

The next morning, after seeing our first ruby throated hummingbird hovering over a thistle on the banks of the Teche River, at the Evangeline State Park, near St. Martinsville, we started east once more. Again we were making a wide sweep along the Gulf, paralleling the advancing wave of spring, on a return to the eastern coast.

Mile after mile the lowland road leading back to New Orleans was bordered by wide ditches choked from bank to bank with water hyacinths. That morning a newspaper headline had announced that a Louisiana congressman had introduced a bill in Washington, D.C., to appropriate $25,000,000 for clearing southern streams and canals of water hyacinths. This runaway plant was introduced from South America into Louisiana at the time of the 1884 New Orleans Cotton Exposition. Its rapid reproduction has made it a multimillion-dollar pest.

A clump of water hyacinths will sometimes double in size in 20 days. A single square foot of these waterweeds may become 1,000 square feet in six months' time. Ten years after a woman in Florida tossed a few hyacinths from her fish pool into the St. Johns River the descendants of those plants spread in great rafts over 50,000,000 square yards of inland waters. The only natural checks upon the plant seem to be salt water and a temperature below 28 degrees F. It has no serious insect foes. Attempts to poison the hyacinths injured livestock and killed fish. A letter to a Florida newspaper once suggested that the hippopotamus ought to be introduced into the state to eat up the water hyacinths. So far the most successful method of dealing with the swift reproduction of the plant is the circular saws of government launches that chop up the rafts into small pieces which float out to sea or are hauled up on the banks to dry out and die. But as soon as the saws stop the plants gain ground. We passed one government boat moored in a roadside canal. It was completely surrounded by water hyacinths.

At one time, I was told, the army engineers, in their work of maintaining navigable streams, had virtually wiped out the plant in Louisiana. Then a new colonel arrived to take charge. Running down the list of funds appropriated for the year, he came to the item:

"Water Hyacinth Control . . . $10,000."

"What are water hyacinths?"

An assistant explained.

"Let's see some!"

So well had the work been done and so nearly were the plants eradicated that a long drive revealed only a few plants. Declaring that this was the silliest waste of taxpayers' money he had ever encountered, the colonel blue-penciled the whole appropriation. The fight against the water hyacinth stopped. Before it was resumed, the swiftly multiplying plant had got its second wind.

As we drove along we saw how its rapid multiplication—stimulated now by the spring—was playing a role in an endless battle that rages over this lowland region. This is the struggle between land and water. Curiously enough, the hyacinth, a plant that lives in water and depends upon water for its existence, fights on the side of the land. We saw a sequence of events taking place along the old canals. First the hyacinth got control. The canal became more and more choked. Cattails sprang up along the banks. They edged farther and farther out. And finally willows took root. Unless man interfered, the canal was doomed. Eventually its water would be replaced by silt and swampy land.

Fifty miles or so this side of New Orleans we passed an expensive car parked by the side of the road. A wheel of black buzzards revolved lazily over willows and marshland beyond. In the car a well-dressed man, wearing pince-nez glasses, was firing a repeating rifle at each graceful soaring bird as it went by. He was a city man relaxing in the country, diverting himself with senseless persecution.

Long ago scientists of the U.S. Fish and Wildlife Service proved that the old charge that buzzards spread hog cholera was baseless. Their tests, in fact, showed that these birds help confine the epidemic by devouring stricken animals and by killing, with their digestive juices, the cholera germs. Yet in many southern communities the belief that vultures spread disease is unquestioned. Buzzards are birds associated with death and, as such, are widely disliked. Here, as always, ignorance wedded to hatred begets cruelty.

As Nellie and I drove on we talked of how few are the men, in all the written history of the world, who have known a fellow feeling for creatures called wild. The story of St. Francis of Assisi needs no miracles to make it superlative. It is miracle enough to find a man well disposed toward all the living things around him.

THIRTEEN

SPRING ON THE SUWANNEE

W E passed a farm called Lonely Acres and a field where a white-haired Negro stumbled after a plow pulled by a red steer in a harness formed of strips of gunny sacking and overalls. Our road was carrying us north. Boys' kites swung back and forth in the air over country schoolyards. Dogwood, redbud, and peach trees were clothed in clouds of white and coral and pink. And all along the main highways human migrants, trailer caravans, were rolling northward in the wake of spring.

With regret we were leaving, for a final time, the colorful birds, the lush vegetation, the river-bearing springs, the sea-shell islands, the mysterious swamps, the fern grottoes, the floating islands of Florida, that state of unwearying interest for a naturalist. There a student of nature might well spend half a dozen lifetimes. No other state east of the Mississippi has as great a north and south distance as Florida. It is equal to that of all New England. We had already followed spring almost one quarter of the way to Canada by the time we reached the northern boundary of this one state.

Our final memory, before we crossed the Georgia line, concerns a flash of gray and white among the bushes and the darting form of a mockingbird racing beside our car down a long straight stretch of highway. For a quarter of a mile it sped almost within reach of the right-hand window, forging slowly ahead. Then, when hardly more than two car lengths in advance of the rushing automobile, it swerved, dashed across in front of us at risk of life and wing and started back down the road. The bird seemed bewitched. It seemed possessed to gamble its life in front of the speeding car. And everywhere we went other birds played this dangerous game. Song sparrows dipped from telephone wires to swoop almost under our wheels. Mourning doves darted from the roadside to miss our radiator by only a few feet. Sometimes birds on opposite sides of the road would change places on telephone wires, passing each other as they shot before the oncoming car. A thousand birds in a thousand places risked their lives in crossing the road ahead of us.

While the Florida mockingbird raced our machine the farthest, other birds frequently dashed down the roadside to shoot, in a narrow miss, before the car. They seemed attracted to a speeding automobile as a moth is drawn to a candle flame. Why? Why didn't they turn aside or wait until the machine had passed?

These questions puzzled us all during our trip. An ornithologist friend explains that the secret of the birds' behavior probably lies in the nature of the avian eye. With few exceptions, birds see to either side rather than straight ahead. A chicken or pigeon cocks its head to look at you. A robin, pausing on the lawn with head turned in a listening attitude, is looking more than listening for angleworms. A few years ago Victor Keppler, a well-known New York advertising photographer, spent hours trying to get a picture of a dog and a parrot, sitting side by side, facing each other. Standing beside the dog, he waved his arms in an effort to get the bird to turn in his direction. He shouted, he whistled, he jumped up and down. Perversely, the parrot refused to turn his way. Then he realized that all the time the bird was watching him intently out of the side of its head. He changed positions and, standing back of the camera, waved his hands in the air. Instantly the parrot turned, facing the dog, to watch Keppler out of its other eye.

A bird taking off beside the road focuses on the approaching car with the eye on that side of its head. Instinctively it tries to keep the moving object in view as it flies. If it turns away from the highway it loses sight of the car. By flying parallel to it or across in front of it, the bird keeps the machine clearly in view. This, incidentally, probably answers the old conundrum: "Why does a hen cross the road?" The supposedly funny stock answer: "To get to the other side," tells a good deal less than the whole story.

The few birds that look straight ahead as we do, such as the hawks and owls, are birds of prey, the pursuers rather than the pursued. They all possess remarkably flexible necks. An owl can rotate its head through as much as 270 degrees. However, its eyeballs have almost no mobility. They cannot be rolled from side to side. They are fixed like headlights on a car. Experimenters have found that the eyes of a freshly killed owl cannot be turned even with a pair of pliers. Although such birds of prey are only a fraction the size of a man, they sometimes have eyeballs larger than our own. Even small species of singing birds have eyes that outweigh their brains. The largest eye possessed by any land vertebrate, an eye larger than that of a rhinoceros or elephant or hippopotamus, is found in the relatively small head of the ostrich.

The keenness of a bird's vision, however, is explained only partly by the size of the eyeball. In addition there is a high ratio of optic-nerve fibers to visual cells and a particularly dense concentration of cones. In the eye of a Buteo hawk, one experimenter found 1,000,000 cones to the square centimeter. Eagles have a sharpness of vision eight times that possessed by the most "eagle-eyed" of human beings. The instant a baby chick steps from the egg it not only can see clearly, it also can judge distances accurately. The ability to judge speeds and distances with extreme exactness is one possessed by many birds. I have watched a hermit thrush close its wings and, without slackening its speed, shoot bulletwise through the small opening of a woven-wire fence. Only twice have I heard of birds colliding in mid-air. Undoubtedly it is their skill in judging speed and distance that saves the lives of many birds in their perilous dashes in front of speeding cars.

The road where the mockingbird risked its life before our machine led us north into Georgia through a succession of pine woods and cypress swamps. Here the difference of a few feet in elevation changed the whole character of the landscape. Eventually, near the village of Fargo, we came to a long, ramshackle bridge of planks. Beneath it black water slid away from the western edge of the Okefenokee Swamp. This flow marks the beginning of the best known river of the South, the Suwannee, immortalized in Stephen Foster's "Old Folks at Home."

Beginning its long journey to the Gulf, the slow-moving water appeared out of the vastness of the Okefenokee, flowing with lazy swirls around the gray trunks of moss-hung cypress trees. As we watched, the wildest horse we had ever seen came snorting and splashing through the shallows. Long hair hung down over its eyes. Its shaggy flanks were caked with mud. Mounting a low island, with water running down its legs in muddy rivulets, it began cropping the new spring grass. Beyond it, in a farmyard on higher ground, two hounds and a razorback pig were fighting. The dogs leaped in and jumped back. The pig, mane erect, using its powerful shoulders as a shield to parry the attack, swung its head from side to side in vicious slashes. In this wild setting, under a clouded and somber sky, we seemed to be watching a prehistoric battle.

But there was beauty as well as wildness here at the beginning of the Suwannee. Suddenly the air above the bridge was filled with a sound like the slurring of many violins. Bright bird music enveloped us. Bright birds swept around us. More than a hundred migrating goldfinches alighted in the cypresses. In flashes of gold and black these thistlebirds, associated with hot summer days in northern states, darted between moss-hung boughs. They arrived among the gray trees, under that gloomy forbidding sky, like a smile breaking on a lowering face.

"There is," wrote W. H. Hudson in *Afoot in England*, "no more fascinating pastime than to keep company with a river from its source to the sea." In our travels we had kept company with the Suwannee almost in reverse, touching it from point to point—at Demory Hill, Old Town, Branford, Ellaville, Suwannee Springs, White Springs—and now coming to its beginning last.

The river, coffee-black with leachings, follows a zigzag, 250-mile path to the sea. Only 35 of those miles are in Georgia. From its head, on the Sunderland Terrace in the Okefenokee Swamp, it moves southward, at times tumbling over limestone shoals, to meet higher land and be deflected west near Lake City. At various times the river flows northwest, west, south, southeast, and southwest. So wandering is its course that it encloses Suwannee County, in Florida, on three of its four sides, north, west, and south. At one time the Suwannee, a natural boundary between the Florida panhandle and the eastern part of the state, served as the division line between two Indian confederations. Along much of its course its bed is eroded from Ocala limestone.

To the Indians the Suwannee was the River of Reeds; to De Soto, who crossed it in 1539, it was the River of the Deer; to those who traveled the Old Spanish Trail it was the San Juanito or San Juanee—the Little St. Johns—a name that is said to have been corrupted in early days to the Suwannee. Indian guides leading the Spaniards up the river told them the stream was paved with gold. It is, in fact, paved with an almost continuous line of springs. Few of the tributaries of the Suwannee are visible on the map. They flow underground through channels in the limestone. Between White Springs and Ellaville, a distance of about forty miles, springs in the bed of the Suwannee add 600 second-feet to the flow of the stream. By the time it pours into the Gulf, near Demory Hill, it is a river 300 feet wide.

To those whose sole knowledge of the Suwannee is based upon Stephen Foster's song, the river must seem bounded by stately mansions and sunny cotton fields. In truth, during most of its course it is a dark and lonely jungle stream. Otters make slides along its banks and alligator snapping turtles reach their largest size in its waters. At only a few points is it touched by civilization; only rarely is it crossed by speeding cars on concrete highways.

A few miles above Old Town, once the site of the largest Indian village on the peninsula of Florida, we spent two days in a cabin on the bank of the river. The opposite shore was a colorful tapestry of greens and reds and grays—the delicate green of new leaves, the dark green of ferns, the red of swamp maples, the frosty-gray of lichen-covered trunks. It was a tapestry of spring, its colors deepening day by day. At night, when the glitter of the sky was reflected in the river, we used to see Orion riding high and the Great Dipper making its slow scythe-like swing above the treetops. Its handle, low on the horizon, almost touched the ebony mass of the farther bank. The constellation had sunk with the season and with our travels south. Its nearness to the treetops emphasized our position at the southern edge of the continent.

And all around us, in the dank lowlands along the stream, frogs calling in the dark suggested the jingling of a multitude of little sleigh bells. We went to sleep with this chorus in our ears. And we awoke in the darkness before dawn with the calling of barred owls, the "eight-hooters," carrying up and down the Suwannee River. Far away they suggested the remote barking of foxes; close at hand they demanded—with a kind of throat-clearing "Arf! Arf!" before the question—"Who cooks for you-all-l-l?"

During its final miles the Suwannee widens, flowing through almost trackless swamps to divide at its delta and pour in a double-river into Suwannee Sound on the Gulf coast between Dead Man's Bay and Cedar Key. At the edge of the delta a cluster of low, unpainted houses huddles on a slight elevation that lifts it a few feet above the level of the surrounding swamps. This is Demory Hill.

Soon after breakfast one morning we started for Demory Hill. For a mile we sped down a wide, paved road. Then the pavement ended, dropping us onto a sand road. The sand road degenerated into wheel tracks wandering aimlessly through palmetto scrub, pine woods, cypress stretches, mudholes, and here and there islands of higher, richer soil shaded by live-oak trees. Along the more than fifty miles of this road, going and coming, we saw not a single human being. It is a land still inhabited by bears and deer, otter and wildcats. We saw deer trails crossing the primitive road where, in the heat of midsummer, the fine, dry sand flows like water down the ruts ahead of advancing wheels. Twice we came upon pigs, as wild as the deer, roaming small clearings. They are marked by their owners and turned loose for later rounding up. In this isolated region also live some of Florida's biggest rattlesnakes.

Diamondbacks are rarely out of the thoughts of dwellers at Demory Hill. All the men I saw were shod in high-topped leather boots. I stopped to talk to one elderly man, wearing a broad-brimmed black felt hat, and his son, a jovial young man with a pouting expression. Our conversation quickly veered to rattlesnakes.

People, the old man explained, don't understand about rattlers.

"They think a snake can strike ahead more than its own length. It can't. It can't strike much more than half its length."

Here, I thought, is somebody who knows what he is talking about.

But I thought too soon.

"That is," the old man went on, "when the snake is striking ahead. But when a rattler strikes *backwards*, it can strike *twice* its length!"

"Another thing," he said a little later. "Maybe you've heard rattlers swallow their young when they are in danger?"

I said I had but I didn't believe it.

"You're right! It isn't true. A rattlesnake never swallows its young."

This time, I said to myself, he has got it straight.

But I had hardly said it when he produced his trump card.

"What really happens is this: The female has pouches on either side of her head. The young rattlers crawl into these pouches when they are scared. The mother snake *never swallows* the young ones."

Thus it went on. One after the other, he exploded popular misconceptions only to top them with bigger misconceptions of his own.

Curiously enough, in this land of dangerous reptiles one of the most dreaded creatures is a harmless blue-headed, striped lizard that lives in bushes. Locally it is known as the lightning snake.

Near the mouth of the Suwannee the signs of spring most noticed are the blooming of the dogwood and the reappearance of the cardinals. The redbirds seem to move inland during the winter months, returning in the spring. On the day we visited Demory Hill, a great concentration of flickers was going through. Their white rump-patches flashed among all the trees.

Above the lower reaches of the river, perhaps a mile above the treetops, we noticed a cloud of glittering white forming and re-forming in the sky. It was an immense flock of white ibis, half a thousand birds or more, riding the updrafts. As they turned in the sunshine they twinkled like flakes of purest white, the shining cloud continually altering its form until it moved away beyond our sight.

The dark river, flowing so far below them, was carrying the blackness of its waters a full mile out into the Gulf. Among the innumerable islands at its mouth and in the shallows of Suwannee Sound, beyond, pelicans and cormorants were diving for fish. At one time racks were constructed in Suwannee Sound as perching places for the sea birds in an attempt to reproduce, in artificial form, the famous guano islands off the South American coast.

Seen from the air, the smudge on the blue of the Gulf, where the ink of the river flows into it, varies with the season, extending or contracting according to the volume of water in the flow of the stream. On this fluid calendar spring is marked by a longer line in blacker ink.

Part of that ink, the leachings of the swamp, was passing beneath the plank bridge at the edge of the Okefenokee as we recalled these other contacts with the Suwannee River in the springtime. For two days rain had swelled the flow from the great swamp. For two days rain had been moving from west to east. We had driven from the Mississippi with rain ahead of us all the way. It had done more than lift the level of the Suwannee. It had turned the dirt roads around Fargo into quagmires. We had planned to drive 12 miles into the swamp, to Lem Griffis's camp. But the road—like that other road down the levee along the Mississippi—was impassable.

Later we turned south from Charleston, South Carolina, and drove 200 miles out of our way in an attempt to get in a second time. And again a deluge stopped us. We had hoped to visit Floyd's Island, Big Water, and Billy's Lake—the very heart of the great morass. But we were forced to change our plans. It was at the opposite side of the slough, at its eastern edge, that we made the acquaintance of the trembling earth of the Okefenokee.

FOURTEEN

THE TREMBLING TREES

LAND of the golden mouse, land of the unstable earth, the great Okefenokee Swamp spread away under the heat of the spring sun. From the top of the 75-foot tower on Cowhouse Island we looked down into cypress treetops where parula and myrtle warblers fluttered amid the filmy green of new foliage on frosty-white branches draped with Spanish moss. Flickers loped past in the sunshine and that greater flicker, the pileated woodpecker, drummed like a woodchopper on a hollow limb. A tufted titmouse repeated over and over again, without tiring, the "Wheedle! Wheedle! Wheedle!" of its song.

Below the trees we could see three alligators and a dozen black-shelled turtles, as large as dishpans, sunning themselves beside dark, sphagnum-filled water. Carpenter bees swept past us, fanned our faces, darted at high-flying dragonflies, hovered where the sunshine glinted on the polished, patent-leather blackness of their bodies. Spring had brought these bumblebee-sized insects from their winter hibernation in tunnels in the logs of the tower and they were as exuberantly alive as the warblers. On this day the vast shallow bog of the Okefenokee —once a depression in a prehistoric sea—was extending its 400,000 acres in an immense caldron of life, a caldron beginning to seethe as spring turned up the heat.

Spring begins in a swamp—the Everglades. The earliest sign of its approach in northern states is found in a swamp—the appearance of the skunk cabbage. All along the line of its advance the most sudden changes, the swiftest growth, the most exuberant outpourings of life occur in swamps.

There were sounds of life as well as sights of life all around us in the Okefenokee. To our north we heard the grunting of pigs and the hammering of some swampman building a sty on an island of higher ground hidden by the trees—or so at first we imagined. Then we realized that we were listening to the famed batrachians of the Okefenokee. There was no island, no pigs, no hammering swampman. The grunting was the call of the alligator frog, *Rana heckscheri*; the hammering—a kind of batrachian hiccough: "K-hick! K-hick! K-hick!" that sounded for all the world like the stroke of a hammer on a board followed quickly by an echo—was made by the brownish-backed sphagnum frog, *Rana virgatipes*. Twenty different species of frogs and toads live in the Okefenokee. Each day, as spring advanced, the chorus of the batrachians increased in volume.

We heard some of these calls close at hand the following day when Will Cox, the big, soft-spoken, ex-otter trapper and cypress logger who acts as guide at the Okefenokee Swamp Park, poled us out along one of the water trails. These narrow lanes of water are the highways of the swamp.

"I have followed the same trail across the swamp that my grandfather used a hundred years ago," Cox told us.

Original Seminole trails, which alligators help keep open, are still in use in the Okefenokee. They were there when the first white pioneers arrived. These water roads are older than America's written history.

The trail we followed had recently been sliced out of the swamp, laying bare a cross section of its teeming life. Lizards, some brown, some brilliant green, raced with a scratching rattle over the bark of waterside trees. Whirligig beetles, the "mellow bugs" of the Okefenokee, spun like pinwheels on the brown water. About the top of a pipes-of-Pan cluster of pitcher plants small flies gyrated. A banded watersnake sunned itself on the decaying wood of a stump. And each time we approached and passed the masses of white, dangling flowers on the thickets of titi bushes the drone of honeybees swelled and diminished. Bees seemed everywhere that day. Overwintering in hollow cypresses in the swamp, they were busy with the honeyflow of spring.

The water trail turned. It carried us among cypress trees. And suddenly we found ourselves in the midst of a new and glorious experience—the first prothonotary warbler wave of our lives. Nellie saw the first bird. A male, with blue wings and head and breast of orange-tinted gold, it paused for a moment in the spotlight of a patch of sunshine. We held our breath as other warblers joined it. The whole cypress wood seemed full of prothonotaries. Darting and pausing, darting and pausing, the restless little birds trooped past us. Feeding as they went, they kept low among the trees and bushes until the one-pitch song of the males—a song that sounded like "Sweet! Sweet! Sweet! Sweet! Sweet!"—faded away in the swamp behind us.

Beyond the cypresses we came out into an open, treeless stretch. Cox poled his boat close to the edge of the water trail. A foot or so above the ground, in a clump of weeds, we saw a ball of dry vegetation. It was the home of a golden mouse. This relative of the familiar deermouse of northern woods is clad in thick, soft, reddish-gold fur. Cox has seen one dive into a swamp canal and swim across underwater. When it climbed up the far side the water streamed from its fur, leaving it almost as dry as an emerging duck. Like its northern relative, the golden mouse often makes its home in an abandoned bird's nest, doming it over muskrat-wise with a mound of dry vegetation to provide a snug little house with a roof.

The first sign of spring Cox notices each year in the Okefenokee is the "flowering out" of the cypress trees. Spring has really arrived for him when the alligators reappear from hibernation. During the winter otters play along the water trails. But as soon as the alligators come from their winter sleep they move back into the swamp away from the deeper water where the danger is greatest. Nothing in the Okefenokee is faster than an alligator in the water. Even the speed of an otter is insufficient to save it. Swimming snakes are easy prey and one old saurian that was lord of the waterway we followed had cleaned out most of the moccasins along its banks.

Alligators and otters are Cox's main interests in the swamp. Not long before, he had guided a scientist from the U.S. Fish and Wildlife Service into the depths of the Okefenokee on a trip to Big Water. The Washington man saw 3 alligators; Cox saw 119. During another trip a companion saw 9 alligators while Cox saw 97. His eyes have been sharpened by special interest and long experience. Yet these same eyes, so keen at picking out well-camouflaged saurians in the swamp, had noticed only two kinds among the innumerable butterflies of the region: "yellow ones" and "speckled ones." Similarly, Cox divides all the turtles of the Okefenokee into two groups: "gator turtles" and "snapping turtles."

Ahead of us we heard an odd, guttural croaking call. We looked up. An American bittern was alighting with a mud snake in its bill. It held the serpent about six inches back of its head. Writhing, twining, and untwining about the head and neck of the bird, the reptile sought to escape. Then we noticed that it had buried its teeth in the neck or neck feathers of its captor. Cox stopped poling. We watched events through our glasses.

Repeating its throaty call at intervals, the bittern shook its head like a puppy worrying a slipper. The mud snake hung on. The bird jerked and tossed its head with increasing violence. The serpent retained its grip. Again and again the bittern hurled its head from side to side through a wider and more violent arc. Yet several minutes passed before it could free itself. The instant the serpent's hold was broken the marsh bird dropped it to the ground, caught its head in its bill, crushed it, shook it, dropped it, caught the head again, crushed it, and shook it once more. Then it transferred its attention to the snake's body. Pinching it, shaking it, crushing it, it progressed from head to tail and from tail to head again, breaking the bones and softening its victim before swallowing it.

The way of a bird with a snake is always interesting to watch. Several species of birds have developed special stratagems for dealing with serpents. At Orange Lake, for example, the Florida gallinules build their nests of the dried stems and leaves of pickerelweed on floating tussocks near the water. Here the fledglings would fall easy prey to the venomous cottonmouth moccasins except for the courage and alertness of the parent birds. Whenever a moccasin comes slithering over the lily pads in the direction of the nest, one of the gallinules runs toward it.

Dancing over the wide, flat leaves, it maneuvers to the rear of the snake and gives its tail a hard whack with its bill. The snake whirls, white mouth agape, attempting to strike. The gallinule scurries out of reach. But the instant the reptile swings back and heads toward the nest again the bird rushes in for a fresh attack upon its tail. This continues, the bird avoiding the venomous front end of the snake and concentrating on the harmless rear end until the cottonmouth is vanquished and swims away.

The tail is frequently the Achilles' heel of the ophidian. I have read that mockingbirds sometimes attack and blind diamondbacks in the West by flying from the tail forward along an extended, crawling serpent and striking for the eyes as they dart past its head. In California ground squirrels begin at the tail when they overcome a snake in their own peculiar way. When these rodents come upon a small gopher snake, a foot and a half long or less, they sometimes dart in and bite through the backbone at the tail, then leap back, then make a second attack, biting through the backbone a little ahead of the tail, then jump back again. In this manner they work progressively forward, immobilizing the snake vertebra by vertebra. By the time they reach its head the serpent is paralyzed and helpless.

Writing in the *Wilson Bulletin,* for June, 1949, F. W. Preston tells of seeing a catbird vanquish a blacksnake by an attack upon its tail. On a July afternoon, near Slippery Rock, Pennsylvania, he noticed a blacksnake, about two feet long, resting in the crotch of an apple tree. Whenever it attempted to climb the trunk a pair of catbirds, with fledglings out of the nest, darted to the attack. They concentrated on the serpent's tail. The snake was mounting straight up, about ten feet from the ground, when one of the birds swooped down, seized its thin tail and jerked. The blacksnake, yanked loose from the bark, plunged to the ground.

The bittern finished its meal and then took wing as we approached. To the Georgia swampmen the bittern is the "sungazer"—just as the Cooper's hawk is the "striker," the black bear is the "hog bear," and cat briers are "bamboo vines."

Even the darkest, most villainous-looking water in the swamp, Cox told us, is perfectly safe to drink. Apparently the leachings that stain it brown also sterilize it. There are no malarial mosquitoes in the Okefenokee Swamp. Cox, nearing sixty, has never visited a doctor in his life. A friend of his, John Craven, spent half a century in the swamp without even catching cold. For years it was his habit to roll up in his blanket and sleep on the nearest higher ground when night overtook him.

"When he was past sixty," Cox related, "he was called to Waycross to serve on Grand Jury. He slept in a hotel room for the first time in his life. And the next morning, for the first time in his life, he woke up with a cold!"

Cox thinks of the swamp as a natural health resort. Many other men have praised its virtues since that long-ago day when William Bartram described the Okefenokee as the "most blissful spot of the earth," a "terrestrial paradise," and the home of Indian maidens, incomparably beautiful, called Daughters of the Sun. Bartram never visited the swamp himself. His information was hearsay. But it reflected the attitude of the early traders and explorers.

Writing in the late seventeen hundreds, Bartram spelled the

name "Ougquaphenogaw." On a map drawn in 1790 it is "Ekanfinoka." On another, which appeared six years later, the spelling is "Afenfonogo." On other pioneer maps of Georgia, preserved in the Library of Congress, the name of the great swamp appears as "Eokenfonooka," "Oquafanoka," and "Oke-fin-o-cau." In all nearly half a hundred spellings have been given to the name before the official spelling, "Okefenokee," was adopted.

Regardless of how its name was spelled, this great swamp on the Georgia-Florida line remained a paradox. A conventional swamp is a lowland area into which water from the surrounding country drains. But the Okefenokee is, like the Mississippi at its delta, higher than much of the land around it. Streams flow from it rather than into it. It is a vast sphagnum-bog sponge pouring its dark water into the St. Marys River, which flows to the Atlantic, and the Suwannee River, which flows to the Gulf. A low ridge running through the depression of the swamp forms the watershed. The trail along which Cox poled us was part of an imperceptible flow working westward toward the slide-off into the channel of the Suwannee.

Ages ago, when America's newest land, the southeastern tip of the continent, rose above sea level, the saucer-shaped basin of the Okefenokee became a shallow lake. During the millions of years since, debris of decaying vegetation has formed the unstable land of the swamp, underlaid with spongy, water-filled humus. At one point, before we turned back along the water trail, we stepped off onto a relatively solid portion of the swamp. It recalled the floating islands of Orange Lake. At each footfall nearby plants and bushes quivered. I stamped my foot and the tremors of a miniature earthquake spread away across the vegetation like ripples on water. In some parts of the Okefenokee high trees are set quivering by the stamping tread of a man below. In the days of the Seminoles the swamp was the Land of the Trembling Earth. It still is.

While the Okefenokee has isolated areas of solid land, such

as Billy's, Black Jack, and Bugaboo islands, most of it, like the *prairies tremblantes* of the Cajuns, is unstable, watery semi-land. Its depths present such eerie sights as will-o'-the-wisps and marsh-gas blowups and such visions of beauty as acres of blue flags blooming at once. Its dark lakes, its islands, its quaking prairies, its "houses" of massed vegetation, each has its own special inhabitants. Sandhill cranes nest on the prairies, their trumpeting carrying far over the lonely stretches. Since 1937 the Okefenokee has been a federal wildlife refuge. In a country where 100,000,000 acres of marshes already have been drained, this greatest swamp of the eastern seaboard promises to retain permanently the fascination of the untamed.

Around us, as Cox poled the shallow boat back along its course, the insects, the lizards, the birds were as active as before. The prothonotary warbler wave had moved off among the cypresses. But where it had been, yellow-throated and parula warblers searched through Spanish moss for insects. Throughout the great morass life was spawning prodigally under the warm spring sun. And behind all the life we saw we sensed other life, veiled and secret. The swamp has curtains behind curtains. No matter how far we penetrate, the unseen outstrips the observed; the sense of mystery is never entirely left behind.

The very smell of a swamp in the springtime is filled with mystery. That smell, rising around us as we climbed out of the shallow boat at the end of the trip, was growing with the season, increasing as warmth stimulated the bacteria of fermentation and decay. For me, at least, that smell is profoundly moving. It is exciting and unfathomable, as though it were stirring memories beyond memories, as though the cells of my body rather than my brain remembered.

Guy de Maupassant, perhaps, has touched the secret. "Nothing," he writes in his short story *Love*, "is more troubling than a morass. Is it the vague rumor of the reeds, the strange jack-o'-lanterns, the profound silence that causes the morass to resemble some dream country hiding a secret, impenetrable and dangerous? No: another mystery floats in the thick fog, the very mystery of creation, perhaps! For was it not in the stagnant, muddy water, in the heavy humidity of saturated lands, under the heat of the sun, that the first germ of life moved, vibrated and opened itself to the light?"

FIFTEEN

BARRIER ISLAND

BEFORE dawn we heard a low, faraway, fluttering call, musical and repeated over and over. It came through the darkness, an elfin sound, the calling of an owl mellowed by distance. Soon afterwards, about two hours before daybreak, a clapper rail by Awendaw Creek raised its voice and beside the tidal stream other clapper rails began to clatter. Then all was silence again.

During the previous days we had drifted more than two hundred miles northward from the Okefenokee. We had crossed the Altamaha River and the Savannah. We had followed low-country roads almost to the delta of the Santee. Beside the highway Carolina wrens had called their run-together "Come here! Come here! Come here!" With green, freshly cut bamboo poles, Negroes were out for the spring fishing, angling for "stump-knockers" in brimming roadside ditches. And along the way, even in the wildest places, we had run a gantlet of signs and admonitions: Drink Coca-Cola; Stop for School Buses; Where Will You Be in Eternity?; Use Sweet Dental Snuff; Eat at Sam's 100% American Cafe; Do You Feel Nervous? Take Dr. Pierce's Favorite Remedy; Rush, Rush for an Orange-Crush; Watch Out for Cattle. On this morning, awakening in a cabin beside Awendaw Creek, 30 miles north of Charleston, South Carolina, we were at the start of a dreamed of week on a barrier island.

Along the coast of the Carolina low country, between the

marshes and the sea, barrier islands, long and narrow, parallel the shore. They extend from the Santee delta southward more than a hundred miles. One, Sullivan's Island, is the setting for Edgar Allan Poe's *The Gold Bug*. Long a haunt of pirates and smugglers, these islands fronting the sea are still believed by some to hold buried treasure. For the naturalist they hold unburied treasure in the form of wonderfully diverse plant and animal life. And this was the season of the year when the charm of the islands is greatest. As Herbert Ravenel Sass writes: "Spring comes with especial exquisiteness to the long, narrow, barrier islands stretching up and down the low country."

At the northern end of the chain is celebrated Bull's Island. For several generations its ocean beach, its dunes, its tangled jungles, its fresh-water ponds, its marshes have been a Mecca for naturalists. Lying about three miles off the mainland, Bull's Island—about six miles long and three-quarters of a mile wide —is now part of the Cape Romain National Wildlife Refuge. At the time Gayer G. Dominick, New York broker, turned the island over to the government for a nominal sum, he also turned over with it a large manor house built under live oaks. Here the official in charge of the island lives and here guests, who make previous arrangements, may obtain board and lodging, roughing it smoothly in the midst of jungle surroundings.

We looked up our letter of instructions: "Turn off U.S. Highway 17 onto a dirt road known as the SeeWee Road. At the schoolhouse, turn right onto another dirt road. An abandoned telephone line of palmetto poles runs along this road. It will lead you to Moore's Landing Dock, east of Awendaw. The boat will meet you there at eight o'clock on Monday morning, April 7." Before eight we had reached the weathered jetty and a few minutes afterwards, Joseph Moffitt, a naval officer in World War II and now in charge of the island, was heading back along a tortuous channel in the Fish and Wildlife motorboat, the *Cape Romain*. Crossing the Inland Waterway, we wound past tidal flats where, among massed oyster and mussel shells, ruddy turnstones, greater yellowlegs, Hudsonian curlews, and oystercatchers, with great lacquer-red bills, fed, rose, circled, landed, and fed again.

Most of the day was still before us when we docked. And beyond that was a whole week of island life in the spring. We awoke mornings to the gobbling of wild turkeys—in itself a sign of spring. We heard a Cooper's hawk give a cry almost like the high-pitched clucking of a hen as it skimmed over an opening among the trees. This, too, was a sign of the season. For spring is nesting time and calling time for Cooper's hawks. Parula warblers and yellow-throated warblers and blue-gray gnatcatchers flashed from limb to limb among the live oaks and laurel oaks, sweet gums and cucumber trees. One day there were blue-winged teal on Summerhouse Pond; the next day they were gone. They had flown north in the night. The mockingbird, South Carolina's state bird, apparently leaves the island in winter and returns in spring. Behind the beach dunes one morning, we saw the first mocker of the new season flitting through a thicket of sweet bay. All across the interior of the island trails and puddles were coated with the spring pollen of the loblolly pines. Each day our shoes grew yellow with this arboreal dust. And over masses of wax myrtle, beside the path to the ocean beach, yellow waves of blooming jessamine filled the air with the perfume of spring.

It was our good fortune to have the island visited during our stay by someone we especially wanted to meet, William Baldwin, a young field biologist with the Fish and Wildlife Service. We had heard of him as a tagger of sea turtles. In the late spring these monsters of the deep drag their ponderous bodies out of the surf and onto the sand to lay their eggs. They come from the waves in the night and disappear into the sea before dawn. This is almost their only contact with the shore. In an effort to learn more about these creatures and their travels, Baldwin had been spending spring nights on the outer beaches. Above high-tide line the loggerhead turtle, a species that sometimes reaches a weight of 450 pounds, scoops out a hole and deposits from 80 to 150 eggs. As many as 600 loggerhead egg nests are thus formed in one season on the Cape Romain beaches. When Baldwin came upon one of these turtles busy laying her eggs he would bore a small hole at the rear edge of the shell and attach a numbered aluminum band. Already he had proved something previously unknown to science, namely, that the same turtle may visit the same beach two or three times in a season to bury successive batches of eggs.

One of these returning sea turtles, revisiting the shore by moonlight, gave Baldwin an exciting few minutes on the outer beach of Cape Romain. He came upon it just as it finished covering its eggs and began dragging its ponderous bulk toward the breakers. Struggling to get the aluminum band off, Baldwin attempted to hold back the turtle. He might as well have tried to restrain a caterpillar tractor. Then he tried to roll the monster over on its back. It was too heavy, weighing more than two hundred pounds. Steadily clawing its way toward the surf, the sea turtle dragged Baldwin to the very edge of the breakers before he succeeded in freeing the band. Its number revealed that this same turtle had been tagged on this same beach a few nights before.

Baldwin's trip to Bull's Island, while we were there, was made to sample the water at various depths in Summerhouse Pond. Coontail, a fluffy, rootless waterweed, had been increasing, replacing other vegetation of greater value to wildfowl. In refuge management the forces of nature are juggled to achieve desired results. By raising or lowering the water level only a few inches, by increasing or decreasing salinity only slightly, striking changes in vegetation are achieved. Before additional salt water was pumped into the pond to control the coontail, Baldwin was making an exact check on its salinity. At the head of a tidal creek, Summerhouse Pond has been dammed off from sea water for decades.

Among its claims to distinction is the fact that it is the home of one of the biggest saurians on the Carolina coast, a bull alligator fully 14 feet long. Two years before, two Fish and Wildlife men were pushing a shallow duckboat along the edge of Summerhouse when the big gator rushed them. The boat capsized. But the men were able to splash through shallow water and cattails to safety. This was the only instance Baldwin knew of an alligator attacking a boat. He thought the craft might have been near the alligator's nest and its upsetting more an accident than a direct attack.

This was a comforting thought as we launched a jittery cockleshell of a boat and I rowed about the pond while Baldwin took samples. Near a small island where egrets perched, I had noticed a long black log floating on the water. My glasses transformed the log into the largest alligator I had ever seen. It was, Baldwin said, the "big one." Even as I watched, the saurian sank out of sight leaving hardly a ripple on the surface.

A few months before, Baldwin had come upon the front half of a large raccoon floating on the pond. The jaws of the gator had snapped shut, cutting the swimming animal cleanly in two. As we zigzagged about the pond, among banana water lilies and beside cattail thickets where Worthington's long-billed marsh wrens set up their high-pitched clatter, we watched sharply on all sides. Once we passed directly over the spot where the big alligator had disappeared. But it did not appear again. And, although I swept the pond with my glasses on other days, I never caught a second glimpse of the "long black log."

However, events of interest were occurring wherever we looked on the ponds of this barrier island. The waterfowl that overwinter here had left for the north. But other birds were coming in from the south. The heron population of the island was building up. One blustery morning at Summerhouse Pond we spent an hour watching Louisiana herons and American egrets and little blue herons come scudding hawk-like down the wind to make thrilling turns, to be carried backward, to labor ahead, to parachute to a landing with downcurved wings. On another morning, calm and bright, as we stood near the masses of needle rushes that rise like great green fountains on the western shore of Moccasin Pond, a glinting of sunlight caught our eye. Through our glasses we saw an otter sporting in the sunshine, looping above the surface, appearing and disappearing like a porpoise while the water glinted and sparkled around him.

On a later day, at the far northern end of the island—where pirates once rendezvoused in Jack's Creek, where treasure hunters have dug most often on the island, and where the decaying tabby walls of an old fortification are so ancient that nobody is sure when or by whom they were built—we came upon another creature in its way as unexpected as the otter, as outstanding as the alligator. It flew up from a sandy trail with a loud chitter of parchment-dry wings. It thumped against the sounding board of a dry palmetto frond. It clung there, *Schistocerca americana*, one of the largest grasshoppers on the North American continent. With its reddish-brown body and spotted wings, this bird locust was nearly as long as my forefinger. We came upon this grasshopper only a few times, always on sandy trails. Usually it whirred away high among tree branches when we alarmed it.

Everywhere we went along the trails we saw hoofmarks in the sand. They were all over the island. And they were all the tracks of the same horse. A few years before, a garden had been started near the house and a surplus army horse brought to the island to pull the plow and cultivator. The garden was soon abandoned. But Solo, the horse, stayed on. Without work to do, he roamed the island by day and by night. The wild turkeys knew him and paid no attention to his approach. We once came upon him feeding with three white-tailed deer at the edge of a pond.

Isolated from his kind, this equine Crusoe led a morosely solitary existence. He seemed to enjoy a saturnine sense of humor. One evening he overtook me walking along a narrow roadway between two marshy ponds; he gently but steadily tried to nuzzle me off into the mud and water. A bright spot in his lonely life came when a retired army officer visited the island. He discovered that Solo was a trained cavalry horse. Riding him bareback, he had him turning, wheeling, maneuvering at his signals and commands. Then the army man departed. Solo, his specialized abilities unemployed, resumed his disconsolate wandering. When Joseph Moffitt tried to ride him, Solo indignantly bit him. He was an army horse and would have nothing to do with the navy.

Only once on the trails, during all that early-April week, did we meet another human being. This was a snake hunter from St. Louis who arrived after breakfast one morning and left with a bag of half a dozen reptiles to catch a plane home in the evening. There are only four kinds of snakes on Bull's Island: a blacksnake, a harmless watersnake, the lined chickensnake, and the cottonmouth moccasin. Only the last is poisonous. Visitors often assume that a fifth species, the copperhead, lives on the island. This is because young cottonmouths are similarly banded and colored. Lying on fallen live-oak leaves, these snakes are amazingly well camouflaged. On the Turkey Walk, leading to Summerhouse Pond, I stepped over a log and set my foot down less than fifteen inches from a coiled but sluggish young cottonmouth. Its pattern blended so perfectly with its background of small crisscrossing leaves that my eyes missed it entirely. These snakes grow darker as they grow older. Cottonmouths live as long as twenty-one years. Old individuals are often so black that all evidence of a pattern has disappeared.

The only permanent residents on Bull's Island at the time were two of the most congenial people we met on the trip, Mr. and Mrs. Moffitt. The migratory urge of spring was in the air and Moffitt was spending his spare time studying trailer catalogues. Our faith in southern cooking, badly shaken by restaurants along the way, was restored by Mrs. Moffitt's hush-puppies, conch stew, fried sea trout, and sweet potato pie. But most of all I remember one breakfast when whole-kernel hominy appeared on the table. Ever since my boyhood in the Indiana dunes, white, plump, flavorful kernels of hominy, fried in bacon fat until each is coated with a crisp, delicious shell, has been a food favored above 99 per cent of everything I have tasted. Simple, nourishing, filled with long-lasting flavor, it is a food supreme for the start of an outdoors day.

Usually after breakfast we started out with sandwiches in a knapsack to spend the whole day drifting over the island, stopping whenever something of interest caught our eye. One time it was a chameleon changing its skin; another time it was a duck hawk balancing itself in the wind at the top of a Spanish bayonet; at other times it was Florida gallinules giving grating little calls as they fed or white bluets beside the trail or a shining blacksnake that lifted its head higher and higher to watch us pass.

Day after day we paused at the same place to watch a running battle near a willow tree clothed in polleny catkins. Flies and bees hummed about the branches and they, in turn, had attracted insect hunters, lizards and birds, to the tree. A kingbird had established its perch on the dead limb of a neighboring tree. Each time it swooped to pick an insect from the air a ruby-throated hummingbird would shoot to the attack, seeking to drive it away.

Deer, raccoons, and wild turkeys had been down many of the trails ahead of us, leaving their tracks in the sand. April showers of live-oak leaves and, some days, April showers of rain sprinkled down around us. Along one moist stretch of trail near Moccasin Pond live oaks, probably rooted there when George Washington was president, spread massive, fern-covered limbs above us, while all around us the trunks were splotched with the red and pink and brown and green and purple of brilliant lichens.

The 12 miles of trails and roads on the island carried us

through widely varied surroundings. In 1940 Baldwin worked out a detailed habitat map of Bull's Island. Its 5,135 acres are divided thus: woodland, 1,515; salt marsh, 2,123; brackish ponds, 685; fresh-water ponds, 213; wax myrtle brush, 284; beach, 160; dunes, 93; food patches and strips, 40; Jack's Creek dikes, 16; headquarters clearing, 5. In its wooded areas the island represents a hammock habitat.

Although we were only three miles from the mainland, with shallows and tidal flats between, the life of the island is singularly isolated. The mainland is rattlesnake country; yet not a single diamondback lives on Bull's Island. The deer we surprised along the trail or saw bounding away across marshy shallows are a distinct subspecies, the product of inbreeding, found nowhere else in the world. There are no foxes on the island because there are no marsh rabbits. Why are there no marsh rabbits? I do not know. It is a perplexing riddle why storms and other natural disasters have not carried some of these creatures across to add to the population of the island. Perhaps the fact that the most violent storms in the area sweep from the sea onto the land may offer an explanation. Or it may be that life has become so balanced on the island that a new species has special difficulty in gaining a foothold.

However, at least one creature has found a place in spite of natural restrictions. This is the dark fox squirrel that peered down at us with bright little eyes set between white nose and white ears. Every squirrel on Bull's Island has descended from one pair of fox squirrels released about twenty years before. This Adam and Eve of the island squirrels were brought from the mainland by Gayer G. Dominick. Scientists have found in this community of related rodents an opportunity to study such things as the effects of interbreeding and population spread under natural conditions.

Scientists also journeyed to Bull's Island to study another, less attractive inhabitant, the tick. In one three-month experiment to discover the best repellent for use in the armed services, half a dozen men roamed the area wearing clothing impregnated with different chemicals. The barrier island was chosen for the test because it is one of the most heavily infested spots in the country. On my first day on the island, as I was reaching for an eyed-elater beetle on a decaying stump, my wrist seemed to develop a small mahogany-colored blood blister before my eyes. A tick had dropped and already secured itself so well that my fingernail slid over its body several times before I could dislodge it. So sensitive to warmth that they can almost be said to see with their skin, the ticks cling to leaves until some warm-blooded creature passes below. If necessary, they can fast for months while they wait. Laboratory tests have shown that some species of ticks can live for years without food. All those we encountered on the island had a single small silver spot on the back. This is the mark of that widespread species, the lone-star tick, *Amblyomma americana*. Each day, as we roamed over the island, we attracted a larger accumulation of ticks. Their increasing numbers formed a kind of arachnid yardstick that measured the advance of spring.

We wondered if the frayed tip of a wild turkey feather, which we picked up on one of the trails, also recorded the advance of the season. During the winter the gobblers and the hens separate and occupy different parts of the island. With the return of spring they come together again. Along the trails we passed places where they had scratched and dusted. Once a gobbler raced across a small opening ahead of us, its neck outstretched, its head held low, its beard almost scraping the ground as it ran. At the edge of another clearing, under a great live oak at sunset, we watched the whole pomp and pageantry of gobbler courtship. Slowly the magnificent bird paced back and forth beside a feeding female. It swelled in size. Its body feathers fluffed out, shining in metallic colors in the sunset light. Its chestnut-edged tail spread like a fan. Its wings drooped until they touched the ground. Its powder-blue head lifted. Stiff legged it strutted in stately parade. From time to time it paused, uttering its loud gobbling call, then resumed its pacing.

That sound was one we heard at every sunset and at every dawn. It was the island's most arresting voice of spring. Each night, as the light faded into darkness, it ceased, to be replaced by the chorus of the frogs, swelling and diminishing, coming through the darkness like the confused clamor of thousands of flying brant. Then, far away or near at hand, sometimes where the moonlight flooded through the shaggy branches of a live-oak tree just outside our window, the chuck-will's-widow began the steady repetition of its song. Our memories of those April nights are among the most vivid of all, particularly one night, the next to the last we spent on Bull's Island. It was a night on a barrier beach.

About sunset we packed our knapsack with extra sweaters, sandwiches, oranges, and a thermos bottle of hot tea and, after a day of uncertain weather, set out for the ocean beach. Beside the road a Carolina wren sang, sounding loud and shrill so close at hand—as though someone were sharpening shears on a lop-sided grindstone. Once we walked through an island of perfume beside a mound of jessamine, and just before we reached the shore we came to stunted trees behind a low ridge of dunes, trees with their tops sheared flat by the wind and all their twisted branches flaring away from the sea. Beyond was the barrier beach. It stretched away, deserted from end to end, as lonely as some primitive shore facing a pre-Columbian sea.

We sat down on the warm sand and leaned back against a beam from a wrecked ship, half buried in the beach. The play of sunset colors changed moment by moment over the expanse of water before us. Two hundred yards from shore a long raft of scaup rode the breakers, rising and falling, appearing and disappearing, as the waves rolled under them. The tide was out. Veils of falling rain, rain that had circled and missed us, increased in number over the sea. The east was serene and blue while in the west the sun was setting in a wild and broken sky.

We wandered along the shore, examining shells and gathering firewood for the night. Twice in succession, shells I reached for began sliding away down the wet sand, propelled by the feet of hermit crabs. High on the beach, where a dead palm tree had been thrown by storm waves, I broke off a decaying frond and discovered the massed white bodies of termites riddling the interior. Steadily the pile of wood increased beside the weathered timber. Gathering driftwood for a fire is a comforting occupation. It is direct and obvious in a world of confusing complexities. The benefits are seen at once. There are no lost or hidden links in the chain of action. Cause and effect, effort and result, are apparent at a glance.

A sprinkle of fine rain ran across the sand and then passed out to sea. A moment later the last rays of the sun streamed suddenly through a long gap in the clouds just above the black trees on the western horizon. Horizontally they shot over the sea, tinting the wave tips pink. They struck the fine shower that had passed us and the colors of a rainbow swiftly brightened. One end of the arch rested on the sea, the other on the northern end of the island. A faint band of red strengthened below the green—the beginning of a rainbow within a rainbow.

Rarely have I seen a more brilliant arch in the sky. The distinctness of its colors probably resulted from the fact that the sheet of falling rain contained an unusual number of small droplets of water. The finer and more numerous the water droplets in the air the more distinct is the rainbow, just as in a halftone illustration the finer the screen—the more and smaller the dots—the more distinct the picture.

A small cloud of shore birds scudded past us; they seemed to fly in and out of the arc of the rainbow. They were followed by three least terns, flying single-file. These dainty, butterfly-like creatures were so persecuted on Bull's Island, half a century ago, that feather hunters from the North, in a single season, wiped out the entire breeding colony. The scaup, more than one hundred of them among the outer breakers, rode the rise and fall of the darkening water—under the sunset, under the rainbow, as they would ride it under the stars. Finally their bobbing forms grew indistinct, part of the vast darkness that was enveloping us.

The tide had changed. The turn of the tide and the turn of the day had come at almost the same time. The waves were advancing on the shore; the night was advancing on land and sea alike. By our flickering campfire we sat on the edge of two mysterious realms, the realm of the sea and the realm of the night.

At seven-fifteen the first star became visible to our eyes. It was Sirius, the Dog Star. From then on, the glint and glitter of the stars and planets increased. Clouds rimmed the horizon where sheet lightning brightened and faded; but the great dome overhead was clear. Infinitely far above us, lost among the stars, we heard a lonely plane thrumming across the sky. Once in the dark, as we gathered fresh firewood, we debated without decision whether a light on the ocean's rim was a rising star or a ship standing offshore. Even our field glasses failed to dispel our uncertainty. Later two ships, like luminous hyphens an inch apart, crept northward along the horizon line.

This was Saturday night. All over the country, in cities and villages, in stores and theaters and dance halls, along Main Street and Broadway, Saturday night was something special. On our barrier beach, with the sea and the dark for our companions, it was something special too. The city man, in his neon-and-mazda glare, knows nothing of nature's midnight. His electric lamps surround him with synthetic sunshine. They push back the dark. They defend him from the realities of the age-old night. A hundred years after he asked it, the answer is still "yes" to Henry Thoreau's question: "Is not the midnight like Central Africa to most of us?"

When the postmidnight hours came, faint clouds formed in streaks or furrows or shoals of vapor. They seemed thicker to the south, and above Charleston, 20 miles away, the reflected light from thousands of street lamps formed a luminous patch on the sky, a kind of celestial lighthouse marking the site of the city.

Each time we piled driftwood on our fire the flames leaped high, brilliantly colored by salts of the sea impregnating the flotsam. They lighted the dunes and the ribbed sand of the beach and the white waves of the flood tide. With our fire as the hub of our activity, we wandered north and south along the beach. Swinging the beams of flashlights over the sand, we stalked ghost crabs, watching them scuttle back into their burrows at our approach. From grass clumps fringing the dune-tops came the metallic bandsaw buzzing of seaside grasshoppers. And beyond, just over the low ridge of dunes, a chuck-will's-widow called hour after hour.

It had fallen silent by the time we packed up and threw sand over the embers of our fire. The night was far gone and "the world and all the Sons of Care lay hushed in sleep." We started back through a gap in the dunes. We had gone no more than a hundred yards before a grayish, dusky bird leaped into the air from the sandy ground. It was the chuck-will's-widow. I caught it in the beam of my flashlight and held it for thirty feet or so as it fluttered upward. This voice of the night was silent as it rose on rapidly beating wings, shining and ghostly in the spotlight.

A still stranger sight was to greet us farther on. Cottonmouth moccasins—the "mackasin snake" of William Bartram—hunt in the night. We moved with caution along the narrow road bordered on either side by water and marshy tracts. We played the beams of our two flashlights along the path ahead of us. Lizards rattled over the palmetto fronds with a dry hissing sound. Frogs leaped from the grass over our feet. Once our flashlights picked out a huge shape bearing down upon us with shining eyes. It was Solo on one of his nocturnal rambles.

It was under such conditions that we came on a scene of eerie beauty. Twenty yards ahead of us we caught sight of a half-moon of green, glowing light shining in the darkness of the roadside. It appeared to be about the size of a silver dollar half thrust into the earth. At first I wondered if it was some animal eye reflecting back the rays of our flashlights. We swung the beams down. The spot glowed as eerily green as before.

Approaching closer, we discovered a large, whitish grub bearing luminous spots along its sides. Almost two inches long, it was nearly out of its burrow, curving in a semicircle. With both flashlight beams concentrated on it, it began backing into the ground. I pried it out with a bamboo stick. It curled up like a cutworm, lying on its side, the row of glowing dots shining as brightly as though formed of Neon tubes. We watched it for a long time, then placed it back on the soft earth where its tunnel had brought it to the surface.

This glowing apparition was the wingless, larvaform female of a beetle, a relative of the familiar firefly. To scientists it is *Phengodes*. To people in parts of the South it is the "neon worm." To us, appearing as it did when the new day was almost beginning, it was the final memory of our night on the barrier beach.

SIXTEEN

UNDERGROUND RIVER

THE year stands still in a cave. There is no summer, no winter there. Time is not divided into night and day, into four seasons of the year. The rising and setting of the sun is something remote and unreal. Calendars are meaningless in this moonless world of damp and darkness. Just outside the mouth of a cave wildflowers may bloom in May, their leaves may wither in August heat, they may be hidden beneath January snow. But within the cavern such extremes in weather are unknown. The year is one long unvarying season of even temperature. The position of the mercury hardly changes winter, summer, fall, and spring. It marks almost exactly the mean yearly temperature of the region.

Driving 500 miles—from Bull's Island south to Savannah and then angling northwest across Georgia to Chattanooga, Tennessee—we had traveled in brilliant, million-flowered spring all the way. Wisteria grew everywhere, even in the tops of lofty pines. It hung in lavender curtains or descended in pale-purple waterfalls from trees, from windmills, from fences. Blood-red thistles and sulphur-yellow thistles flowered beside the highway. Cherokee roses and zephyr lilies bloomed in yards. Redbud and dogwood bordered the road and ran up wooded hillsides. But we left all this behind, as we left spring behind, as we left even daylight behind, when we entered the cool darkness of Nickajack Cave, near Shellmound, Tennessee, 20 miles west of Chattanooga. Within this cavern the

annual range in temperature is only a few degrees. The thermometer stands at between 54 and 56 degrees Fahrenheit virtually the year around.

Four hundred years ago, De Soto visited Nickajack Cave.
Indians followed an ancient warpath for uncounted generations past its entrance. Soldiers of the Civil War fought for
the cave and its saltpeter deposits. Dancers, in the 1890's,
waltzed to orchestra music under its vaulted roof. Now, as we
approached it, the cave was deserted. Its mouth, 175 feet wide
and 60 feet high, yawned in the side of Raccoon Mountain. A
thick stratum of blue-gray Warsaw limestone ran in a flat
ceiling across the top, extending as far as we could see back
into the cavern. Out of the darkness toward us flowed a river
of cool air. We could feel it around us while we were still in
sunshine. Also out of the darkness flowed a river of cool, green-
tinted water, a subterranean stream issuing from the heart of
the mountain. It emerged among great rocks at one side of the
cave to wander away westward in the direction of the Nickajack
Narrows of the Tennessee.

Just inside the cave we stopped to look around. Sixty feet
above us the masonry globes of cliff swallow nests clung to the
limestone ceiling. On the walls beside us, where, eighty years
before, Civil War soldiers had cut their names in the rock,
masonry tubes, each several inches long, were cemented side
by side like the pipes of an organ. They were the nests of a
dark mud-working wasp of the genus *Trypoxylon*. Below them,
in the fine dust at the foot of the wall, ant lions had formed
the inverted cones of their pits.

A hill within the cave lifted us nearer the ceiling, then let us
down in a steep descent into galleries beyond. Light from the
entrance decreased in a kind of sunset behind the hill. In semi-
darkness we entered the largest corridor and switched on our
flashlights. The beams slid along water-worn limestone,
hopped across gaping side openings, revealed connecting galleries ahead. Like ants stealing along the branching corridors

of a riddled tree trunk we moved deeper into the cavern.

The rock walls around us had once been, quite literally, alive. Three hundred million years before, in the Mississippian period of the Paleozoic Era, in a time of towering fern trees and giant club mosses, the calcareous remains of unnumbered small invertebrates had collected underwater to form a deep layer of limestone. Condensing the activity of aeons that followed into a swift succession of events, we imagined the limestone lifted in the making of mountains; imagined rain water falling through the air, collecting carbon dioxide, becoming weak carbonic acid as it fell; imagined it seeping into small openings, forming calcium bicarbonate, dissolving limestone, enlarging cracks, forming sinkholes, hollowing out galleries, spreading in branching corridors deeper and deeper into the mountain, finding an exit, forming a channel through which a flow of water made its way. Thus the cave and the subterranean river were born.

The corridors we followed are considerably above the level of the river now. Those of a still higher level are dry and dusty. Far back in Nickajack, we were told, a great room beyond a "crawl," 200 feet long and hardly eighteen inches in diameter, a room that once held a lake, is ankle deep in dust as fine as talcum powder. One cave explorer who stirred it up in passing reported that part of the dust still hung in the air when he returned four days later. What is supposed to be the biggest stalagmite in the world is said to rise from the floor of this room. It measures 174 feet around its base. Another Tennessee cavern, a cave at Elk Valley, contains a lethal passage so devoid of oxygen that the bodies of rats that have made their way into it and have been suffocated remain for years without decomposing.

The corridor we were following, winding and narrow, suddenly expanded into an immense room, a chamber roughly circular with the arch of its ceiling rising 60 feet above our heads. Sweeping across the curve of this ceiling, the beams of our flashlights picked out dark smudges on the limestone. They were formed by the close-packed bodies of hibernating bats. The lofty chamber was the main bat room of Nickajack.

A curious feature of the bat population of this cave is the fact that it changes winter and summer. Different species inhabit it at different seasons of the year. All the hibernating bats we saw that day belonged to the same species, *Myotis sodalis*. They arrive in October and leave before the middle of May. During the summer they are replaced by several species: the little brown bat, *Myotis l. lucifugus*, Trouessart's little brown bat, *Myotis keenii septentrionalis*, the pigmy bat, *Pipistrellus*, and the little gray bat, *Myotis grisescens*. This last species, described by A. H. Howell in 1909, was originally discovered at Nickajack Cave.

The winter bats were gone and the summer bats were back, a month later, on the 15th of May, when we swung south on our trail to pay a second visit to this remarkable cavern. As we followed the same narrow corridor on that later day it was filled with a faint sizzling sound, like grease in a frying pan. The air was heavy with a smell suggesting a poultry house. Each foot we advanced the sound grew in volume. It was joined, as we neared the end of the passage, by another sound, a sound like the rushing of wind in the cavern. Yet the air around us was stirred by only the faintest of breezes. We reached the doorway of the vaulted chamber once more and swung our flashlight beams upward. The air was filled with the wheeling forms of disturbed bats, their dim, indefinite shapes, like shadows of bats rather than bats themselves, becoming suddenly bright and sharp as they momentarily flicked across the beams of light. Their beating wings, a thousand tight-stretched membranes striking the air at once, produced the illusion of a great wind.

Above this wheeling multitude the dome of the cavern was decorated with continents and islands and archipelagos of black—masses of bats, bats beyond our counting or calculation. Around them the stone of the ceiling seemed studded with specks of shining silver or diamonds in the rock where drops of condensed moisture reflected back the rays of our flashlights. Continually, from the hanging clusters, fresh bats dropped to join the confused merry-go-round in the air. Immeasurably magnified, the sizzling sound we had heard in the corridor had risen into a metallic, grating, high-pitched climax—the sum total of an infinite number of squeaking calls given off by the flying mammals.

Besides the sounds we heard, we knew there were others, so high-pitched that our ears were unaware of their existence. These ultrasonic cries have a frequency of roughly 50,000 cycles per second, 30,000 cycles above the range of the human ear. Bats' ears, it has been shown, can hear up to 100,000 cycles. During flight the sensitive ears of these aerial mammals catch echoes of the high-frequency sound waves that warn them of obstacles ahead.

In a laboratory at Harvard University, where I visited Donald R. Griffin and Robert Galambos when they were making their pioneer researches in "bat radar" in 1940, I heard a Pierce apparatus catch and translate these ultrasonic cries into audible sounds. A bat flying about the room uttered a quick series of squeaks as it approached an object ahead. So rapid is this succession of "soundless sounds" that the records of the Harvard experimenters showed that as many as thirty, or even fifty, cries a second are sometimes uttered by the flying bat.

Ever since the eighteenth century, when Spallanzani hung strings from a ceiling with a little bell at the end of each, and demonstrated to his own mystification that a bat flying in the dark could avoid striking the strings and ringing the bells, the navigational skill of these animals has been a source of amazement. The key to this ability is the short wave length of the ultrasonic sound. The bat's radar would be far less effective if it employed only the longer wave lengths of sounds we can hear. They would not echo back from small objects as do the short wave lengths of the high-pitched cries the bats use.

At a cave in Pennsylvania, Charles E. Mohr once observed a striking instance of the effectiveness of this system of sound navigation. In an attempt to capture bats for study, he stretched a tennis net across the mouth of a small cavern. It completely blocked the opening with the exception of a slight gap that a forefinger would have bridged, a gap less than three inches wide. Yet, every bat in the cave, flying at full speed in the dark, avoided the net and shot through this one small opening!

Several times, as we retraced our steps along the water-worn corridor, alarmed bats rushed by us down the passageway. They never touched us although, each time, they swept so close that we could feel on our faces the breeze that formed momentarily in their wake. On the wall of the corridor, within reach of my arm, a little brown bat hung upside down, wrapped in profound slumber, dead to all the excitement around it. I ran the tip of my forefinger gently along its back. It stirred in its sleep. Under my finger its fur was soft and velvety. It recalled the robe of bat skins worn by Atahualpa, the last of the Inca kings. Behind us the cries of the multitude of disturbed bats sank again to a mere sizzling noise. This sound, the sound of the active bats, was one of the few indications, in this seasonless world of the cavern, that spring had come.

Later that day, on the underground river in the cave, we observed another sign. We were riding in a small boat in which a farmer living nearby took us far back into the cavern on the subterranean stream. The only sounds on that silent, glassy flow were the startled exclamations of falling drops of water. Moisture collected on the rock overhead, swelled to a larger and larger drop, let go, struck the surface of the river with a liquid "plop!" that echoed in the stillness, magnified by the walls of stone. The sound of dripping water is the voice of the cavern. When spring replaces winter outside the cave, our companion told us, dripping increases in Nickajack.

Aristotle, who classified metals as "water in a sense and in a sense not," believed that winds rushing through subterranean caverns caused earthquakes. Around us, on this river in a cave, the air was unmoving. Here, even the smallest fluting of the wind is stilled. Twice we ran through "storms" along the way. But they were storms without wind and without violence. Each time, for a dozen yards or so, we passed through a kind of loose mist where innumerable droplets of water drifted in the air.

Where the stream that flows through Nickajack originates, nobody knows. After a heavy rain on the other side of the mountain, its flow increases. At such times its water becomes slightly milky. Normally it is so clear that in one of the lakes, where the stream spreads out in a wider cavern, an aluminum dipper can be seen distinctly, although it lies on the bottom under 30 feet of water.

Half a dozen times we floated across subterranean lakes surrounded by water-carved stone, fluted, rounded, sculptured into grotesque shapes in which an active imagination could see faces and cathedrals and animals, all immobile, all unchanged for centuries. Stalactites, those icicles of stone, all seemed icicles of ice here; all seemed melting, each with a large drop of water pendant at its tip. Wherever our electric searchlight turned, we saw the eerie scenery of the cave double, its inverted image below, mirrored on the unmarred surface of the water. But sometimes, as we looked, the image wavered, the mirror was shattered by the plunge of a large drop from the tip of a stalactite.

Both the carved stone and the stalactites around us were the product of unhasting change, of such vast stretches of time that they brought to mind the Oriental's definition of eternity: "When the Himalayas shall be ground to powder by a gauze veil floating against them once in a thousand years."

Nearly a mile in from the mouth of the cave we came upon a single bat attached to the rock wall above the river. All around it the limestone had been fashioned by the water into a subterranean badlands or Grand Canyon. Below, the water shallowed away above a bar that projected into the lake and there Nellie caught sight of a ghostly creature. It was a snow-white crayfish. Like other members of the white fauna of the cave depths, this crayfish was blind. The unvarying night of Nickajack curtains a continual struggle between the sightless. White, blind fish seek the eggs of white, blind crayfish that devour white, blind isopods in the dark. Specially sensitive hairs project from the claws of the cave crayfish. They partly compensate for its blindness, supplementing its antennae as organs of touch.

In its wanderings our subterranean stream carried us directly under the point where three states meet. About a mile and a half in, just before a great rock slide prevents a boat from going farther, the river spreads out into Mirror Lake. Above it the state lines of Georgia, Alabama, and Tennessee join. We circled the underground pool in a tristate boat ride before we started back. As our light swung through a full circle it illuminated a parade of bizarre shapes, gleaming with moisture, carved from the rock around the edge of the lake. It also illuminated something else.

Suddenly the beam was filled with flying motes. Pale, ghostly little fungus gnats swarmed above the water, drifting on the motionless air. They came out of the dark into the searchlight beam, shone white in its rays, disappeared into darkness again. These frail creatures, living in the heart of a mountain, had never seen sunlight. Theirs was the world of a subterranean passage, damp, dark, and silent. We had seen a few pale gnats living dangerously in the very bat room of the cavern. But here, where their minute wings carried them from state to state as they fluttered over the water, they were concentrated in such numbers that we rode through clouds of them.

Into one of these assemblages I swept a makeshift insect net—a small glass vial with an open mouth no more than three-quarters of an inch across. Two of the gnats were imprisoned inside. One now rests in that Westminster Abbey of the Insects, the collection of the American Museum of Natural History, in New York City. Dr. C. H. Curran, dipterist of the institution, places it in the genus *Orthocladius* (*Wulp*). A North Carolina relative of the Nickajack fungus gnats is one of the most remarkable of all the insects. Its larva is not only luminous but, spider-like, it spins a web in which it captures the tiny insects on which it feeds.

On our return trip we moved with the almost imperceptible current of the underground river. Our voices echoed hollowly when we spoke. We passed rounded mounds of yellowish deposits where stalagmites were building up. We counted seven distinct layers of rock as our eyes followed a beam of light mounting the 167-foot wall of the Echo Room. We drifted past the place where a pole bridge once carried Confederate soldiers across the stream to the saltpeter mines. At one time, more than one hundred men worked these deposits. Daylight came suddenly and we drifted out on the green-tinted stream, past immense rocks, under the wide flat ceiling of the entrance, out into sunshine again.

Near the mouth of the cave the dripping of water had increased noticeably. On days before a storm, our companion told us, the condensation of moisture here is greatest of all. These falling drops in the cavern proved accurate weather prophets. For that evening a deluge, accompanied by thunder and lightning, continued for hours. It provided another memorable view of cavern bats in action.

Behind our cabin at the Interstate Tourist Court, half a dozen miles west of Chattanooga, that night a neon sign 20 feet long faced a wide valley. Its glowing red and green tubes spelled out "INTERSTATE" in letters three feet high. As soon as dusk had fallen, moths began to assemble at the sign. They whirled and rose and fell, tinted by the neon glow. Smaller insects joined the dancing throng. At times they rose above the sign like sparks swirling upward from a fire. All the

winged throng congregated before the green letters and ig-
nored the red. It is the blue end of the spectrum that has the
greatest attraction for nocturnal insects.

In the grass below the sign fireflies flashed on their tiny
lamps, the greenish tinge of their luminescence almost exactly
matching the greenish glow of the neon tubes. Beetles from
time to time thumped against the sign and fell kicking to
the ground. We noticed the next morning that mockingbirds
came early to feast on the dead and injured insects. But before
that another harvest had been reaped by the flying bats.

They came in the dusk, soon after the moths arrived. Sweeping in a straight run past the sign, tinted now green, now red,
they plowed through the swirling cloud of insects. They appeared from the dark and disappeared into the dark, only to
reappear going in the opposite direction. As one light-gray bat,
almost luminous in the neon glare, fluttered past, a jagged
thunderbolt behind it transformed it for an instant into a black
silhouette. Lightning flashed with increasing frequency. At
each glare the blackness of the rain clouds seemed greater.
The first drops fell and then the deluge began. But the charmed
insects danced unheeding before the light, and the bats rushed
back and forth undeterred by the downpour. Hour after hour
this show went on.

During one period of two minutes when I kept track a bat
passed the sign every three and a half seconds. The largest
number of bats I saw rushing past at one time was four. Each
flying mammal would dart down and, like a racing plane
streaking past a grandstand on the straightaway, rush down
the length of the lighted sign. And, all the while sheets of rain
were sweeping across the valley, the lightning came in rapid-
fire stabs and around the horizon thunder seemed caught
among the mountains, unable to escape, rolling and rever-
berating continually.

Far into the night, even after the storm had passed, we sat
watching this strange show—the tinted, whirling insects and

the shuttlecock of the bats—while all around us were the fresh smell of the rain and the coolness of the spring night and the perfume of the washed flowers. This was the odd, exciting climax of our day associated with a world without spring, with Nickajack cavern and the unforgettable stream that flows in silence and darkness through it.

SEVENTEEN

THE POISONED HILLS

ALL that morning, in the April sunshine, our road had carried us through mountain forests, green and lush. Then, like a pleasant dream sliding into a nightmare, the country swiftly changed.

The forest thinned away. The trees grew smaller, became stunted, disappeared altogether. Bushes shrank and vanished. Grasses died away. Blighted land replaced the forest. All around us dead hills, red, raw, ribbed by erosion, stood stark in the sunshine. Hardly two miles from dense woodland we were in the midst of a moonscape on earth. Ahead of us the road led through a land of desolation, through a man-made desert, through a hundred square miles of poisoned earth.

We were in the southeast corner of Tennessee, in the Ducktown Desert of the Copper Basin. Chattanooga lay 70 miles to the west behind us, Gatlinburg and the Great Smoky Mountains more than a hundred miles to the north and east along the Tennessee–North Carolina line. Like Nickajack Cave, which lies at the junction point of three states, the Ducktown Desert occupies a position where three states—Tennessee, Georgia, and North Carolina—join. The boundaries of the three commonwealths meet near an old church on a desolate elevation which bears the ironical name of Pleasant Hill.

All the hills were pleasant here less than a hundred years ago. What had happened? What had left these slopes around us sterile and lifeless? What had produced this desert in the midst of a green landscape? We pulled in for gasoline at a filling station perched like an oasis on a barren hilltop. Our questions were an old story for the proprietor. Ten thousand times a year he had heard them. Bewildered tourists had interrogated him so often that he had had a pamphlet printed in self-defense. From it and from other sources we learned the history of this tragic area. It is a classic tale of land abuse. It is also, in its way, a murder story. For it deals, literally, with the murder of a countryside.

Until about 1840, Cherokee Indians occupied the land. Hardwood forests clothed the hills and shaded brooks meandered toward the Ocoee River. Then General Winfield Scott, carrying out orders, rounded up the Indians and herded them west. White settlers moved in. Not far from the village of Ducktown copper was unearthed, and a scramble of fortune hunters began. The village boomed. It was at one time more prominent than either Knoxville or Chattanooga. It had a newspaper, the Ducktown *Eagle*, before the Civil War. During the war copper from Ducktown played an important part in keeping Confederate armies in the field.

At first ore was hoisted to the surface with a hand-operated windlass. The bellows of the smelting furnaces were powered by old-fashioned water wheels. And the refined metal was packed on mules 70 miles to the railroad at Dalton, Georgia. By 1853, however, gangs of laborers had cut a road through the Ocoee Gorge to the west and for decades thereafter ironshod wheels of heavy wagons rolled behind straining horses to carry copper 40 miles to the railroad at Cleveland, Tennessee. We had followed this same route, now U.S. Highway 64, that morning as we passed through the Cherokee National Forest.

In the early days of copper mining, it was a custom to roast the ore under large log fires before placing it in the furnace. This eliminated the sulphur. As the Ducktown area developed, the demand for wood mounted. One company alone consumed 20,000 cords of wood and 500,000 bushels of charcoal annually. Convict labor was pressed into service to chop wood. Axes rang all day long. The forests receded in an expanding circle. At the same time the flaming piles of wood, sending up their showers of sparks night and day, ignited the surrounding grass and bushes. Behind the receding forests, in times of dry weather, almost daily fires ran across the open spaces. Over and over again, year after year, flames swept the earth bare of vegetation. Always it came back. But always it was consumed again.

Even worse than ax or fire, however, was a third enemy of the vegetation. This was the clouds of sulphur-dioxide gas that rose from the roasting piles and hung in a noxious pall over the hills of the Copper Basin. It attacked the grass and plants and bushes that remained. It damaged the breathing pores of the leaves. Evergreen needles became brown. Leaves on deciduous trees turned white, red, red-brown, or yellow. Growth rings in the trunks of the dying trees became thinner with each succeeding year.

Different kinds of vegetation respond in different ways to the poison of this gas. Blue violets, for example, when enveloped in sulphur dioxide, lose their blue and turn green. Larch trees are highly susceptible to the fumes in spring but more resistant in fall. Hemlocks, white pines, and sycamores are easily killed by the gas; red maples, white oaks, and black gums are more resistant to it. On still days, when there is fog or high humidity, the damage is greatest. Vegetation on hillsides facing the roast yards and smelters of the Copper Basin was first affected by the fumes.

In addition to attacking the growing plants, the sulphur dioxide entered the soil, either directly by absorption or indirectly by atmospheric precipitation or through absorption by vegetation. This tended to increase the acidity of the soil.

By the end of the roast-yard era, that is, about the turn of the century, all the trees were gone from the region and all the lower forms of vegetation were going. The hardy sedge grass, which had withstood the attack longest, was giving way before the endless burnings. The protecting skin of the earth, vegetation, was being sloughed away. Patches of bare soil expanded. Those twin instruments of erosion—the chisel of the rain and the hammer of the wind—did the rest. The climatic extremes and the heavy Appalachian rainfall of the region speeded the destruction. Swiftly the fertile topsoil slipped away down Potato Creek, down Bushy Creek; millions of tons of it washed away as silt down the Ocoee and the Tennessee, down the Ohio and the Mississippi. Left behind, like a red flayed carcass, were the raw hills of sterile undersoil.

They rose around us as far as we could see. They formed a nightmare region, symbolic of all the erosion-ridden fields, all the dust bowls man has created on this continent. Only a few minutes before, we had stopped by a mountain spring amid woods to listen to a hooded warbler sing high in a yellow birch. Small birds had been everywhere. The forest edge along the roadside had swarmed with them. There life was at an exuberant peak. Here it seemed almost entirely absent. We heard the faraway jingling song of a field sparrow on one of the patches of sod that still clung to an eroding hillside. We saw three English sparrows picking on the bare ground before a clapboard house that huddled disconsolate on a treeless plain, its roof tinted pink by dust from the desert hills. But in all that accursed red land we saw only one wild songbird among the millions then migrating north.

It was drinking from a small streamlet of clear water that flowed down the groove of a deep gully. Even there, where water was plentiful, the sterile soil supported hardly a single plant. Beside the rill, bending down, then lifting its head high as it drank, was a white-throated sparrow. Its crown was brilliantly streaked, its throat patch snowy, the yellow before its eye vivid in the intense sunlight. In this bleak setting this

migrant, pausing on its journey to damp, mossy, shaded northern woods, looked incomparably beautiful.

Near the edge of the desert, where the patches of sedge grass
were larger, half a dozen cows wandered about, feeding as
best they could on the sparse pasturage of these shrinking islands in a sea of erosion. A few meadowlarks, I was told, still
return to nest on these patches that hang like pieces of slough-
ing skin to the hillsides. During the time nestlings are being
fed the larks fly from patch to patch, as though among the
islands of an archipelago, in their search for insects.

But insects, like other forms of life, are scarce in the Ducktown Desert. We saw a few small blue butterflies, azures of
spring, drifting along the roadside. And once, when we stopped
on a hilltop to view the dead landscape around us, we discovered minute red ants swarming over the red soil. They were
racing wildly, bumping into one another, milling about a
small caterpillar a few inches from the anthill. Here was a
great prize in this austere land. Never have I seen ants of a
similar size running with greater speed. The untempered glare
of the sun beat down upon them. Its heat shifted them into
high gear.

I laid down a thermometer beside the anthill. Its mercury
slid swiftly upward until it touched the 115-degree mark. What
would a midsummer reading be? Without the balance wheel of
vegetation, the bare hills of the Copper Basin heat up rapidly
under the sun and cool off just as rapidly with the coming of
night. Between midafternoon and night on a September day
the thermometer may fall as much as 35 degrees. The greatest
daily range of temperature known is found in parts of the
Sahara Desert, where the mercury often plunges 110 degrees,
and sometimes as much as 130 degrees, between midafternoon
and night.

In other ways the disappearance of vegetation has modified
the local climate in these badlands of the South. During summer months, for example, the heat is usually greater at the

eastern edge than at the western edge of the area. The prevailing winds are from the northwest. They flow across the vast griddle of bare ground and are heated as they go. Moisture in this red soil also evaporates at an abnormally rapid rate. When scientists of the U.S. Forest Service made tests they found that the speed of evaporation on the naked hills was five times as great as in the neighboring forest.

As we drove past the great smelter of the Tennessee Copper Company, at Copperhill, in the heart of the Ducktown Desert we looked up and saw lofty stacks discharging their fumes high in the air above us. After years of litigation, the U.S. Supreme Court, about 1907, ruled that the copper companies of the area were responsible for controlling the sulphur dioxide that had previously been liberated into the air. In consequence, special equipment was installed to recover sulphuric acid from the smelter smoke. The result is that today the Copper Basin is the largest producer of sulphuric acid east of the Mississippi. To aid in dispersing what fumes remain in the smoke away from the immediate neighborhood, higher smokestacks were built. One of the stacks that towered above us was 400 feet high.

Can the Ducktown Desert ever come back? Can this moonscape ever be made fertile again? Extensive researches were carried on in the area before World War II by the TVA and the Tennessee Copper Company. The Tennessee Valley Authority was concerned because erosion among the naked hills threatened a rapid silting up of some of its dams. Under the direction of the Civilian Conservation Corps hundreds of thousands of trees were planted. Check dams, formed of brush and hogwire, were set up in gullies. Hilltops were mulched to retain moisture and prevent runoff. From Africa, Japan, the Mediterranean countries, plants were brought to Tennessee and tested as cover for the poisoned hills.

In nearly a hundred different plots, scattered over the area, the scientists tried out plants with strange names and remote origins—kudzu, Sudan grass, trailing lespedeza, Italian rye grass, crown vetch, Bermuda grass, bird's-foot deervetch, Bahia grass of the Pensacola strain. And one by one they crossed them off the list. A single plant, *Eragrostis curvula,* or weeping lovegrass, a native of South Africa, proved useful in the completely denuded areas. Among the innumerable trees tested, black locust showed itself most effective in the gullies and pitch pine on the exposed hillsides.

Before World War II virtually brought to a halt efforts at reforestation, more than 2,400,000 trees were set out. We looked around us. A few small clumps of pines huddled together amid the waste. These were the trees that had survived, an almost negligible number. The vast majority had succumbed to the insurmountable conditions of life in this desert produced by man. So far man has failed to undo the damage he has done. The problem of the poisoned hills—a classic instance of forest and soil destruction—remains unsolved. Unless more effective aid is forthcoming from man, the desert has only the long hope of nature's slow repair.

We drove on through this land no spring could awaken. Here no showers could stimulate probing roots and rising stems. Here no sun could contribute to the production of chlorophyll. The hills were stricken and the land lay dead. But, as we drove on, grasslands reappeared. Small trees, at first widely scattered, grew more numerous. They gained in size. Then we were in woodland once more, the desert left behind. All the lushness of spring surrounded us as we climbed on winding roads through mountain country to the east. But in our mind's eye, all the way and during days that followed, we saw the bare ribs of the earth, that strange, dead, red earth which spreads away over the tragic hills of the Ducktown Desert.

EIGHTEEN

TRILLIUM GLEN

ONLY 120 miles, air line, separated us from the desolation of Ducktown. Yet we might have been half around the world, so great was the contrast.

We had driven down a dusty road that afternoon and walked past silvery trunked beeches and among robin's plantain and violets and star chickweed, into the soft, leaf-filtered light of a mountain glen. The glare and heat of the denuded hills were far away. The coolness of a grotto surrounded us. The air of the glen was perfumed with the scent of thousands of woodland flowers. It was murmurous with the music of falling water. We were at Pearson's Falls, near Tryon, North Carolina, at the southern end of the Blue Ridge Mountains.

Like the leaves of a partly opened book, the walls of the narrow glen rose steeply on either side. They were tilted flower fields, starred from top to bottom with the great waxy pink and white blooms of immense trilliums. Changing color as they grow older, some wake-robins range from snowy white through pink to deep purple-pink before their petals wither. Our first and most lasting impression of the ravine was this trillium tapestry that ascended on either hand.

But there were other flowers too: hepatica, columbine, Dutchman's-breeches, bloodroot, lady-slipper, spring beauty, wood anemone—just to name them over is to bring to mind the sight and smell and feel of woodland loam. Nowhere else along the way did we find so glorious a wild flower garden as in this hidden nook among the North Carolina mountains.

Half a century ago John Muir tried to buy a section of prairie land at his boyhood farm in Wisconsin, hoping to turn it into a sanctuary where the pasque-flower would bloom in the spring and conditions that existed in pioneer times would be maintained for future generations to see. He was unable to acquire the land. But, more and more, local groups are carrying out Muir's idea. They are performing invaluable service by preserving representative areas in different parts of the country. Habitat areas, as well as species of birds and wildflowers, can become extinct. Conservationists have grown increasingly conscious of the importance of these small, "type-specimen" sanctuaries. There is no finer example in the country of the value of such a preserve than the glen at Pearson's Falls. Since 1931 it has been a sanctuary maintained by the Garden Club of Tryon.

Our lives touched it at this one point, at this one time in spring when its magical beauty was unrivaled. Along the path to the falls we hardly advanced a foot without pausing to delight in some new wildflower. White violets blooming among hepaticas; the umbrella leaves of the mandrake sheltering the forming May apples; the massed plants of the false Solomon's seal crowding together on a rocky ledge; the white Dutchman's-breeches and the red columbine—the Jack-in-trousers—these, each in turn, attracted our attention. We bent close to see foam flowers that enveloped their upright stems in little clouds of white. The tip of each tiny floret seemed dipped in wax of a delicate apricot hue.

Up the slopes the striped flowers of the jack-in-the-pulpit rose among the trilliums. Like the skunk cabbage, the jack-in-the-pulpit blooms before its leaves appear. It also is a plant that changes its sex, becoming female after storing up food for three or four or even five years. Another oddity among the familiar woodland flowers around us was the bloodroot. Each year it consumes the rear portion of its root and adds a new section to the front part, thus continually renewing its root-stock. Theoretically a bloodroot should be immortal. However, it requires special conditions for its existence. It dies, for instance, if the trees around it are felled.

It is no accident that most of the spring's earliest flowers bloom on the woodland floor. This is the time, before the leaves of the trees are completely unfolded and the shadows have grown dense, that the maximum amount of light for the growing season reaches the plants. It is then that they complete their most important vegetative and reproductive functions. Just as there is a direct relationship between the amount of light reaching the interior of a forest and the character of the vegetation growing there, so there is a direct relationship between the amount of light at different seasons and the time of blooming of these woodland plants. Of necessity, wildflowers of the woods bloom early.

In several places the sides of the glen were dripping like the walls of a grotto. Where a continual trickle of water ran down saturated wicks of moss on one little ledge beside the path, a half-circle of maidenhair ferns clung to the disintegrating rock. In A *Natural History of Pearson's Falls*, an early book by Donald Culross Peattie that did much to arouse interest in preserving the glen, thirteen different ferns are listed as native to the ravine. They include the walking fern, the rattlesnake fern, the sensitive fern, and the ebony fern. Nine species of violets also grow in the glen. We saw—below the troops of trilliums, the trout lilies, and the lady-slippers—violets of many kinds: white violets, yellow violets, blue violets. During almost the whole length of our trip we found violets, like the multitudinous footprints of spring, scattered over the map before us.

At the head of the glen the path brought us to the white lace of Pearson's Falls. It is lace formed of water by gravity on a loom of granite. In a thin, foaming layer the water of Pacolet River slides down the face of successive shelves of rock. The sound of this falling water is murmurous, calming, companionable. Here is no mighty, roaring Niagara, no deep-tongued bellow. This was a sound for a glen to enclose.

Red-gold sand forms a little bar at an edge of the pool into which the cascade falls. On this bar I picked up one perfect wing of a yellow swallowtail butterfly. Perhaps it had fallen into the ravine when some bird stripped it from the body of a captured insect. Lying there in the full brilliance of its colors, it recalled the Guiana Indians, in the South American jungles, who cling to the poetic belief that the most beautiful butterflies contain the souls of their ancestors.

Night and day the falling water of Pearson's Falls generates a cool, moist breeze. It stirred the ferns and the lady-slippers and the pendant white flowers along the underside of branches of the silver-bell tree that leaned out over the pool. It blended together the perfumes of many wildflowers. Sometimes, as we slowly walked back along the trail, we came to areas where one scent predominated as when we passed strawberry bushes and caught the overwhelming spilled-wine fragrance of their dark-red flowers.

The perfume of the wildflower is never a product of the nectaries. It comes from special cells holding the essential oils that produce the fragrance. When you break open the skin of an orange you see similar cells near the surface. Oftentimes the essential oils are waste products of the plant. They are occasionally stored in scentless chemical compounds within cells in the flower buds. When the flowers unfold, the compounds are chemically changed so that they produce fragrance. The cells that contain the essential oils may be in the leaves, the petals, or even the stamens of a plant.

It is the petals of the yellow jessamine, for example, that is the source of that flower's famous perfume. Thyme, equally famous, has its oils stored on the surface of its leaves in flask-shaped cells that are easily broken. It gives off its perfume at a touch or under the hot sun. The cells of rue lie just beneath the surface of the leaf and are roofed over with a thin layer that is pierced in the middle by a narrow slit. These lids on the cells swell, bend down at the edges, and thus—at the same time—enlarge the opening and press the fragrant oil out onto the surface of the leaf.

Writing more than three hundred years ago, an English herbalist noted the earlier observation that the seat of the perfume of the musk rose was in its stamens. "Some there be," he declared in the quaint wording of his day, "that have avouched that the chiefest scent of these roses consisteth not in the leaves but in the threads of the flower." This observation has since been verified by scientific tests.

Students of orchids have discovered a curious fact about their perfume. The elaborate specialization of some of these flowers includes giving off different scents by day and by night. *Pilumna fragrans*, for instance, is said to have a vanilla smell in the morning and a narcissus smell in the evening. *Dendrobium glumaceum* suggests heliotrope during the day and lilac at night. *Cattleya bogotensis* resembles in its scent a carnation in the morning and a primrose in the evening. It is the lily-of-the-valley in the daytime and the rose in the nighttime that is suggested by *Phaloenopsis schilleriana*.

So powerful are the perfume oils of flowers that 1/120,000th of a grain of oil of rose is all that is required to affect our sense of smell. That sense, incidentally, can be cultivated. After World War I a number of blinded French veterans were trained by Paris perfumers and became experts at analyzing scents by nose alone.

At one time, in France, it was believed that the smell of mint was the basic scent from which all others were derived. Psychologists today divide smells into six elementary odors: spicy, flowery, fruity, resinous, foul, and scorched. Because each perfume produces its own peculiar effect upon the olfactory cells, just as each musical note has its own characteristic effect upon the ear, a European scientist, several generations ago, sought to arrange all the odors of the world in a scale corresponding to a musical scale. He actually worked out such a scheme, assigning low notes to the heavy perfumes, such as vanilla, and high notes to the sharp odors, such as peppermint and citronella.

Below the pool where I had found the butterfly wing and where the breeze from the falls swayed the silver-bell flowers Pacolet River plunges down a rocky bed along one side of the glen. The foaming stream is broken and rebroken; it swerves, slides over tilted slabs of granite, batters huge brown boulders; it is hurtling, tumbling all the way. If, instead of turbulence, calm had marked its flow, with quiet pools along its path, they would have reflected the beauty of flowering trees. For down all the course of the river through the glen redbud and dogwood and silver-bell trees lean out over the water. The white of the bellflowers and the dogwood matches the white of the foam. Rhododendrons are there too, laden with their 5-petaled white flowers with golden dots spattering the top two petals. We noticed that over and over again bees that came to the flowers alighted on the top two petals. We wondered if the insects were led there through mistaking the golden spots for pollen.

As we accompanied the river back to the mouth of the glen, with the perfume of innumerable wildflowers sweet in the air, I recalled an old inscription engraved on the tombstone of an early American naturalist:

"Lord, 'tis a pleasant thing to stand in gardens planted by Thy hand."

It was already past sunset when we walked under the beeches and among the star chickweed once more. The coolness of evening was increasing in the glen. From somewhere ahead, on a forested slope, came the bell music of a wood thrush. The memory of this rare and beautiful place we were leaving—its water music, its flower perfume and flower color—was one that often, in later recollection, brought us special pleasure.

NINETEEN

A HUNDRED MILES OF WARBLERS

FOR hours that April Friday we went in and out of spring.
Our road led through mountain country, over a long series
of ridges. It rose and fell, climbed and tobogganed down again
like a roller-coaster a hundred miles in length. Each time the
road lifted us to a new summit we found ourselves amid trees
with buds hardly opened. Then, like a swimmer diving downward into foaming surf, we would swoop into a world of white
dogwood, of fruit trees clouded with blooms, of grass freshly
green. Spring would be all around us in some valley fragrant
with flowers.

The season was advancing swiftest along the valleys; its high-
water mark was lifting little by little up the mountainsides. Like
floods of water, the floods of spring follow a lowland course.
They race ahead down the long valleys, climb slowly, as though
struggling with gravity, up the slopes. In the mountains the
streams, the highways and the railroads go through the gaps
together. And with them goes spring.

We had awakened early that morning in a cabin beside a
rushing mountain brook, 20 miles east of Asheville. It was still
dark when we heard, high overhead where the flying bird was
already touched by the sunrise, the wild, lonely voice of a kill-
deer. Then the valley lightened and wood thrushes, mockingbirds, and cardinals sang all up the slope of the mountain that
climbed steeply behind us. Their notes descended in varying
volume. Those of the topmost singers reached us in fragments,

during lulls in the lower chorus, as mere fairy songs, whisper songs, echoing down the slope. These were the first of innumerable birds we heard that day.

During the night a great warbler wave had poured over the Appalachians, spilling its gay, colorful migrants down the ridges that, in gigantic waves of granite, descended toward the east. The fluttering wings that had carried them from islands of the Caribbean, from Central or South America, from Mexico, had lifted them over the barrier of this ancient range. Before we had started our trip, Ludlow Griscom, Harvard's famed field ornithologist, had told us:

"Be near Asheville, North Carolina, the third week in April and you will see the warblers pour across the mountains."

This was the third week in April. And these were the warblers he had promised. Nearly one-third of all the species of warblers found east of the rockies were about us that day.

We never knew whether we were in the beginning, the middle, or the end of the wave. We drove for more than a hundred miles, from east of Asheville south to Hendersonville and west to Highlands, and there were warblers, pockets of warblers, trees swarming with warblers, warblers beyond count, along the way. These rainbow birds of spring, like other manifestations of spring, increased and decreased as our road tobogganed or climbed. They were most numerous in the valleys; absent almost entirely on the higher summits. Wood warblers come north as the leaves unfold. They feed on the forest caterpillars that feed on the new green leaves. Their northward flight keeps pace with unfolding bud and expanding leaf. The sequences of nature, the timing of the tides of migration, are exact. Buds burst, new leaves unfurl, larvae hatch, and warblers appear.

South of Asheville the road descended a long decline with climax forest on either side. For an hour we swept the hardwoods with our glasses, watching the warbler show.

No other family of North American birds travels more in mixed companies than do the wood warblers. Redstarts darted among the branches, fanning their brilliant tails. Ovenbirds called from the woodland floor. Prairie warblers endlessly went up the scale in the thin "zee-zee-zee-zee-zee-zee" of their song and chestnut-sided warblers ended on a whiplash "switch you!" As they appeared and disappeared among branches and bushes, we saw the rich lemon of yellow warblers, the black raccoon masks across the faces of Maryland yellowthroats, the flash of yellow rump patches as myrtle warblers swooped and rose. We watched hooded warblers opening and closing their tails—birds that to Frank M. Chapman seemed to say: "You must come to the woods, or you won't see me!" The final notes are almost as explosive as those of the chestnut-sided. High in the oaks and maples the parula, smallest of all North American warblers, hung from twig tips like a chickadee or flashed among the new leaves the brilliance of its yellow throat and breast, its white wing bars, and the old-gold shield on its bluish back. And every bird was in perfect plumage. This was the season of the new and unmarred leaf, the time of the bird at its best. This was the unblemished world of the spring.

A little later we pulled up near a huge tulip tree. Its billowing cloud of pale-green new leaves was a world of succulent plenty for larva and warbler alike. Magnolia warblers and black-throated blues and parulas and redstarts and myrtles swarmed through this arboreal land of plenty. Nothing in the world is more alive than a warbler in the spring. Surely it must have been a warbler that James Stephens described in *The Crock of Gold* as being "so full of all-of-a-sudden." All of a sudden a warbler starts and stops. All of a sudden it flashes from branch to branch, peers under leaves, snaps up small caterpillars, darts on again.

One black-and-white warbler, a little striped mouse of a bird, left its caterpillar hunting to hawk after a pale-brown moth gyrating beyond a lower branch. It fluttered, hovered, spurted ahead, missed the moth in its erratic course time after time. In the end it became discouraged and suddenly zoomed upward, back to the trunk among the gray-green leaves of the tulip tree. By the time we drove on, our necks ached from looking up at the strenuous little treetop birds.

In the White House, in Washington, D.C., on May 4, 1906, Theodore Roosevelt wrote to John Burroughs, at Slabsides, that he had just come in from walking around the White House grounds and had wished heartily that Burroughs had been there to tell him what the various warblers were. Most of the birds had been in the tops of the trees and he could not get good glimpses of them. But there was one with chestnut cheeks, with bright yellow behind the cheeks and a yellow breast thickly streaked with black, which had puzzled him.

This same warbler that perplexed the twenty-sixth President of the United States at the White House danced among the upper branches of a maple near the cemetery at Fletcher, North Carolina, where Bill Nye, the humorist, is buried. It was a Cape May warbler, the only one with chestnut cheeks. This warbler, incidentally, has little to do with Cape May, New Jersey. It does not breed there. I have never seen one there. Its name resulted from the fact that, during migration in 1809, the individual from which it was described happened to be shot on Cape May. Breeding almost as far north as the Great Slave Lake of northern Canada, these warblers concentrate in winter in the West Indies, especially on the island of Haiti. The path of their migration is wide at the top and funnels down to form, roughly, an inverted pyramid.

In contrast, the redstart—the "firetail," the warbler the Cubans call the "little torch"—has a particularly broad front throughout both its southward and its northward movement. As these warblers near their southern wintering grounds, their flyway still has a width of more than two thousand miles, extending all the way from Mexico on the west to the Bahamas on the east.

Near Druid Hills, North Carolina, we pulled up beside an apple orchard in bloom. The trees descended a long slope in tumbling clouds of white. Bees hummed. The air was fragrant with the perfume of the apple blossoms. Sunshine filtered among the branches, where a myriad white petals glowed, luminous in the backlighting. And here warblers—myrtles, magnolias, Maryland yellowthroats, prairies, and black-and-whites—darted amid blossom-laden boughs or flicked, in flashes of living color, from tree to tree.

There were other moments of especial beauty that day. Where a mountain road turned sharply on the way to Highlands, a black-and-white warbler flitted past us over a shining, glittering waterfall of mica that streamed down an embankment from decomposing rock. Then there was the hooded warbler we saw, singing with face lifted to the sunny sky, beside an upland pasture blue with bird's-foot violets. Once we came upon a prairie warbler, its yellow breast edged with streakings of black and its tail bobbing about, balancing itself on the fiddlehead of a cinnamon fern. Another time a long finger of sunshine descending through a treetop spotlighted a Maryland yellowthroat, brilliant in contrasting yellow and black, swinging on a low cluster of red maple keys.

John Burroughs thought the yellowthroat's song said: "Which way, sir? Which way, sir? Which way, sir?" In a less genteel modern day it is usually set down as: "Wichity, wichity, wichity, witch." And so it sounds in the North. But here some of the birds seemed substituting an "s" sound; seemed to be singing: "Seizery, seizery, seizery." We wondered if this was a warbler dialect, a local accent given by birds that originated in the same area. Several times on our trip we encountered regional variations in song.

Blue jays in the South seemed to have a higher-pitched, thinner, less full-bodied call. Acadian flycatchers, in a cypress swamp near Wilmington, North Carolina, called "*Squeak*-it!" In Rock Creek Park, at Washington, D.C., the accent seemed shifted. There it was "Squeak-*it!*" In Europe ornithologists have recognized that chaffinches from the continent and from the British Isles sing in a different way. One is said to have an English accent, the other a Continental accent.

Later, as we drove north, we were tantalized by a ringing bird call from the woods. It was a monosyllabic "Teach! Teach! Teach!" It immediately suggested the ovenbird. But it was so different from the rounded "Teacher! Teacher! Teacher!" of the northern ovenbird that we thought it must be made by a different species. Finally, near Lynchburg, Virginia, we saw the singer in the act of singing. It was unmistakably an ovenbird. Through the southern part of its range, below the Mason and Dixon Line, the warbler drops the final syllable from its song. Roger Tory Peterson has noted that along the old canal that by-passes the Falls of the Potomac, near Glen Echo, Maryland, he can distinguish the resident from the migrant ovenbirds, when they return together in the spring, by this difference in their song.

Each time we crossed a brook among the wooded ridges, on that day of warblers, we stopped. For there we were sure to find a pocket of migrants. The trees beside such streams were always filled with the song of the spring woods, the small and varied music of the warblers.

During one such stop we were impressed by the way the bright yellow rump patches of the myrtle warblers disappeared almost instantaneously when they alighted, leaving only grayish plumage that blended with the tree bark behind it. The effect was similar to that produced by the sudden disappearance of the brightly colored underwings of an alighting *Catocala* moth. This swift eclipse of the yellow rump patches produces the impression of watching a creature vanish into thin air.

During another stop, beyond Lake Toxaway, we fell into conversation with a native of the region. He had noticed the swarms of birds that day. But he assured us that migration had nothing to do with it. Why? Because there is no such thing as migration.

"The birds are here all the time," he said.

"Why don't we see them in the winter?"

"That's simple. They're just farther back in the woods."

Surrounded by uncounted migrants, standing on one of the great, immemorial flyways of the East, he was unalterably convinced that migration did not exist. He reminded us of Thoreau's farmer who, while contending a diet of vegetables could never make bones, was being hurried along behind his oxen which, with vegetable-made bones, were jerking along both him and his heavy plow.

Somewhere near Frozen Lake we stopped for half an hour where ancient hemlocks receded into gloom beside the jumbled boulders of a mountain torrent. The trees were hoary with usnea lichen. In small gray beards, like lesser Spanish moss, it waved from branches and the rough bark of the tree trunks. Usnea is the chief nesting material of the parula warbler. And, appropriately, here we found half a dozen parulas. They danced from limb to limb, alternately in sunshine and shade, the males singing their buzzy little trill that has been aptly described as resembling the winding of a watch.

Perhaps for these warblers the hemlocks were home, the goal of their northward migration. Driving among migrating birds along the Gulf we had assumed, before we thought about it, that the earliest flocks contained the birds with the farthest to go; that those with only a short flight ahead of them would wait until last. The reverse is true. As spring moves northward, birds return home behind its advancing front. Each bird, as Ernest Mayr so well expresses it, seems attached to its breed· ing area by a rubber band. No matter how far the autumn migration stretches the band, when spring comes it draws the bird back home again. Georgia birds return to Georgia and Maryland birds to Maryland. The farther south their breeding ground, as a rule, the earlier they come home. Conditions are right for the return of the songbirds in Virginia weeks before they are in Massachusetts. Thus, returning migrants leapfrog up the map. Banding has shown that the successive waves in the tide of migration carry birds over and beyond those already at home.

Late starters in the migration parade tend to catch up with the spring. The yellow warbler, for example, winters in the tropics and reaches the Gulf coast about the first week in April. Some of these warblers nest as far north as Manitoba. During the last fifteen days of their journey they traverse an area that spring requires thirty-five days to cross. The average progress made by all species of spring migrants ascending the Mississippi flyway is said to be 23 miles a day. Blackpoll warblers, one of the last warblers to come north, exceed this rate by a dozen miles a day. Between Louisiana and Minnesota they average as much as 35 miles every 24 hours. Beyond Minnesota the blackpolls that nest in western Alaska increase their speed as they follow the Mackenzie Valley until they are making 200 miles a day. They require only half the time consumed by the initial 1,000 miles to cover the final 2,500.

As the road climbed nearer to Highlands, among these ancient ridges that are a relic of the early paleozoic continent, snowdrops were in bloom beside the mountain road. Riding west we seemed transported north. Hardwoods and open meadows set among dark evergreens were around us. The Low Country of the coast had the charm of the exotic; the High Country of North Carolina had the attraction of the familiar. The forest openings might well have been in Maine. But the sun was the sun of the South. Through the clear air of the heights, unhindered by vapor, its rays beat down with full intensity. This same clear atmosphere, when we came to vantage points above the valleys, enabled us to see for immense distances across the green panorama that spread away to the east.

In the dawn of that morning, what a host of warbler eyes had glimpsed that very scene!

During the hours of the night, with tiring muscles, with consumption of stored-up fat, the little birds had followed, in the dark, the sky highway of their ancestors. They had threaded

through gaps, climbed over ridges, mounted to cross the continental hump of the Appalachian range. Rocks untouched by
glaciers, plants of older lineage than any in the North, had
passed unseen beneath their wings. Their aerial trail had cut
across the path of the early Spaniards who in 1567—so many
warbler generations ago—had pushed northward among the
mountains. Some of the migrants, perhaps, had passed in the
night above the very spot on Bear Camp Creek, near Highlands, where in 1886 Charles S. Sargent, of Harvard, redis-
covered Michaux's *Shortia*, a flower that had been lost for a
century.

Now the little birds were scattered over the descending
ridges, feeding, resting, regaining their strength, just as their
ancestors had done in pre-Columbian springs. We wondered
how many times in each bird's life it stopped at the same spots
while journeying from its winter quarters to its summer home.
Audubon's phoebe, marked with a loop of silver wire about its
leg, proved that songbirds return to the same nesting areas in
the spring. White-throated sparrows, banded at Thomasville,
Georgia, have returned in successive winters to the same identical garden, revealing that southward migrants also may have
specific goals. But what of the vast spaces between? Do the
birds tend to come down at regular stopping places, at way
stations along the route?

So far as I know, no final answer is available. The area of
migration is so great, the number of migrants so astronomical,
the percentage of individuals banded so infinitesimally small,
the chances of recovery so slight that exact and accurate in
formation is difficult to obtain. But it seems logical to conclude
that the eastern slope of the Appalachians in North Carolina
is an ancient annual resting ground of the songbirds, offering
sanctuary after strain. And of this we were sure: the descending
ridges for many miles that day were providing food and rest
and shelter and new strength for a host of homegoing warblers.

TWENTY

MOUNTAIN MEADOWS

F IFTY miles northwest of the ridges where the warblers
fed and rested, the Great Smokies straddle the North
Carolina–Tennessee line. Sixteen of their peaks rise above
6,000 feet. Five overtop famed Mt. Washington. To climb the
highest of these, Clingmans Dome, in the spring is equivalent
to moving backward more than a month in time or jumping
northward more than half a thousand miles in space.

Each hundred feet of elevation, theoretically, represents one
day's advance of spring. In mountain country, however, the
wheel of the seasons speeds up. Spring advances faster the
higher it goes. For more than a decade Arthur Stupka, head
naturalist at the Great Smoky Mountains National Park, has
recorded the blooming dates of various wildflowers. This provides a simple and accurate yardstick for measuring the arrival
of spring. The season we followed north, Stupka told us, had
come to the valley around Gatlinburg, Tennessee, almost
two weeks late. Yet by the time it reached the 5,000-foot
mark in the mountains it had caught up with itself and was
running on schedule.

Our first sight of the Smokies came in April. Later, after
mid-May, we cut back for a longer look when spring had come
to the heights as well as to the lower slopes. The second time
we were accompanied by a guide, philosopher, and friend, Ben
Richards. During innumerable lunches, when he and I worked
in the same editorial office in New York, Ben had regaled me

with stories of the southern mountains. He had been born in the Cumberlands of eastern Tennessee, son of a Welsh coal engineer, and had been familiar with the region of the Great Smokies from boyhood. Our long-standing date to see the mountains together, during the spring trip, was fulfilled when he landed at the Knoxville Airport and we drove east to Gatlinburg.

A lively cricket of a man, weighing about 115 pounds, Ben Richards speaks with a ready wit and a loud, commanding voice. Once he spent three weeks on a boat trip with a deaf companion. He had to talk loud to be heard. At the end of the trip he entered a store and, without realizing it, spoke as though to his hard-of-hearing companion. Clerks snapped to attention. Service was prompt. This result was so gratifying that he has talked the same way ever since. Taking command of the situation, he had us painlessly installed in the vast, brown Mountain View Hotel by midafternoon and during the all-too-short days that followed showed us the wondrous beauty of the Great Smokies in the spring.

The morning we started our trip to Silers Bald, it was May 19, according to the calendar. It stayed May 19 all day long in Gatlinburg. But, according to the calendar of the seasons, time ran backward as we drove upward on the winding road. In fifty minutes it rushed backward more than fifty days—or so it would if each hundred feet represented a full day's delay in the advance of spring. At the top of Newfound Gap, 3,582 feet above Gatlinburg, we were—according to the calendar of spring—at April 14, and at the top of Clingmans Dome, 5,180 feet above the start, we were at March 29. Descending at night we raced forward the same number of days and were back at May 19 again before we went to sleep.

Morning fog clung in a mile-high cloud to the side of Clingmans Dome when we reached it. Through the dense mist we heard the same bright bird voices we had heard below the Tamiami Trail, in Florida—the calling of goldfinches. Dimly we could see the migrants fluttering from tree to tree, their good cheer undampened in the heart of a cloud, their vivacity undiminished at the top of this lofty mountain. As we left the car and climbed the path to the Appalachian Trail, the fog and the woods were filled with a sound like a musical creaking axle, a long unwinding bird song, sweet and tumbling forth, a song that went on and on as though it would never end. All through the upper Smokies we heard this song repeated without once seeing the singer. Then we heard it no more until the very end of the trip when, near timberline on Mt. Washington, in dark, fog-filled woods by Hermit Lake, it was all around us again. It was the song of the winter wren.

A mile and a quarter in the air, we followed Ben along a trail through dim, wet woods, through a cloud forest on a mountain-top. Every leaf was dripping; every tree trunk was hoary with moss and lichens. The trees were trees of the North—spruce and fir and yellow birch. Beneath them, extending in waves over rocks, over moldering trunks, over the path before us, was a thick plush carpet of russet-green moss. We moved down this cushioned trail as silent as the fog. In the dim, gray light, in the heavy, saturated air, we seemed making our way through a realm that was half land, half water; half night, half day. Snails and slugs and brown millipeds with yellow legs moved, wet and shining, over the dripping moss. Every dogtooth violet and trillium was decorated with glistening drops of water. Once a strange tree, twisted like a piece of taffy, loomed up out of the mist beside the trail. A trunk beyond was scarred by the clawing of a bear. At intervals ahead of us, on other trunks, the metal tags and white blazes of the Appalachian Trail marked the way.

This trail, 2,050 miles long, follows the highland route all the way from Mt. Katahdin in Maine, to Mt. Oglethorpe in Georgia. Long before the Appalachian Trail was thought of, that remarkable Swiss geographer, Arnold Guyot, had climbed all the peaks along the way. Enduring a thousand hardships and dangers in primitive conditions before the Civil War, this friend of Louis Agassiz measured ridges and mountains to assemble an exact picture of the Appalachian chain. Appropriately, the most massive peak in the eastern Great Smokies is named Mt. Guyot. The long path that follows the line of his pioneer labors traverses fourteen states. How many times, under what varied conditions, we crossed the Appalachian Trail during our travels with the spring! Its lowest point is the Bear Mountain Bridge over the Hudson, about 45 miles north of New York City. Its highest point is the mossy path along which we walked at the top of Clingmans Dome.

Something like five miles away, over mountaintops in the direction of Georgia, the Appalachian Trail crosses Silers Bald, a mysterious upland meadow shaped like the head of an arrow or lance. This was our goal that morning. For a mile or so we worked ahead beneath high-piled fog, like beetles creeping under cotton batting. We had descended the rocky western slope of Mt. Buckley and had threaded our way into a dim maze of fallen, long-dead trees when the enveloping cloud began to break up. The fog tore into long, windblown shreds. Blue sky appeared. And we found ourselves walking in sunshine along a razorback ridge with stupendous views unfolding on either side.

To our right was Tennessee, to our left North Carolina. For 50 miles the Great Smokies lift a high wall of rock in a barrier-boundary between the states. We walked this line at times, no doubt, with one foot in North Carolina and the other in Tennessee.

Unending wind blew up the long slope of the North Carolina side. We sat down on a weathered tree trunk to rest and a towhee flitted to the top of a wind-polished stub, singing snatches of song as it was tossed and buffeted by the gusts. It kept its position with difficulty. Once it nearly toppled over backwards and saved itself by thrusting its tail hard against the stub, bracing itself woodpecker-wise. For a minute or so it faced the wind and its gymnastics continued. Then it scudded away over the ridgetop into the protection of the lee. In more sheltered places Carolina juncos sang. Fledglings in nests on this high gap west of Clingmans Dome never know a day of calm. All their early lives are surrounded by the wind.

At times that day we looked down on lesser wooded ridges so far below us that they seemed undulations covered with moss. Even through our glasses the trees appeared midget puffs of green. Where Steel Trap Creek flowed away at the bottom of a long descent, spots and waves of white ran through the green. There the shadbush, the "sarvice berry" of the Smokies, was in full spring bloom. Pausing at one point along the ridge, we watched a small cloud floating on a level with our eyes. Suddenly it ripped downward hundreds of feet, yanked toward the earth by a powerful downdraft. Far below, other cloud fragments galloped over the lower ridges, rushing up the sides and skimming over the summits like white horses clearing hurdles.

Wherever we looked, to right or left, mountains and ridges extended away in tumbling waves, blue in the distance, green closer at hand. The Great Smokies occupy about 780 of the 3,026,789 square miles of the United States proper. Yet in this relatively small area there are more species of trees than in the whole of Europe. Europe has 85 species of native trees, the Great Smokies have 131. Here 200 different kinds of birds are seen, almost half the total for all of Great Britain. Fifty kinds of fur-bearing animals and eighty kinds of fish live in the Great Smokies. Here also are 1,800 kinds of fungi, 1,300 flowering plants, 330 mosses and liverworts, 230 lichens, and 26 orchids.

Our long trip with the spring continually underscored the prodigal variety of American nature. Where else in the world does nature offer such striking contrasts in the spring? Or such bountiful profusion? And nowhere along the length and breadth of our zigzag course was spring more dramatically beautiful than in these ancient mountains of the South—home of the richest flora and the most luxuriant deciduous forests on the North American continent.

The plants of the Great Smokies, unlike those of the northern areas, extend back in an unbroken line far beyond the Ice Age. When the glaciers moved down from the polar icecap, like vast, implacable white erasers they rubbed out the work of aeons of evolution. But the plants of these southern mountains remained untouched. Moreover, their numbers were augmented by northern species driven south by the advancing ice. There are today, in the heights of the Great Smokies, plants found nowhere else south of northern Ohio. They are racial relics left from glacial times.

We took our time along the trail, stopping often. The long finger of the Appalachians carries the Canadian Zone a thousand miles southward. On this high ridgetop we were in the realm of mountain ash, of beech, of red spruce, of yellow birch and balsam fir. Around us were flowers associated with a northern spring, dandelions, violets, spring beauties, wood anemone. Fiddlehead ferns rose beside the path, still sheathed in soft and silvery envelopes.

Once, where the right-hand side of the ridge dropped away in a dizzying, almost-vertical descent, a frail lacewing fly fluttered in a wide circle on the pale-green gauze of its wings. Part of the time it was over the ridge and hardly a foot above the ground; part of the time over the chasm, with half a mile of space below it. Occasionally, where the trail passed among sheltered trees, we would come upon a mile-high pocket of birds. Robins would dart down the trail ahead of us and chestnut-sided warblers would sing in beech trees with buds just unfolding.

As we emerged from one wooded section of the trail, and a magnificent panorama of mountains spread away before me, I had the sensation I had already experienced half a dozen times in rounding turns or coming over ridges in the Great Smokies, the feeling:

"Why, I have been in this very spot before!"

But I knew I never had. Each time I was remembering a picture instead of a place, an illustration made where I stood among much-photographed peaks. In these days of television, motion pictures, and an ever-growing number of elaborately illustrated magazines, such vicarious experiences are rapidly multiplying. If we actually go down in a submarine or up in a jet plane—or, presumably, on a rocket to the moon—we will have the feeling we are repeating an experience already familiar through the screen. If we see, in person, a president or a prime minister we have to think twice to be sure all those other glimpses were only in the newsreel. During recent years the actual and the vicariously experienced events have become more than ever mixed in our minds. Not only the present but the past, not only life but memory as well, has taken on a new complexity.

A little after noon we came to the last steep ascent that led to Silers Bald. Pulling ourselves from tree to tree up an almost vertical climb, we reached the mountain meadow. There we sat down, panting, our backs to a granite rock that shouldered up out of luxuriant turf, and looked around. We were 5,620 feet above sea level. Shaped roughly like an arrowhead, the grassy opening extended for five acres around us. Forty miles to the south, as this arrowhead points, lay Highlands, North Carolina. Between stretched the blue waves of the lesser ridges.

We ate our lunch, leaning back against the rock. A "cloud spring" at the edge of the bald supplied cold and transparent water. Its flow is derived from the heavy fog that daily envelops the mountaintop. About four hundred miles north of the Gulf, about three hundred miles east of the Mississippi, the Great Smokies receive abundant moisture from those rivers without channels, the clouds. Now the clouds were scattered, drifting in a blue sky, some of them below the level of our eyes, and all of them trailing their shadows up and down the slopes of the ridges. Across the green expanse of the bald, wildflowers bloomed—yellow cinquefoil, blue violets, and the white stars of the star chickweed. The rising tide of spring had reached and engulfed this mysterious mountaintop meadow on which we sat.

Its mystery—the mystery of the open balds found only in the southern Appalachians—is a riddle of long duration. The earliest white men found them there. The Indians, long before that, had linked them with fabulous creatures and events in their legends. The King of the Rabbits, a rodent as large as a deer, was supposed to make its home on Gregory Bald. Another open space was known as the Lizard Place. Here, according to Cherokee folklore, an immense lizard, with glistening throat, could be seen sunning itself on summer days. A number of balds were taboo. One was believed to be the dwelling place of a gigantic snake so big that it could swallow fifty warriors at a time. The Nunnehi, a race of spirit folk, "The People Who Live Anywhere," were said to camp on the higher balds. The Indian word for balds, "udawagunta," appears often in the folklore of the Cherokees.

Two of the Indian legends offer supernatural explanations for the origin of the mountain pastures. One tells of a giant, with a head shining like the sun, who descended from the sky and rested for a time on a mountaintop. When he vanished, two balds remained where his feet had been planted.

The second legend, quoted at length by James Mooney in the *Nineteenth Report of the United States Bureau of Ethnology*, published in 1898, concerns the Ulagu, a mythical monster which assumed the form of an immense hornet. Swooping down on Indian villages, it would snatch up children in its claws and swiftly vanish. Where the Ulagu lived, no one knew. Sentinels placed on the mountaintops finally traced it to its lair, an inaccessible cavern on a precipitous mountainside. In their extremity the Indians prayed for divine help. The Great Spirit hurled a thunderbolt from the sky. At one stroke it split off the whole mountainside and threw down the stunned Ulagu. The Indians, attacking it with axes and spears, hacked it to pieces. So pleased was the Great Spirit with their initiative in tracing the Ulagu to its cave and their courage in attacking it that he decreed that thenceforth various mountaintops should be bare of trees and covered with grass the better to serve as lookouts for the sentinels.

Such legends, although they offer little help in solving the riddle of the balds, do attest to the great antiquity of the open spaces. How did they begin? How have they lasted so long? Why have they not been engulfed by the surrounding spruce and balsam, rhododendron, laurel, and dog hobble? These are riddles that have interested generations of scientists. Botanists, geologists, ecologists, foresters, all have studied the areas. Many theories have been advanced but none with conclusive proof. The enigma of these lofty pastures remains to be solved.

Obviously, the explanation is not altitude, not timberline conditions. The mountaintop meadow on which we sat was more than a thousand feet lower than Clingmans Dome, which is wooded to the top. Gregory Bald, one of the largest of the score or more balds scattered through the Smokies, is lower still. Not one of the three highest peaks—Clingmans Dome, 6,643 feet high, Mt. Guyot, 6,621 feet high, or Mt. Le Conte, 6,593 feet high—has a grassy bald at its top. Thus height is eliminated as the cause of the balds or as an important factor in maintaining them. Why, then, do balds appear on certain mountains and not on others?

J. W. Harshberger, in 1903, and Mrs. Helen R. Edson, in 1894, advanced the theory that balds are the consequence of ice-storm injury. In these particular locations, they thought, abnormal ice conditions destroyed woody plants and permitted grass to take their place. W. H. Camp, years later, suggested another "local weather" theory. The key to the riddle, he decided, was the hot, dry southwesterly winds that strike these areas with special effect during dry seasons, killing the trees but letting the grass remain. It has been noticed that many of the balds slope to the south and are near mountaintop springs. But not all. And the fact that some are not proves that neither factor is indispensable.

Fire damage or a combination of blowdowns and fires has been put forth by some scientists as the secret of the balds. Others have leaned to the theory that they were cleared by Indians in prehistoric times as lookout stations or game lures. A few years ago a southern scientist suggested that an abnormal population of gall wasps might have killed the trees in these areas by laying their eggs in the tips of the twigs.

On Silers Bald the only wasps we saw were two yellowjackets. They were probably overwintering queens, busy that spring day with the work of founding new colonies. Bears, late in summer, sometimes come to the bald to dig out yellowjacket nests and eat the grubs. For days afterwards the insects rush to attack any animal that comes near. Several times horses have been stung and riders thrown.

Among the roots of the thick grass bumblebee queens were starting the nests of the new year. We watched these furry, bustling insects seeking nectar from even the smallest blooms. We saw them alighting on violets, riding down the flowers with their weight. Near one mossy rock four bumblebees at the same time were busy in a blue harvest field—a mat of blooming violets nearly a yard across. Beyond, a dip in the bald enclosed a pale-blue lake. The depression, from rim to rim, was filled with a solid sheet of bluets. Wild strawberries and dandelions bloomed amid the meadow grass and around the edges we found trillium and yellow wood betony, fiddlehead ferns, high-bush blueberries, and stands of blackberry canes. Shadbush branches were white with flowers. Their heavy, plumlike perfume carried far downwind across the bald.

All told, 125 different species of plants have been found on the balds of the Great Smokies. In May these lofty meadows bloom with wildflowers as though they were pieces of prairie lifted thousands of feet into the air. But the dominant plant on most of the balds is a species of grass, the remarkable mountain oat-grass, *Danthonia compressa*. Its requirements are a cool climate and abundant atmospheric moisture. It grows so densely that tree seeds have little chance of reaching the ground and taking root. It provides competition too severe for bushes. And it is able to hold its own against other plants.

In 1936 a severe drought killed much of the grass on Silers Bald. The bare spots were filled in by goldenrod and other plants. But in the intervening years the oat-grass had come back. It is the climax plant of the balds. Botanists who watched its return saw the luxurious grass engulf the goldenrod and gradually reduce it in size until it became so suppressed by competition that it was able to put forth only two or three leaves in a season.

On some balds, where the soil is more moist, sedges become predominant. This is the case on Andrews Bald, a square opening surrounded by balsam and spruce, about two miles south of Clingmans Dome. Besides the grass and the sedge balds, the Great Smokies contains heath balds, or "laurel slicks." From a distance they appear soft, green carpets; close at hand they are almost impenetrable jungles of twisted trunks and branches where rhododendron and laurel are solidly massed together. In June these slicks become sites of spectacular beauty. Then all the Catawba rhododendrons are covered with rose-purple blooms.

Coming along the ridgetop trail to Silers Bald, we had passed through a small grassy opening edged with wild blackberries. It was hardly a quarter of an acre in extent. This was High Spring Bald, the smallest in the Great Smokies. In contrast, the largest, Roan Mountain Bald, extends over a thousand acres. Arnold Guyot, writing of his pioneer mapping operations, noted: "The level space between the two main peaks of Roan Mountain, a mile in extent, I found to be a beautiful prairie, covered with grass a foot high and interspersed with bright·

colored flowers and an abundance of ripe strawberries."

Pioneers who pastured their cattle on this bald undoubtedly enlarged it somewhat by felling trees around its border. When Asa Gray visited the spot in 1840, and discovered there the beautiful orange lily that was named in his honor, he assumed that the bald was entirely the work of early settlers. In pioneer times a number of balds were employed as summer pastures. All so used developed the same distinguishing mark. This was the presence of the path rush, *Juncus tenuis*. The abundance of this rush, botanists have discovered, is a measure of the amount of grazing that has been done on a highland meadow.

Where the eastern edge of Silers Bald dropped steeply away we found a dense growth of young beech trees. Their silvery trunks advanced to the top of the rise and there stopped, running like an irregular fence along the edge of the grass. Somewhere down the slope and among the beeches a towhee called over and over again: "Time-for-teeeeeee!" Overhead chimney swifts went crackling by. We looked up. When we looked down again, a dark butterfly with buff edgings on its wings—a mourning cloak—was fluttering from among the trees to sail away across the grassy open.

Insects of many kinds were active in the spring sunshine as we walked about this mountaintop arrowhead of grass. Red ants explored the tiny bellflowers of the high-bush blueberries. A lacewing fly crawled over a ladybird beetle in reaching the top of a grass blade. There it looked about through eyes that shone in the sunlight as though plated with burnished gold. Once a brownish grasshopper, a giant almost as big as the *Schistocerca americana* we saw at Bull's Island, leaped from under our feet and sailed away like a wind blown leaf. Strangely out of place on this mountaintop, remote from ponds and streams, a large, dark dragonfly hawked about above the grass and the bordering trees. Even more surprising was the black-and-yellow carrion beetle, *Silpha americana*, creeping beneath the droppings of a black bear. It had been attracted unerringly to this lonely, mile-high mountaintop meadow by a specialized sense of smell, incredibly keen.

Three other carrion hunters jockeyed about in the windy sky above us. A trio of turkey vultures swept back and forth or circled away only to return again. They had spotted some dead animal invisible to us. We had gone hardly a quarter of a mile along the homeward trail when we looked back and saw the dark birds, rocking wildly in the ground gusts, drop to the bald. Later on, where the trail turned and entered trees, we looked back again for a last glimpse of Silers Bald. It had grown small and dim in the distance. But the question mark it represented was as large as ever. The balds of the Great Smokies are mere dots in the expanse of the mountains. They are widely separated, scattered here and there among the peaks. The riddle is: Why are they *here* and why are they *there*? Why are they at these particular spots rather than elsewhere?

Nearly five miles and an ascent of a thousand feet up a higher mountain faced us when we started home. Amid the beauty and strangeness of the mountain meadow we had forgotten time. We had forgotten our fatigue. Now the miles stretched out and time ran swiftly. It was sunset when we stopped at a spring to drink. Below us, amid the dead trees of the ridge-side, an olive-sided flycatcher repeated over and over its exuberant call. Nearer at hand Carolina juncos hopped from branch to branch among bushes, making small smacking sounds like miniature brown thrashers in the underbrush. It was at this spring that a gray daddy longlegs popped into a collecting bottle and so began a series of events that resulted in its spending the rest of its days in a phalangid collection at Purdue University, in Indiana.

Along the gap where the wind had boomed in the morning the wind was booming still. The valley below had sunk into twilight. In darkening woods we worked our way up the side of Mt. Buckley with, all the way, veeries singing their throaty songs in the deepening dusk. We had left Clingmans Dome enveloped in fog. We returned to it enveloped in twilight that was close to night. Before we started down the long decline to Newfound Gap and Gatlinburg we stood for a moment beside the car. Somewhere above us the same song that had come out of the mist in the morning came out of the shadows—the long, sweet, unwinding song of a winter wren.

TWENTY-ONE

A NIGHT IN A CLOUD

WE take about 2,000 steps to the mile. Each step makes use of a motor mechanism that weighs in the neighborhood of 80 pounds: 60 pounds of muscles and 20 pounds of bones. To balance our heads we employ 20 muscles; to balance our spines, 144; to take a step ahead, about 300. Every one of these hundreds of muscles—all 60 pounds of them—ached as I crept from bed the next morning at six. I stretched. I seemed to have hardened during the night. I felt stiff as though encased in a chitin shell like an insect. Nellie winced as she rolled over. Mountain climbing by motorcar, we agreed, had been a poor conditioner for mountain climbing on foot.

Ben was depressingly chipper as we ate our early breakfast. He seemed to have no chitin shell at all. He talked with gusto of our coming climb to the top of LeConte, a mountain 305 feet higher than Mt. Washington. At Newfound Gap, where Nellie drove us before returning to well-earned rest, his motor mechanism seemed all warmed up and ready to go. He started off briskly while I trailed behind, struggling up the "rises" leading to a trail mockingly named the Boulevard. Gradually I limbered up. But for the first mile or so an unusual number of things seemed to call for a pause and a closer look.

"What's the good of being a naturalist," Ben jeered, "if you can't stop and look at things and rest yourself?"

In truth, there was a wonderful variety of things to stop and see. This was the time when, in the Great Smokies, wildflowers of the forest floor were at their peak. Masses of the fringed white flowers of *Phacelia fimbriata* extended like long patches of foam beside the trail. Trilliums and violets and showy orchises intermingled in the rich loam. Twice we came around bends in the trail and found ourselves among spring beauties, acres and acres of them. The whole mountain slope, above and below us, was white with their blossoms. They swept in a wide waterfall of flowers that fell away beneath the trees, pouring down the mountainside as far as we could see.

Mountain bumblebees, queens searching for nest sites, 5,000 feet above sea level, droned past us to alight and investigate holes in the dense green carpet of moss. And once, stealing silently along the trail, we came within a few yards of a blue-headed vireo singing in a dead birch. It slid away down the slope from tree to tree, bursting into its sweet, slurring song at each new perch. Everywhere around us we saw signs of a mountain spring.

The day had started clear and sunny. Now the sky grew grayer. A lid of somber clouds extended from rim to rim of the heavens by the time we reached the shelter at Ice Water Spring. Near here the trail forked. The Boulevard mounted Le-Conte; the Appalachian Trail turned right. Leaving our packs at the log lean-to shelter, we started down the right-hand trail leading to Charlie's Bunion, that spectacular promontory created by a geologic slip ages ago. For a time the trail slanted downward and gravity hustled us on.

"You take the lead," Ben suggested. "Then you will get the full force of a first impression."

The trail emerged from trees and rocks. It curved in a narrow ledge around the face of a peak whose sheer side plunged in a power-dive descent more than a thousand feet to the Greenbriar Wilderness below. A knob projected out beyond this ledge with a vast chasm beneath. This was Charlie's Bunion.

Once we became accustomed to the dizzying drop we

climbed onto the Bunion. Ridges, covered with red spruce and balsam fir, extended away until they blurred into dark, smudgy lines in the distance. Seen from above, mountains become different mountains in different lighting. Under top-lighting, cross-lighting, flat-lighting, back-lighting they present varying pictures to the eye. The scene changes with every movement of the sun. On this morning, under a leaden sky, in the breathless silence before a rain, the dull gray lighting stressed the wild and lonely character of our surroundings. In all the sweep of mountains and sky around us we saw no single sign of life. Almost naked rock slid downward into the chasm. Here and there some ancient, wind-polished conifer clung, its hold on the rocks unshaken by death.

Then life appeared—life most fitting to that somber scene. Over the crags and blasted trees two dark birds, a pair of ravens, flapped past us. Their hoarse calls carried hollowly across the empty mountain spaces. I followed them in my field glasses until they grew small and the sound of their voices died away altogether. At intervals one of the birds would dive and twist in a wild display of aerobatics. There were times when the stunting bird was completely inverted, flying upside down. In the ecstasy of spring a number of birds loop or stunt or sail in inverted flight. As Charles L. Broley had recalled, pairs of bald eagles grasp talons and pinwheel down through the sky. Male marsh hawks loop-the-loop and barrel-roll. Wood ibis roll over and sail for distances upside down. Male peregrine falcons loop and stunt before the females. But here, amid these crags that appeared as lonely as a moonscape and as devoid of active life, the aerobatics of the raven were superlatively impressive.

Beyond the ledge and Charlie's Bunion the Appalachian Trail wandered along mountaintops into the northeast. Half a mile away, where it traverses the sawteeth range, it passes over craters blasted in the rock by lightning. The following spring a lone hiker, with a 40-pound pack on his back, passed the spot where we were sitting and headed toward the sawteeth range.

He was Earl V. Shaffer, of York, Pennsylvania. Starting from Mt. Oglethorpe, in Georgia—the southern end of the Appalachian Trail—on April 4, 1948, Shaffer walked an average of 17 miles a day for 123 days, lived largely on corn bread which he cooked in a pan, wore the same pair of shoes throughout, and reached the northern end of the trail, Mt. Katahdin, in Maine, on August 5. He was the first man in history to cover the entire 2,000 and more miles of the Appalachian Trail in one continuous hike.

Back at the shelter, Ben and I ate sandwiches and drank some of the purest, coldest water to come from any spring. Then, with the threat of rain increasing around us, we started up the Boulevard. In the distance we heard a low, muffled, reiterated sound, like faraway cannonading, increasing in tempo. It was another sign of spring—the drumming of a ruffed grouse. We heard it at intervals that afternoon, echoing through the heavy air. Once, as we rounded a trail bend, walking noiselessly on moss, there was a windy roar and two grouse launched themselves down the slope.

Our trail steadily tilted into a steeper ascent. At times it skirted the edge of abysmal drops and once it narrowed to a path along the knife-edge of a ridge where the graywacke and conglomerate of the mountain dropped away on either hand. Beyond it mounted through dark fir forests. Under the interlacing trees, mosses and lichens formed a continuous carpet, thick and russet-green. Here the silence of the evergreens was broken only infrequently by the little bells of the Carolina juncos or the long, rambling musical monologue of a winter wren.

We had almost reached the ragged lower edges of the rain cloud when the first drops pattered around us. Then we were climbing through the cloud itself. Damp and darkness enveloped us. Gradually the light increased; the mist grew luminous and thinned away. Then suddenly we were out in sunshine. Like a slowly climbing plane, we had ascended through the cloud ceiling that had darkened our sky. Below us it was raining.

A little farther up the trail we sat in the sunshine, our backs to a rock, and looked down on the shining whiteness of the mist. It filled all the valleys. It spread away to the horizon with ridges and peaks thrusting up, dark islands in a snow-white sea. As I gazed on these islands in the fog my mind somehow went back to an entry in John Josselyn's record of his voyage from London to New England in the year 1638: "June the First Day. In very thick foggie weather, we sailed by an enchanted island." I have often wondered what Josselyn saw just as I have wondered what an Eskimo hunter meant when he told Peter Freuchen, the explorer, that he sometimes roasted and ate a lemming just "for the sake of a memory."

Above us other clouds floated in a blue sky. Their shadows trailed across the fog-fields below. These cloud shadows on clouds increased in number. New masses of mist formed above us as we watched. They joined into larger masses. The cloud factory of the Great Smokies was in operation and a second ceiling, a ceiling above a ceiling, was being formed. It closed around the top of Mt. LeConte and moved down the trail to meet us. Again we labored upward in mist and the rain began in earnest.

Late in the afternoon we reached the last steep ascent. The wet woods had taken on an early gloom. Everything was saturated. Moss, growing on the rocks, on the fallen logs, on the trees from top to bottom, formed a great sponge filled to capacity. Little waterfalls descended amid the ferns. A thousand tiny rivulets ran down stringy wicks of moss. A wind was rising and we slogged along, slashed by gust-driven sheets of rain. Near the top we paused in the shelter of a massive cliff. Across its face ran brilliant, sulphur-colored lines and patches, lichen or alga growing on the rock.

Soaked and weary, we climbed the last yards on feet of lead. Somewhere amid the roaring of the wind and the drumming of the rain the strange "musical axle" song of the winter wren went on and on. At the log lodge that Jack Huff had built for overnight guests on the summit of LeConte, we dried out before the fireplace, turning around and around like chickens on a spit. Our long climb was over. Tomorrow would be easy— all downhill.

After supper I sat in the warmth of the blazing logs—my body half asleep but my mind wide awake—and listened to Huff recall Old Tom, the big black bear that tried to carry off a whole barrel of bacon and cheese, and Old Joe, the first horse to reach the summit of Mt. LeConte. Even before the earliest regular trail was cut up the mountainside, Huff led this sturdy pack animal to the top. Later, when the lodge was built, everything used except wood—hardware, cement, stoves, bedsprings —had to come up the 6,593-foot mountain on the backs of horses. One hundred and fifty pack trips were required to bring up the cement alone. Almost every day, during those trips, a ruffed grouse, entirely unafraid, used to appear from the woods and walk part way up the trail ahead of the horses.

When Huff first came to the top of LeConte, natives avoided the spot, believing it was infested with panthers. The peak was, in fact, as wild as it had been before the Civil War, when Arnold Guyot climbed it and named it in honor of a Charleston, South Carolina, scientist who lent him instruments used in his work of mapping the Appalachians.

Before we went to bed, about nine, we looked outdoors. Rain smashed against the windows. Gust-driven fog swirled over us like seething breakers. We were in the heart of a cloud and in the heart of a storm. All that night, as we slept in rustic bunks on mattresses and springs that had ridden up the mountain on horseback, the storm buffeted the cabin. It was still booming outside when I awoke a little after five. The leaden-colored fog grew slowly brighter in the early dawn. Amid the storm a robin began to sing. A little later, at each lull in the great wind, I heard the sweet, bell-ringing jingle of the awakening juncos.

All night long, more than a mile above sea level, they—and we—had slept in a cloud—a cloud that enveloped us still.

After a breakfast of scrambled eggs and popovers, we sat by the fire, hoping the storm would die out and the clouds break to give us a view of the vast panorama that spreads away from this "Grandstand of the Smokies." The rain stopped and began again. The fog grew thin, then dense. About nine o'clock the clouds parted momentarily and we saw spreading away below us range on range, a grandeur of green mountains fading into blue distance. Then the window in the sky slammed shut. The clouds darkened. And the wind rose.

On the chance that the clouds might break again, Ben and I climbed over the moss amid dripping, shaggy trees, to Cliff-top. At the top of this prominence the gusts were at their maximum, the fog more dense than ever. We could see only a few yards in any direction. The cliff was a wind-swept island in the sky. Treetops behind us, seen dimly through the blanketing fog, writhed and lashed as the immense gusts hurled themselves over the mountain. Ben's poncho streamed straight out sidewise in the wind. We held our ground by clinging to small trees and bushes. An ex-army airman, on LeConte at the time, estimated the velocity of the gusts at 70 miles an hour. The bellow of that tempest of wind and fog was so great that we had to shout, straining our lungs, to be heard a dozen feet away.

Laboring along the edge of the precipice, clinging to laurels and rhododendrons, we saw the low sand myrtle, already in bloom, tossed and pounded by the wind and rain. Dizzying plunges yawned below us at every lightening of the fog. Down there, invisible now, were coves and prongs and ridges with comb-teeth tops formed by the red spruces. Down there was the tangled wilderness of Huggins's Hell. And straight below us, clinging somewhere to the sheer face of the cliff, was the narrow ledge along which we would have to make our way, buffeted by the wind, in descending by a different route, this time by the Alum Cave Bluff Trail.

For a long time I stood close to the brink, clinging to a stunted Fraser fir. Hardly a dozen feet high, it had been twisted and distorted by the wind. All its branches streamed in one direction, back from the edge of the escarpment. Like some green Winged Victory it clung there, bearing the brunt of the storm. I could feel the tremors running down its toughened wood as the great gusts struck. This was an old story for it. Its world was a harsher, windier world than that of the lowland trees. It was blighted, but still alive; it had endured, altered but unbroken by adversity. I have often thought of that steadfast tree. A fragment of one of its twigs lies before me as I write. On that day, with fog streaming past us, with the wind howling over us, feeling the tremors run through the fibers of its trunk and down my arm, facing the gale as it had faced so many gales, I felt an overpowering oneness with this storm-racked tree. And never have I felt myself in better or more noble company.

Exhilarated by the fury of the mountain blasts, we made our way back to the cabin. The day held little promise of better weather. So, with sandwiches and a thermos bottle of hot coffee in our packs, we started down the long descent. At first the trail led through sheltered woods where robins and juncos fed under trees that had their tops in wind-blown fog. Then our path skirted the cliff and cut downward across its face along a narrow ledge of rock. Above us, brown siltstone rose in a towering wall until it disappeared in the mist. Below, a precipice plunged in a vertical descent hundreds of feet beyond the limits of our fogbound vision. Between the two was the ledge on which we walked, streaming with water, frequently narrower than the breadth of my shoulders, and open to the full onslaught of the wind.

Wryly I recalled my thought of the evening before:

Tomorrow would be easy—all downhill.

Six thousand feet up, we were above the neighboring mountains. Unhindered in its sweep across the sky, the wind met the wall of rock head on, shooting up its face in tremendous updrafts. My main concern was the possibility that a violent gust might cease suddenly, or produce a suck-back, and upset our balance on the narrow ledge. While the gusts sometimes pushed us hard against the siltstone of the wall, this was their only effect. Three times in half a mile, as we worked along the ledge, we passed through waterfalls where runoff from the storm poured down the face of the cliff. More than once we passed over spots where the rock was pegged down with iron spikes to keep it from disintegrating and once we stepped gingerly over a V gaping at the outer side where a landslip had carried away the edge. At times the ledge was no more than eighteen inches wide. The next morning I discovered that my left hand was sliced along the side and palm with tiny cuts. They had been made, without my being aware of it, as I slid my palm along the support of the wall in edging past the narrowest spots.

Every hundred feet that the trail carried us down, the wind lessened. In the shelter of a fir forest the ledge widened and became a broad and easy path. We stopped to catch our breath. Then we went on side by side. We were below the greatest wind, but even here trees were uprooted and thrown across the path. In favorable surroundings the Frasers fir of the Great Smokies becomes a magnificent tree. One such conifer attained a circumference of 6 feet 7 inches.

Our respite from the wind soon ended where the trail led out across a great landslip on the side of the mountain. From the highway to Newfound Gap, this bare spot looks like a brown patch on a green coat. I had imagined that great boulders littered the scene of the landslide. Instead, we emerged on an expanse of smooth, undulating siltstone, pitching steeply downward. Here, if a foot slipped, there was nothing on the weather-smoothed rock, streaming with running water, to halt a long descent. Once more we were out in the open, exposed to the full pounding of the wind. We moved slowly and carefully and eventually reached the protection of the trees beyond.

From now on, the wind could blow as it would. There was shelter all the way.

Just before we reached Alum Cave Bluff we traversed a gloomy stretch of spruce forest. In the wet, midday twilight beneath the fog-filled trees, snails and glistening slugs fed beside the trail. Suddenly a black apparition flapped up before us. It was a turkey buzzard that had been sitting out the tempest on the protected trail. Tossed and buffeted by the gusts, it struggled upward into the treetops. Here the shifting wind struck it first on one side, then on the other. Fighting to maintain its balance on a limb, it twisted, shifted position, thrust out a wing to keep itself from falling. This lightly loaded soaring bird was ill equipped for fighting storms of wind. Once it was thrown on its side among the spruce twigs; another time it lost its hold completely and tumbled to another branch. When we had gone a hundred yards or so down the trail I turned. The vulture was dropping downward to the shelter of the path once more.

Under the overhanging rock of Alum Cave Bluff we ate our lunch, protected from the veils of falling rain. Water ran from the eaves of the rock in rivulets and cascades and occasionally stones, loosened by the downpour, came crashing to the trail and in great leaps bounded away down the slope. Chickadees were in their element in the storm. They flitted past us, called, fluttered from spruce to spruce. They seemed the only thing alive; everything else was lying low.

By the time our lunch was over, the rain was a steady drumming. The drops had increased in size. They were liquid bullets fired by the wind. Fog, the smoke of the Great Smokies, veiled the scene wherever we looked. In fog we wound downward through a rhododendron slick, walking as through a tunnel and peering to either side into a wilderness of twisted trunks. Beyond, the trail ran through a natural rock garden flowering in the spring. All along the edge of a bluff the ground was white with the blooms of the sand myrtle—a plant I was to see later, under vastly different surroundings, seven hundred miles away in the pine barrens of New Jersey.

We slogged along in the downpour. Hours before the time Nellie was to drive up and meet us with the car we reached the Alum Cave parking field. We decided to walk the ten miles to Gatlinburg. Bedraggled and soaked, with the rain slashing us in the face, in the back, and from either side as the road wound and the direction of the gusts altered in the ravines, we plodded on. The insole of one of my shoes began slipping and wrinkling under my foot. Cars raced past us, going downhill, their whirling tires filling the air with flying spray.

It was under these conditions that the Knoxville *Journal* became my favorite paper of the South. I had never seen a copy before. That didn't matter. For it was a Knoxville *Journal* truck that slowed to a stop beside us; it was a Knoxville *Journal* driver who invited us aboard. In fog, in blizzards, on icy roads, it was his job to get the papers over Newfound Gap to towns on the North Carolina side. He rode alone with the wilderness at night, returning to Knoxville by day. Not infrequently, he told us, his headlights picked out the shambling forms of black bears beside the highway. Thus entertained and vastly contented, we rode down to Gatlinburg—to a hot bath and a good supper and a long, long sleep. The next morning, bidding Ben and the Great Smokies goodby, we moved on with the spring.

TWENTY-TWO

VERTICAL MIGRATIONS

―――――――――

IN the mist, in the rain, under cliffs vivid with sulphur-colored lichen, in the wet, mossy mountaintop woods of the Great Smokies, I had glimpsed again and again the fluttering form of a blue-gray bird, the Carolina junco. Nellie and I saw it now beside the road a few miles from Blowing Rock, in the Blue Ridge Mountains of northwestern North Carolina.

It perched on the top rail of a fence that wandered as an insubstantial barrier along the rim of a roadside cliff. Beyond, blue-tinted mountains extended away, fold on fold, to the west. The bird picked at a high grass blade. It darted into the air. It hovered like a flycatcher. It swept, with a flash of white outer tail feathers, to the tip of a balsam bough. It sent the bell jingle of its song down the granite face of the sheer descent. It was home. Its migration was over. While slate-colored juncos, the snowbirds of the North, had traveled half a thousand miles and more to reach their breeding grounds, this southern relative, *Junco hyemalis carolinensis*, had climbed the stairway of the mountains in a vertical migration back to its summer home. For the Carolina junco migrates up and down while billions of other birds migrate north and south.

In the valleys of the Southern Appalachians the spring migration of the Carolina juncos may represent a horizontal journey of no more than a dozen miles. Winter and summer they remain in almost the same spot on the map. Yet their ascending flight is as truly a migration as the long trek of the golden plover or the flight of bobolinks from Argentina to New England fields.

Around Gatlinburg, in the Great Smokies, the snowbirds of the North and the snowbirds of the South—the slate-colored juncos and their subspecies, the Carolina juncos—intermingle in the valleys during midwinter months. Experts tell the two apart by the larger size, the grayer hue, and the horn-colored bill of the southern bird. The back of the northern junco has a brownish cast and its bill is flesh colored. But to the casual eye the two birds are indistinguishable. Yet each spring the flocks split apart along the cleavage of an ancestral pattern of behavior. They separate like oil and water. One migrates horizontally, the other vertically, to return to their separate breeding grounds.

By the 15th of April, Arthur Stupka told us, all the juncos in the Great Smokies are Carolina juncos. The northern birds have gone and the southern juncos have climbed the mountainsides in their altitudinal migration. They breed almost entirely above 3,500 feet and nests have been found above 6,500 feet. The Canadian Zone is the main breeding area for both northern and southern juncos. One reaches it by flying up the map, the other by flying up the mountains. In terms of the advance of spring, a flight to the top of North Carolina's Mt. Mitchell, the highest peak in the East is the equivalent of a northward journey of almost a thousand miles.

The range of the Carolina junco extends up the Southern Appalachians from Georgia to Virginia and West Virginia, with a few pairs even being found across the Maryland line. Each winter, along the eastern flanks of the Great Smokies and the Blue Ridge Mountains, in North Carolina, the birds fan out over the Piedmont Plateau. They return, flying west and up, with the coming of spring. During summer, Carolina juncos are one of the most common and characteristic birds of the hill towns in the western part of the state.

We saw them in Highlands, in Asheville, at Blowing Rock,

in Boone, and along the high mountain roads between. One evening at sunset, as we were walking down the main street of Boone, a lively flock of a dozen or more juncos swept around us to alight with tinkling trills on a lawn not more than thirty feet away. We saw them feeding like English sparrows along the sidewalks and in the yards, paying scant attention to the passers-by. Some of these mountain juncos even build their nests close to houses in towns, beside clods in garden patches, or like phoebes, in the protection of garages. They are friendly and unafraid. Their jingling song—like that of a more musical chipping sparrow—their repeated, one-note, bell-like "cling-cling-cling-cling," the smacking sound they make—a miniature imitation of a brown thrasher, only more sharp and metallic—and the chitter of small flocks taking off by the roadside—all these became familiar to us.

Where Blowing Rock juts out in a granite cliff 2,000 feet above the Johns River Gorge, we heard juncos all about us. They flitted over the rhododendrons and the gray granite rocks splotched with lichens. They hopped among the clumps of bluets under small oaks, with twigs still bare and some of the trunks sheeted in moss. The unceasing wind sweeping up the face of this towering precipice brought sounds with remarkable distinctness from the slopes and valley below. Our ears caught the faint, faraway sound of a waterfall. We heard the "wicky-wicky-wicky" of a flicker, the calling of a robin, the drumming of a woodpecker on a hollow limb—spring sounds all. And, carried on the wind from nearer trees of the slope, came the unmistakable jingling-bell song of other juncos, singing down the mountainside.

The home of the Carolina junco is also the home of the cloudland deer mouse, the New England cottontail, and the Appalachian black-capped chickadee. We never saw the cloudland mouse. We caught sight of only a few of the mountain rabbits. But in numerous places we encountered the blackcaps trooping through the forests, uttering their double-note calls that seemed a kind of repeated reassurance: "OK! OK! All right! All right!"

In mountain ponds frogs start their calling late in spring. Their concerts begin according to the delayed calendar of elevation. But there is little delay in the nesting of the Carolina juncos. By mid-May eggs are in the nests as high as 6,500 feet above sea level. And the nesting season is a long one. Alexander Sprunt has found fresh eggs in a junco's nest in the North Carolina mountains as late as August 10. This, he thought, was probably a third brood for the season.

During the years since 1886, when William Brewster, the Cambridge ornithologist, described and named *Junco hyemalis carolinensis*, the list of birds known to migrate vertically has lengthened. In the West altitudinal migrations are the rule among a number of species. Fox sparrows and white-crowned sparrows and Oregon juncos move up and down the Sierras with the changing seasons. The mountain bluebird of the Sierras, the Cascades, and the Rockies also moves downward into the warmer lowlands with the coming of winter.

The pipit, which normally nests in the Arctic Zone, on the tundras above treeline in Canada and Alaska, sometimes nests in the high Rockies in Colorado, spending its summer among the peaks and descending in a vertical migration to lower levels for the winter. In the Alpine Zone of the Rockies the rosy finches and pine grosbeaks have a summer breeding ground which is the goal of their upward flight in spring. Red-breasted nuthatches, golden-crowned kinglets, ruby-crowned kinglets, hermit thrushes, and others also engage in vertical migrations among the western mountains. A variation of the seasonal ascent and descent of these birds is found in the life of the Clark's nutcracker, *Nucifraga columbiana*. It nests on the lower slopes of the mountains but, as summer advances, it ascends in an annual movement that has been compared to the postbreeding migration made by some southern herons northward along the Atlantic coast.

It may even be that the few hardy robins that overwinter each year in the cedar swamps along the New England coast are individuals that have nested in mountain areas and have come down to sea level instead of flying south. Almost invariably, vertical migrants are hardy species. They simply find a milder season in the lowlands. But their year contains a winter as well as a summer, while most horizontal migrants, birds that head south as soon as autumn comes, live in warm weather the year around.

During subsequent days of our spring trip, after we had left the Carolina juncos behind, we encountered other forms of vertical migration. Tiny creatures as well as larger ones, plants as well as animals, engage in a seasonal descent and ascent, correlated with the coming of autumn and spring.

One morning we followed a path across a wide, dew-covered field. Ahead of us, as far as we could see, the trodden earth was speckled with the castings of innumerable earthworms. They, in their way, recorded another form of vertical migration in the spring. Earthworms, in the fall, migrate deeper into the earth, below the frostline. Sometimes they ball up to reduce moisture loss—as many as a hundred worms being bunched together—and thus spend the winter in inactivity. When spring comes and frost leaves the soil, the earthworms become migrants again, tunneling upward. They appear at the surface, leaving the first castings of the new season, as soon as the average temperature of the ground reaches about 35 degrees Fahrenheit. At the same time the robin returns from the South. This is part of the endlessly meshing gears of nature's machine—the appearance of both earthworm and robin when the thermometer rises to a given point. All over the North the return of the humble earthworm, the completion of its vertical migration, is a symbol of arriving spring.

During the heavy rains of this season, before vegetation has made much headway, the castings of earthworms play an important part in erosion control. The castings are harder, more resistant to falling raindrops, than ordinary soil. I remember hearing a paper at one of the meetings of the American Association for the Advancement of Science, some years ago, on results of tests made in Maryland by research workers of the U.S. Department of Agriculture. Earthworm castings, they found out, are more than twice as resistant to raindrops as the soil around them. Six drops were sufficient to start erosion in the soil, whereas it required thirteen to produce a similar effect in the worm-casting material. A kind of mesh of harder spots is spread across the surface of bare soil by a multitude of castings. The more earthworms in the soil the more resistant it is likely to be to the erosion of spring.

Moles, feeding on earthworms, also tunnel deeper into the earth when late autumn comes and force their way upward toward the surface in the spring. Similarly, the white grubs of the May beetles burrow deeper to spend the winter below the frostline. More than fifteen times, the periodical cicada makes such an underground migration, downward in autumn, upward in spring, before its final ascent brings it into the open air. Invisible behind the curtain of the soil, numerous earth dwellers move up and down in response to the changing seasons.

The toad, the turtle, and the frog all burrow varying distances into mud or earth for their long, cold-blooded winter sleep and work their way upward again when the spring of another year arrives. This movement is also, in its way, a vertical migration. Many fish descend into the deepest part of a lake during the months of cold. Whirligig beetles and May fly nymphs pull themselves downward along the stems of waterweeds at the approach of winter. And, low on forest trees, certain minute beetles creep along ridges and valleys of bark to spend the winter in the carpet of moss below. They make their way from tree trunk to moss in autumn and from moss to tree trunk in spring. Their vertical seasonal trek can be measured in inches. Yet it is truly a migration.

So, under different conditions, is the rise and fall of the duckweed. All along the way, as we worked north, we saw this unrooted botanical nomad multiplying on streams and swamps and ponds. It was spreading over the surface in spring sunshine. As much as the bloodroot and hepatica and Dutchman's breeches, the earliest duckweed is a plant of spring. On lowland streams in the North, it begins its swift multiplication early in the season—at the end of its odd migration.

The old herbals call the small, flat, green duckweeds, because of their shape, "lentils." In *The Grete Herball*, of 1526, they are "lentylles of the water," or "frogge's fate." Strictly speaking, the duckweed has no leaves and no stem. The plant body, or thallus, floats on the surface while rootlets dangling below obtain mineral food from the muddy water. During spring and summer the duckweed reproduces by "budding" or dividing in two like a plant amoeba. The number of duckweeds thus produced reaches astronomical proportions almost before spring is past.

Using a small pasteboard box, two inches long and one inch wide, as a kind of botanical cooky cutter, I sliced two square inches from a floating mat of duckweed on one sluggish lowland stream we encountered. The mat contained both *Lemna major* and *Lemna minor*. Laboriously I counted the plants. There were 272. This meant there were about 20,000 duckweeds in one square foot or some 175,000 in each square yard. By mid-July, less than a month after spring's official close, I was told, this stream is often covered with duckweed from bank to bank for miles along its course. As the stream averages about fifty feet in width, simple multiplication gives the total for one mile—5,280,000,000 individual plants.

Had this mat contained that most tiny of duckweeds, the smallest flowering plant in the world, *Wolffia*, the number would have been even greater. There are, it has been estimated, about 2,000,000 of these pin points of green in a square yard. It takes 4,500,000 *Wolffia* plants to weigh one pound. Among the duckweeds, rapidity of multiplication makes up for small size. This swift yearly increase, all through the North, is made possible only through the plant's vertical migration.

When autumn comes, almost spherical "winter buds" appear. Air sacs in the thallus of the duckweed make it a natural buoy and keep it floating on the surface. Winter buds, however, have few air spaces and they are heavily loaded with stored-up starch grains. Gradually they sink lower and lower. They seem to become waterlogged. In fact, in *Lemna minor*, at least, something of the kind occurs. Researches have shown that water enters the intercellular spaces which are normally filled with air. As a submarine submerges by taking water into its ballast tanks, so the winter buds, or hibernacula, of the duckweeds increase their load and thus descend.

They may reach the mud of the bottom or remain just above it. Here the tiny living balls spend the winter while ice forms overhead and all the myriad floating plants of the surface are killed. To the uninitiated, the duckweed hosts seem wiped out each fall just as, to one unaware of migration, the innumerable warblers seem destroyed. Yet both warblers and duckweed return with the spring. One migrates northward, the other upward.

Rising temperature in the water stimulates the resting form of the duckweed. It begins to grow. It produces new air spaces filled with gas. Its buoyancy increases. It ascends nearer and nearer the surface. Not long after the ice has left ponds and streams the first returning migrants among the duckweeds appear at the surface. They are the forefathers of the new generation. Their autumn descent and spring ascent—as though riding on an underwater elevator—preserves the species in northern states. This annual trek is an important part in the life cycle of the duckweed, just as vertical migrations in varying form are an important part of the life cycle of earthworm and turtle and mole and beetle—and Carolina junco.

TWENTY-THREE

KITE HOLLOW

"MRS. TOY MILLER. Kite Hollow. Off Happy Valley. On the road to Blowing Rock."

I wrote it down in a spiral-ring pocket notebook.

We were in a huge rambling wooden building at Lenoir, North Carolina. Around us rose the smell of drying plants and roots and barks. The building was the headquarters of the Greer Drug Company, one of the country's largest dealers in medicinal herbs. Mountainfolk in hundreds of lonely spots were out in the spring weather gathering herbs, grubbing out roots, making a wild harvest to sell to the Greer Company. One of the most active of the Blue Ridge plant hunters is Mrs. Toy Miller. She ranges through Kite Hollow, along a mountain stream north of Happy Valley, and over the ridges beyond. I noted the directions for reaching her; for we hoped to go along on a hunt for mountain herbs.

The Greer Company, we found in looking over a price list, is in the market for such odd items as elder flowers, catnip leaves, balm of gilead buds, skunk cabbage roots, wild strawberry vines, mistletoe twigs, horse nettle berries, haircap moss, shonny haw bark, and maypop pops. In the United States there are more than 250 species of roots, herbs, and barks of value in the manufacture of drugs. A bulletin put out by the U.S. Department of Agriculture, *American Medicinal Plants of Commercial Importance*, is a Who's Who of these salable herbs. It is also a dictionary of curious botanical folk names.

The harvest of an American plant hunter may include badman's-oatmeal, truelove, tread-softly, simpler's joy, lords-and-ladies, shoofly, nature's mistake, or mad-dog skullcap. He may bring home Aaron's-rod, Noah's ark, Jacob's-ladder, or Devil's bones. Or he may return with juglans, kinnikinnic, hackmatack, missey-moosey, daffydowndilly, hurr-burr or robin-runs-away.

In the cavernous loft of the building at Lenoir we walked among piles of white pine and wild cherry bark, mounds of mullein leaves and blackberry roots, and rows of burlap bags filled with fragrant sassafras bark—the first product of the New World shipped back to Europe by the Pilgrims. Wooden barrels held Adam and Eve roots. Star grass roots, like small onions, were drying near adjoining mounds of yellow jessamine bark and pokeweed roots. And extending across a wide carpet of cloth lay bushels of balsam poplar, or balm of Gilead, buds. More buds were coming in every day. This was spring, the harvest-time of the budpickers. A waxy substance extracted from these buds is used in salves. For the dried buds, the Greer Company pays 60 cents a pound. Other prices range from 3 cents a pound for birch bark and 4 cents a pound for sumac berries to $1 a pound for star grass roots and $5 a pound for golden seal roots.

The highest price of all is paid for ginseng, from $8 to $10 a pound for the dried roots. Although there is no evidence that ginseng possesses any therapeutic or pharmacological properties, it has been in constant demand in China for centuries. The superstition that it has magic ability to restore virility to the aged has resulted in as much as $700 a pound being paid for especially fine roots in Manchuria. Most American ginseng grows far back in the mountains. The roots are at their best, shrinking least and bringing the highest prices, during a few weeks in autumn. André Michaux records that, in 1793, ginseng was the only product of Kentucky that could be transported profitably overland to Philadelphia.

Mailtime at the Greer Company brings a varied assortment of letters, penciled in unregimented spelling on odd scraps of paper by mountain plant hunters. The morning we were there, a note was deciphered suggesting that the writer should get twice the regular price for his roots because they were dug at a place "where the most dangerous snakes in the world live."

Not all the wild products handled at the Lenoir warehouse go into making drugs. Leaves of deer's-tongue are in demand for flavoring smoking tobacco. Another wild herb is necessary in the manufacture of silver polish. Sassafras bark goes into making perfumes as well as medicines. A recent development has been the collection of pollens for the treatment of allergies. One year, in less than a month, the Greer Company shipped $40,000 worth of ragweed pollen to northern pharmaceutical laboratories. In a kind of nightmare chamber for hayfever sufferers, we saw row on row of glass vials and jars filled with brightly colored dust—pollen from more than a hundred different plants.

Some of the first pollen handled by the Greer Company came from Kite Hollow. The red dirt road that leads into this side valley eluded us that day and it was afternoon before we came to the beginning of the hollow. A mile or so away we had asked directions for finding Toy Miller's house.

"Anybody down there can tell you," we were assured. "They're all kinfolk in the hollow."

The house we were hunting, gray from long weathering, clung to the foot of a steep descent. A dozen rows of peas and a small patch of catnip for the cat occupied a cleared space in the weeds at the back of the house. Chickens, dogs, cats, and children swarmed over the porch and unfenced yard. The herbwoman came to the door—thin, tired looking, her left cheek and lower lip bulging with snuff used "for the toothache." She was, she said, going up the creek that afternoon—the balm of Gilead buds were right for picking—and we were welcome to come along.

While she was getting a basket, Nellie passed around some Beechnut gum to the children. The oldest, a girl of about eight, chewed her stick solemnly for a few minutes. Then, before all the flavor was gone, she stuck it, for future enjoyment, under the arm of a cane-bottomed chair on the porch. A moment later she thought better of it. She returned, unstuck the wad, and attached it high on the frame of the front door, well out of reach of the smaller children.

We started down the hollow. The herbwoman was alert, pleasant, friendly. She had been born near Blowing Rock and was, she said, "a mountain girl from the beginning." She had a kind of natural dignity and her mountain dialect was interspersed with words of an older and better diction. She had been collecting wild plants, roots and barks for fifteen years. Once, when lumbering operations felled a stand of white pines near Kite Hollow, she and her husband skinned the bark from the logs and, in seven hours, earned $41. Another time, in two days, they earned $61—piling up more than 800 pounds of bark at 7½ cents a pound. Those were long-remembered bonanza days.

Where a decaying rail fence staggered along under a load of honeysuckle vines we stopped amid wild strawberries. The ground was white with their blossoms over an area of a hundred square yards. The herbwoman comes here to pick strawberry leaves sometimes. They sell for 20 cents a pound. But she never comes to pick strawberries. By the time they are ripe the rattlers and copperheads that live in the honeysuckle tangle are out and active.

"There's a heap of berries here," she told us, "but you can't get near 'em for snakes."

Once, back in the mountains, she was standing in thick bushes when she heard a buzzing sound and looked down in time to see the brownish body and V-shaped crossbands of a timber rattlesnake slide almost across her foot. The snake, apparently, did not see her. What did she do?

"I made tracks out of there in a hurry!"

In the main, however, when she is hunting herbs in the mountains she gives little thought to snakes.

"Hits a wonder," she observed, "I ain't all eat up."

We followed the creek, swollen with spring rains, until we came to the first of the balm of Gilead trees. Under favorable conditions these balsam poplars reach a height of 100 feet. The young twigs are hairy and the cigar-shaped leaf buds are fragrant and shining with yellow wax. Indians used this wax for sealing the seams of their birchbark canoes. Honeybees collect it to stop up cracks in the hives. Pioneers valued the wax so highly as a healing salve that they planted balm of Gileads near their cabins. It was a medicine tree. Today these "balm buds" still form the source of an important ingredient in many manufactured salves.

We pulled down branches and picked off buds. They rattled into the basket. We went from tree to tree. The sun was warm, the air filled with fragrance. Above the roar of the swollen stream, tumbling over the boulders of its bed, the calling of a cardinal carried far from his perch in the top of a willow tree. The ringing "What cheer! What cheer! What cheer!" was repeated over and over again.

"Hits got a big enough mouth," said the herbwoman succinctly.

The farthest she goes into the mountains in her plant collecting is about four miles. This is for the rarer herbs. The most sought-after of the roots grow scarcer every year. There is only one place now in the mountains where she is sure of finding ginseng. Also rapidly disappearing in the region is the "Noah's ark," the yellow lady-slipper. Its roots, collected in autumn, sell for $1 a pound, dried. The mountains of western North Carolina supply a large part of the nation's medicinal plants. Yet even here, where at one time the supply seemed unlimited, uncontrolled collecting is having its effect. Herb hunters have to roam farther and farther into remote regions to make their harvest. Near settled communities, many species have been completely extirpated.

As we walked along, the herbwoman pointed out plants that she would visit later. Horse nettle—apple of Sodom or tread-softly—grew in a sandy place. Its berries, split and dried in autumn, bring 36 cents a pound. The dried roots bring 25 cents. The spindle-shaped roots of the yellow dock sell for only 9 cents a pound. Mullein, that plant of many names—candle-wick, blanket leaf, Adam's-flannel, old-man's-flannel, hare's-beard, velvet plant, clown's lungwort—was beginning the production of the thick, felty leaves of a new year. The leaves and tender tops of the mullein, picked and dried, have a market value of 10 cents a pound. Once we passed a mound of pokeweed. This was a wild garden the herbwoman visited annually. Pokeberries bring 15 cents a pound; the roots, which unfortunately "dry up to next to nothing," bring only 10. Nearer the stream, in a boggy stretch, skunk cabbage massed its sappy green leaves. Here harvest days come in early spring. The roots and rootstocks are dug up and dried, after being split to hasten the process. The split, dried roots sell for 20 cents a pound.

One of the few things the herbwoman never collects is mistle-toe. These clumps usually grow too high in trees. However, much of the mistletoe that reaches northern states during the holiday season comes from North Carolina, tons being shipped from one county alone. Some modern Daniel Boones, expert with a squirrel rifle, are said to harvest the topmost bunches in their own peculiar way, snipping off the branches with well-directed lead.

Along the creek, as we walked back, willow trees leaned, in clouds of new, pale-green leaves, far out over the rush of the mountain stream.

"I've skinned more willow bark in this place than most people think," the herbwoman volunteered.

In recent years the streamside willows have become a new

source of revenue. The catkins have assumed special importance. For willow pollen has gone to market. Each spring Mrs. Miller collects bushels of the staminate catkins, sifting their floral dust through a fine cloth into a dishpan. The best time for harvesting pollen, she has found, is in the morning just after the dawn mist has evaporated.

The fluffy, greenish catkins of the black willows are as long as a little finger. Sometimes the tassels are more than three inches in length. They represent the largest pollen source with which the herbwoman deals. The smallest is the white flower of the plantain. On one of the hottest days of June, the previous year, she had followed the black-top road through Happy Valley, picking plantain flowers on either side. A score of times cars pulled up and people who thought she must be crazy wanted to know what she was doing.

When R. T. Greer, head of the Lenoir company, needs a new kind of pollen, he frequently puts Mrs. Toy Miller on its trail. Her knowledge of local plants is widely respected. Will Rogers once observed that we are all ignorant; we are just ignorant about different things. Our companion that day had had little schooling; she had never been beyond sight of one small part of the Blue Ridge Mountains. Her knowledge was narrow— but it was deep. She was an expert, an authority in her field.

A century and a half before, when André Michaux was wandering through the wilderness of the New World, collecting plants for Old World herbariums, he had recorded in his journal, in the spring of 1795, that he was "herborising in the Bleue Ridges." We too, that day, had been "herborising" in those same mountains.

As we drove away down the red dirt road heading for Statesville, we reflected on how humbling such a trip as ours eventually becomes. I remembered a famous explorer once saying to me: "The main thing I learn on every expedition is my ignorance." Everywhere we went we met new and unfamiliar things. Everywhere we went we encountered people who had spent their lives reading from one particular shelf in nature's library. They knew more about it—more about their area and their particular field—than we could ever hope to know. We could but sample the books they had time to read in detail.

We were near Hickory, North Carolina, in the sunset that evening when we caught the perfume of the first lilacs of our trip. They bloomed in a farmyard close to the road. A little farther on we ran through a great swirl of apple petals carried from a hillside orchard. And all along the way mockingbirds and cardinals sang in the failing light. It was dusk when we reached Statesville.

TWENTY-FOUR

THE RETURN OF THE ELVERS

THE next morning, before breakfast, we opened a book that would have fascinated Charles Dickens. It was the Statesville Telephone Directory.

In a pocket notebook, Dickens used to jot down unusual names for later use in his novels. As we leafed through the directory we seemed to be going over one of these notebooks. Here were fresh and original names. They stirred the imagination. We amused ourselves, as we drove east that day, by conjuring up characters Dickens might have fitted to such names as Herman Goforth, J. C. Turnipseed, Bess Gant, R. E. Nooe, Peggy Snipes, C. Moose, Laura Jolly, and J. C. Dayvault.

For the next few days our route zigzagged over the Piedmont. We crossed the cedar-bordered Yadkin River, in Davidson County, where hundreds of thousands of northern robins sometimes concentrate in winter. We paused beside a sunken meadow that spread away for half a mile in one vast, brilliant tapestry of spring—red and blue and yellow wildflowers intermingling, with the bright scarlet of the painted cup predominating. Near Concord, North Carolina, we passed our first spring swarm of honeybees. It enveloped a roadside sign, with parts of the cluster descending the post like drippings of yellow wax.

All one day we ran through localized spring showers. Sometimes the rain came down the concrete to meet us, the line of its advancing front as clearly defined as though it were a breaking wave. We could see before us huge raindrops pounding the concrete, the highway glistening with running water, while we rode on dry and dusty pavement. There would be one measurable moment when we were out of the shower, then in it—the great drops drumming on the roof and hood of the car, the windshield streaming with such quantities of water that one end of the arc of the swinging rubber wipers was blurred while the other end was being wiped clean. For several miles we would be enveloped in the deluge. Then it would pass. We would speed for a time along wet pavements; then we would be beyond the storm and the highway would be dry again. Five times in a hundred miles we plunged into such rainstorms. Each time the sensation was like diving head first into an advancing wave.

As we worked east, from the escarpment of the Blue Ridge to the fall line where rivers drop off the Piedmont onto the Coastal Plain, we watched leaves expanding as though we were watching a lapse-time movie. Traveling downhill, we were advancing in the spring. As we proceeded, the same kinds of trees were clothed in larger leaves.

Near Southern Pines the flat and sandy fields lay under a haze of delicate pastel shadings of red and blue where sorrel and toadflax intermingled. Masses of blue lupines rose beside the road; and beneath the long-leaf pines, where giant cones and foot-long fallen needles carpeted the ground, bird's-foot violets lifted thousands of flowers. Farther north, as we neared Chapel Hill to spend two days with our friends, Dr. and Mrs. Raymond Adams, whole hillsides were white with dogwood.

There after weeks associated with swamps and caves and mountaintops, we suddenly found ourselves at lunches, giving speeches, caught up in civilized routine once more. We visited bird-feeding stations. We were shown wildflower gardens. We attended meetings. We looked up Richard L. Weaver, of the American Nature Study Society, and accepted an invitation to join an outing of the North Carolina Bird Club, at Beaufort on the coast. We examined Dr. Adams's extensive collection of Thoreau material and when Walter Harding arrived for dinner, in a dripping green raincoat during a spring hailstorm, we held an impromptu reunion of the Thoreau Society. In Chapel Hill we met old friends and made new ones. There we also met Heine.

Heine was the Adams's engaging dachshund. At eleven, Heine was as old, proportionately, as a man of seventy-five. Several times a day he would be overcome by wheezing fits of coughing. We noticed that these occurred most often when Dr. Adams was talking. The next summer, at Walden Pond, in Massachusetts, when various speakers addressed the Thoreau Society at the occasion of marking Thoreau's hutsite, Heine was in the audience. He remained perfectly quiet until Dr. Adams began to speak; then he was attacked by violent coughing. This was, perhaps, his manner of attracting notice. For pets employ a legion stratagems in bidding for attention.

A Carolina spring heat wave was beginning the morning we left Chapel Hill for Beaufort. Highways shimmered before us. Dragonflies tilted wildly in the heated air. And all across the Coastal Plain, in lowland stretches, the waxy yellow and red flowers of pitcher plants shone in the glaring sunshine. North Carolina is the longest state, east and west, this side of the Mississippi. We had traversed its length, from one end to the other, when we reached the sea at the U.S. Fish and Wildlife research station at Beaufort.

Out of the confusion of meetings and field trips the following day we recall especially the song of a Macgillivray's seaside sparrow and the bright red mud dauber nests formed from dust of disintegrating bricks at old Fort Macon. We met Mrs. Cecil Appleberry, of Wilmington, who promised to show us the natural history of the Cape Fear region, and Charlotte Hilton Green, whose nature column in the Raleigh *News and Observer* has stimulated widespread interest in the North Carolina outdoors. We heard of an albino white-throated sparrow which could be identified only by its song and a female cardinal that battled its reflection in a window like a male robin redbreast at mating time. We also heard of the oddest pet of our experience.

John Pearson, one of the research scientists at the laboratory, told us of his adventures with a pet baby eel which he kept for five years in a glass jar. Whenever he made a trip away from home, the jar and its occupant went along. During the day the eel buried itself in sand at the bottom of the container. There it remained until Pearson came home. The vibrations of his footfalls were sufficient to arouse it. It would pop out of the sand and dart to the surface to be fed. Sometimes it would thrust fully a fourth of its body above the surface reaching for bits of shrimp or fish held at the end of a pair of tweezers. As long as titbits were offered it continued to gorge itself. On one inland trip, when seafood was difficult to get, Pearson fed it small fragments of beefsteak. Soon after this feast the pet eel died. Beef is more fibrous, harder to digest, than fish and is believed to have been the cause of death.

On the back of an envelope Pearson sketched a map. We followed it the next day as we drove south toward Wilmington. Turning off the main highway near Newport, we ran over the pale, anemic sand of a dirt road through pine flats, past a prison camp, into a pocket of crested flycatchers, under nighthawks hunting in the sunshine, and came at last to a wooden bridge below a log dam. The little stream that flowed beneath it was partly choked by boulders and fallen limbs. Its water was the color of root beer. This was the lonely setting for a fabulous event of spring.

Below us, as we looked down, the water fanned out over shoals of light sand tinted amber by the flow. Soon we became aware of little threads of life, hardly as long as a little finger, hardly thicker than a darning needle, moving upstream, wriggling across the shallows, fighting the current. One after the other, a dozen crossed the little sand bar and disappeared into the deeper, darker pool above. These slender creatures were elvers, baby eels, ending a year-and-a-half journey, a journey that had carried them 10,000,000 times their own length across the open sea. Now, so close to their goal, they were traveling by day as well as by night, in brilliant sunshine as well as under the cover of darkness.

We leaned on the rail of the bridge and, with the sun warm on our backs, stared down at this parade from the sea. A procession of elvers, head to tail, was following the sinuous edge of the sand bar. Now a single baby eel was deflected into an aquatic merry-go-round where the water swirled lazily in a shallow depression about the size of a dinner plate. Three times it made a circuit of this miniature lagoon, swimming faster and faster apparently sensing something was wrong. Bursting from this cul-de-sac, it turned, as though on rails, upstream, nosing head on into the current. The nervous system of the elver, during its spring migration inland, seems set like an automatic pilot. The wriggling creature instinctively tries to keep the pressure on both sides of its body equal and in consequence swims head on into flowing water.

All up the coast, on that spring day, baby eels, millions and billions of baby eels, were streaming inland from the sea. They were mounting rivers and creeks and brooks. They were fighting their way up torrents, wriggling over spray-drenched rocks around waterfalls, threading their way into lakes and ponds and reservoirs, penetrating to the headwaters of all the infinitely branched water lanes leading to the sea. No course was too roundabout. No path was too difficult. They were climbing tumbling brooks to reach mountain lakes, working into the depths of the Great Dismal Swamp, even penetrating the aqueducts and mains of the water supply systems of the largest seaboard cities.

For weeks the "eel-fare," as the English term this return of the elvers, had been going on. We stared down with a feeling of awe and respect at these diminutive travelers, so tenacious of purpose, so unwearied by travel. Only the sides of the log dam upstream had to be surmounted and their long journey would be at an end. In the pond behind the barricade they would reach the headwaters of the stream. Sometimes at night, below this dam, John Pearson had told us, the elvers piled up in a squirming mass, temporarily blocked by the log wall ahead of them. It was the final obstacle in an odyssey of obstacles.

Near the edge of the stream, swirls and swifter currents had scoured away the sediment, so that the amber water slid over clear white sand. A chain of such lighter spots, with the sediment dark between them, extended for a dozen feet or so upstream. Each little eel that wriggled across such a spot stood out against its lighter background. Once a parade of elvers passed along the chain of sand spots, appearing and disappearing, becoming successively visible and invisible like forms stealing at dusk before a series of lighted windows.

Sometimes the little migrants speeded up; sometimes they slowed down; sometimes they nosed into quiet nooks and rested. But hour after hour the intermittent procession continued. It wound in and out among the waving flags of green scum that fluttered from submerged branches. It passed beneath whirligig beetles, spinning unheeding on the surface, beneath the shadow of a green-tinted dragonfly that darted and hovered over the stream, through golden meshes of sunlight reflected from the ripples.

This upstream journey was the reverse of the movement that had carried adult eels down this very ravine the autumn before. Migrating to the sea to breed and die, they had traveled by night and rested by day and had ridden with the current instead of opposing it. The Chinook salmon of the Northwest migrates into streams, returns to fresh water to spawn. The eel reverses the procedure. It migrates to the sea, from fresh water to salt. Otherwise it remains sterile. Only in the abysses of the ocean is it able to reproduce its kind.

The breeding eels that had slipped down the stream the

autumn before had been well layered with fat. As summer had merged with autumn, they had ceased to eat. Their bodies had lost their color, had taken on a silvery sheen. All along the Atlantic seaboard of North America, all along the coast of Europe, other silver eels had begun their last journey. On cool autumn nights, eels hurrying to the sea sometimes crawl for a mile or more across dewy meadows to reach streams that will carry them to salt water. Away from the coast, they all turn south, swimming day after day and week after week in the direction of the Sargasso Sea.

For centuries silver eels disappeared and baby eels reappeared and no man knew the events that took place between. Aristotle believed that eels were sexless, that new eels came into being spontaneously in the sea. His opinion prevailed for centuries. Leeuwenhoek, the pioneer Dutch microscopist, mistook parasites for young eels and announced that the creatures gave birth to living young. Sir Thomas Browne reported— as a "strange yet well attested" fact—"the production of eeles in the backs of living cods and perches." Thus science progressed from misconception to misconception until very recent times. Less than half a century has passed since one of the great detectives of science, the Danish ichthyologist, Johannes Schmidt, filled in the blank between the disappearance of the silver eels and the appearance of the elvers. Only the experiments of Karl von Frisch, in the realm of the language of the honeybee, have in modern times rivaled these patient researches of Schmidt.

In his quaint book, *Vegetable Staticks*, published in 1727, Stephen Hales wisely observes: "Hardly do we guess aright at the things that are upon earth; and with labor do we find the things that are before us." With what labor did Schmidt unravel the mystery of the baby eels!

Year after year he put to sea. He was hunting for a needle in a haystack and the haystack was as big as the ocean. His cruises of investigation ranged from America to Egypt, from Iceland to the Canary Islands and the West Indies. For nearly two decades he kept doggedly at a seemingly hopeless task. One of his research ships, the *Margrethe,* was wrecked on a West Indian island. But slowly his accumulating information drew him closer to the solution of this riddle of great antiquity.

In May, 1904, on the research steamer *Thor,* Schmidt hauled in a Petersen's young-fish trawl and found it in the first baby eel ever taken in the open Atlantic. What followed afterwards, Schmidt described in 1923, in *The Philosophical Transactions of the Royal Society of London.* Other baby eels were pulled from the sea. Those near the European coast were larger than those farther out and farther south. Reasoning that the younger the eel the smaller it would be, Schmidt followed smaller and smaller clues into the region of the Sargasso Sea. There, four years in succession, he found minute larvae, less than ten millimeters long. The center of the breeding area, he concluded, lies approximately equidistant from Bermuda and the Leeward Isles.

Here the brown Sargassum weed drifts above the greatest abyss of the Atlantic Ocean. Four miles of water separate the surface and the floor of the sea. It is here that the outward journey of the adult eels is ended. Here they find the right conditions of temperature and depth for spawning. One female will scatter as many as 100,000 eggs in the water. The silver eels breed and die and leave behind a myriad spherical eggs floating in the sea.

These eggs are "bathypelagic." That is, they drift at considerable depths in the ocean. In February the eggs begin to hatch, often a thousand feet below the surface. From them emerge minute larvae, from seven to fifteen millimeters long. They are flattened vertically into the shape of a willow leaf standing on its edge. They are crystal clear. Colorless blood is pumped through colorless bodies. The only pigment they contain is found in the dark pin points of their eyes.

Slowly these larvae work upward through the darkness and

the crushing pressure of the depths. In swimming, they undulate from side to side. When at rest, they maintain their balance by curling up like a loosely coiled watchspring. Biting with minute needle-teeth, they feed on microscopic fare, such as little spheres of algae. As they near the surface they begin drifting with the ocean currents, starting the long, unhurried trek that carries them north. Both American and European eels spawn west of longitude 50 degrees. While most of the billions of eggs released by American eels are to the west of the billions of eggs released by European eels, there is a common overlapping area where the eggs of both float side by side. Side by side the eels hatch out, one destined from the beginning for life in North American waters and the other for a home on the continent of Europe.

Instinct, planted in their tiny, transparent bodies, leads them across hundreds or thousands of miles of watery waste to their respective destinations. The backbone of a baby eel is a kind of ticket revealing its destination to the scientist with a microscope. By counting the vertebrae he can predict infallibly whether it will eventually turn east or west. From the time they hatch, North American eels have from 104 to 110 vertebrae, never more. European eels have from 111 to 118, never fewer. Thus a single vertebra divides the two. If a baby eel has 110 vertebrae, it is destined to turn toward America; if it has 111, it will veer away toward Europe. The journey of the European eel, which matures less quickly, takes three years; that of the American eel only a little more than one. On the Pacific coast of America there are no eels except Lampreys. However on the Oriental side of the Pacific eels are found. They too disappear into the sea in autumn.

Swimming northward in the Atlantic both European and American elvers engage in an ocean odyssey attended by many dangers. The procession of elvers below our North Carolina bridge was made up of the survivors who had safely run the gantlet of fish and jellyfish and squid, of enemies innumerable. At the age of six months, the American eels are about one inch long. European eels are hardly half as long. At that time the two can be told apart at a glance, by size alone.

Strangely enough, during generations while the mystery of the eel's spawning ground remained unsolved, scientists were familiar with the baby eels themselves. They had been pickled in alcohol, examined through microscopes, minutely described, and given the scientific name of *Leptocephalus*—all the while the scientists assuming they were examining another species of small tropical fish, never suspecting that they held in their hands the key to the great riddle.

People who see adult eels pour down to the sea in fall and baby eels appear from the sea in spring assume the latter are the progeny of the former. Instead there is always a lapse of a generation between. The elvers we were seeing were the children of the adults that had gone downstream two autumns before. Each year the silver eels, swimming southward through the ocean to breed and die, pass the elvers, in numbers beyond imagining, working northward. The life of the eel begins and ends in a journey through the sea.

By the time it is one year old the young eel is in wintery seas off the North American coast. Here an amazing change begins. Its knife-blade body shrinks. It contracts both vertically and longitudinally. It assumes the form of a slender, transparent rod. It is known, now, as a glass eel. In this transformation, it loses weight as well as size. A glass eel sometimes weighs only one-third as much as it did in its *Leptocephalus* form.

The earliest days of spring find the transparent elvers moving in across the Continental Shelf toward estuaries and inlets. One of the many mysteries that remain in connection with their return is the manner in which they distribute themselves along the coast. Tagged Chinook salmon return, after five years in the sea, to the very brook where they were born. Their instinctive return to their birthplace distributes them throughout the watercourses of the Northwest. But how are the eels

spread along the length of the eastern coast? Why do they
not pile up with too many in the South, too few in the North?
Do they, like the salmon, carry an instinctive chart within their
bodies, guiding them back to certain streams? Probably not.
For, while the salmon are returning where they have been
before, the eels are entering a new world when they approach
the shore. Perhaps some hatch earlier than others or ride north
in swifter currents, thus lengthening their journey before instinct turns them toward the land. Whatever the cause, the
eels, in their infinite numbers, are distributed all along the seaboard from the sluggish, lowland streams of the rice country to
rocky brooks in Maine.

All the rivers are in spring flood, all the tides are at spring
high, when the elvers throng in toward the surf. They wait until the tides subside from their highest crests; wait, usually, until
some night of warm spring rain. Then they pour into the estuaries. They drive head on into the current and, with fresh
water around them for the first time in their lives, wriggle
upstream.

By now they are no longer transparent. Beginning with small
darkened cells along their backbones, pigmentation has spread
across their backs. This darkened upper surface of their bodies
provides needed camouflage in a new realm of many enemies.
Herons, kingfishers, pickerel, bass, older eels, all gorge themselves on the moving hordes of elvers. Those which survive,
which find themselves in the quiet upper reaches of rivers
and brooks, in lakes and ponds—sometimes as high as 8,000
feet above sea level—feed and grow for at least eight years
before they reach maturity. The females, larger than the males,
many attain a length of five feet and a weight of twenty pounds
before, in silver dress, they begin the last long journey that
rounds out their lives.

We talked in low, almost awed voices, of all the strange
life history of the eel as we stared down at those little travelers
passing beneath us, so close to journey's end. Their minute

bodies were equipped with instincts we could but dimly comprehend, instincts that had guided them north, that had swung their course to the west, that had brought them, at a time of high spring tides, close to shore. Their movement across the coastal shallows was a tide within a tide, a tide of incoming life, a greater tide, dependent upon stronger forces than the attraction of the moon, upon the invisible, all-mysterious forces of instinct.

TWENTY-FIVE

PREHISTORIC TRAPLINE

ALL through that moonlit night, while fireflies shimmered in the white ground mist, a mockingbird spun out the brilliant thread of its song behind our cabin a mile from Wilmington. Whenever we awoke, the passion of its melody filled the night. Moving northward through the South, we had been in advance of the main singing season of these birds. Only here did we experience the full virtuoso performance of a mockingbird in the spring. The memory is indelible: the low-lying mist luminous in the moonlight; the scented air; the trees dark in their shadows; the flashing, greenish pin points of innumerable fireflies; and, unseen in the shadows, the singer, with passion unwearied, pouring forth his tumbling melody hour after hour through the night.

This was our introduction to a region of special attraction. The next morning, at six, we were breakfasting with Mrs. Cecil Appleberry, one of the most enthusiastic and capable amateur naturalists we met on our trip. During the following days she guided us down byways of the Cape Fear region, the original home of the Venus's-flytrap, an area of pine woods and bays and true savannas.

Twenty-five miles north of Wilmington, near Burgaw, we came out upon the vast wildflower garden of one savanna that stretched away for 1,500 acres, flat as a Western prairie, lush as a bottom land. A wash of yellow ran across the whole expanse. Thousands upon thousands of the biscuit-shaped flowers of the pitcher plant, *Sarracenia flava*, were nodding above the grass on their slender stems. As spring advances, a kaleidoscope shifting of tints, a sequence of colors, sweeps over the savanna. At their appointed time, in the procession of the wildflowers, different blooms become dominant.

First come the bog dandelions of March, then the violets, the blue butterworts, the white fleabane, and the great iris show of May when the expanse of the savanna, from end to end, is one wide lake of blue. No wonder foreign botanists come from far parts of the world to see the Burgaw savanna! We envied those who lived close enough to watch the whole rainbow sequence from the beginning to the end. Like Pearson's Falls and the Great Smokies, the Burgaw savanna is a fragment of this nation's heritage that is infinitely valuable and that should be permanently preserved.

Our visit came when pitcher plants dominated the scene. And all over the flat coastal plain of the Cape Fear region, during those days, pitcher plants bloomed everywhere. They were the most obvious of a host of carnivorous plants—sundews, butterworts and those most astonishing of botanical inventions, the Venus's-flytrap—that prey upon insects. Probably nowhere else on the continent are there such concentrations of insectivorous plants as on the coastal plain of North Carolina. For untold millions of years they have been reversing the normal procedure: everywhere, animals eat plants; here, plants were consuming animals. They were trapping them with glue, with slippery surfaces, with mazes of spines, with bending leaves and with leaves hinged at the middle and set to snap shut on the body of the victim. Here, as we wandered over savannas and open pine flats, we were following nature's trapline, a prehistoric trapline, infinitely older than man.

Bats, swooping low, have sometimes been caught and held prisoner by burdock burs. In Oregon, some years ago, a young short-eared owl was discovered held fast by the sticky leaves of the tarweed, *Asio flammeus*. These instances, and others of their kind, were accidents. The plants derived no benefits from them. But here the trapping of small victims was no accident. Here it was being accomplished by means of some of the most amazing ruses and stratagems of the botanical world. And here the plants benefited directly. They were plants that ate meat. They secreted juices. They digested their victims. They functioned almost like animal stomachs. In this way they supplemented a diet deficient in needed elements.

One whole morning, with Mrs. Appleberry leading the way, we wandered down floral traplines that extended for miles across flatland among scattered pines. Often the ground was spongy with sphagnum moss. We would walk for fifty yards at a time on carpets that were thick, moist, and soft. In some places the top of this layer of sphagnum had changed from gray-green to a yellowish hue that made the area seem coated with sulphur. A pair of indigo buntings dashed about, the male brilliant blue, the female brown and sparrowish. And singing somewhere in a pine ahead of us, a Bachman's pinewoods sparrow repeated over and over again its song of one long note and then a trill on a lower pitch.

The slender upright trumpets of *flava* rose in clusters, in rows, all around us. Three of different heights stood side by side, their tops descending like a trio of notes on a sheet of music. I split open one trumpet and found nearly five inches of insects packed in the lower part of the slender tube. All except a few at the top were dead. The fluid in the pitcher, largely secreted by the plant, has been found to drown insects more quickly than ordinary water. It is also thought to stupefy the victims. Physicians who have experimented with an extract taken from *Sarracenia* pitcher plants, have reported that, in some ways, the drug is superior to novocain as a local anesthetic for human beings. Enzymes also are present in the secreted fluid. They assist in digesting the captured insects. Young trumpets, not yet open, are sometimes half full of liquid.

The flow of this fluid within the pitchers is stimulated—
like the flow of saliva—by food. Bits of raw meat, beef broth,
and milk produce an increase; but cheese, casein, and raw
whites of eggs do not. In one series of experiments, two scientists, Frank Morton Jones and J. S. Hepburn, found that the
introduction of small fragments of raw meat increased the
fluid volume within a pitcher by as much as 157 per cent. In
five days after beef broth was introduced, the fluid content
increased 387 per cent. And when milk was used, the fluid increased by one-fifth in a single day and in seven days it gained
by as much as 1,242 per cent. The experimenters also introduced dilute solutions of various acids and alkalis. No notice-
able change in fluid volume resulted. But the tests revealed
an interesting fact. No matter whether the introduced liquid
was alkali or acid, the fluid in the pitcher-plant—as within the
human stomach—soon returned to neutrality. The common
idea that the liquid within these pitchers is nothing more than
rain water is far from true.

In fact, all the thousands of slender trumpets of *flava* rising
around us had a kind of awning or roof above their open
mouths. Another pitcher plant of the area, *Sarracenia minor*,
is equipped with a peaked roof or rain hat that shelters its opening. In both instances, these extensions, resembling the top of
a jack-in-the-pulpit, prevent most of the rain from entering
the pitchers. Except for such a provision, heavy downpours
would fill the pitchers until they overflowed and thus lost some
of the captured insects. This is what happens in the commonest
of sphagnum-bog pitcher plants, *Sarracenia purpurea*, a plant
found as far north as Labrador. We saw its wine-red flowers
scattered among the yellow blooms of *flava*. Extending spokewise out from the center of the plant, its curved pitchers lift
their wide, unprotected mouths to the sky. Every heavy rain
overflows them. In spite of this, the plant thrives for 2,000
miles along the Atlantic coast from Florida northward.

One factor in its success is hundreds of downcurving hairs,

massed together like quills on a porcupine's back along the inside of the top of the pitcher. We ran our fingers over them. Going down, they slid in a smooth toboggan; coming up, they met the resistance of the forest of downcurving spines. The insect that slips down this chute-the-chutes finds it impossible to crawl out again. Its descent is a one-way trip. And slipping is made easy by the smooth, rounded lip of the pitcher. I watched one ant come up on the rim of a *flava* trumpet. It ran along for a dozen steps, then suddenly skidded sidewise and shot downward out of sight. I slid a forefinger over the spot where it had lost its hold. The rim of the plant was polished and waxy.

Even the possibility that some of the winged insects might fly upward and out of the trap has been taken care of in two of the American pitcher plants, *Sarracenia minor* and *Darlingtonia californica*. Each has a thin, translucent spot in the hood that extends over the mouth of the pitcher. The insect, which might otherwise escape, is attracted to the light of this window and flying against it is knocked back down into the pitcher again.

Each pitcher is a leaf, a leaf with its edges grown together. Many are veined with purple, delicately tinted with shadings of yellow and green. They have the beauty of flowers even when the real flowers of the plant are absent. Like flowers, these leaf traps attract insects by means of nectar and perfume. Some pitcher plants are scented like violets, others have a rich fruity odor. One, *Sarracenia minor*, leads ground insects such as ants up the side of the tube and over the rim by means of a path of sweet nectar.

The ant that most often loses its life in pitcher plants is *Cremastogaster pilosa*. Yet, strangely enough, this species sometimes nests in the dry tubes of the very plants whose green pitchers are bringing death to large numbers of its kind. Other small insects live even more dangerously. They dwell within the active traps themselves. The scientific name of one small

carrion fly, *Sarcophaga sarracenia,* indicates its close association with pitcher plants. It lays its eggs on the mass of decaying
insects in the tubes. The larva, apparently immune to the
digestive acids and enzymes of the fluid, feeds and grows and
when it reaches full size bores through the side of the tube and
pupates in the ground. The larva of a minute gnat has a somewhat similar history. And in the North the mosquito, *Wyeo-
myia smithii,* spends its larval life in the fluid within *purpurea*
pitchers, hibernating frozen in ice during the winter. Remaining frozen in solid ice for months on end and surviving
in the vegetable stomach of a pitcher plant are both common-
place events in its remarkable life cycle.

Predatory creatures also haunt these predatory plants.
Spiders lurk near their open mouths, catching insects attracted
by the perfume and nectar, before the plant can trap them.
A tiny tree toad and a small lizard not infrequently make their
home in the carnivorous plants. And minute parasitic wasps
descend within the tubes to lay their eggs on moth larvae that
feed on the inner tissues and spin their cocoons within the
dangerous confines of the pitchers. Each hollow leaf, so cun-
ningly fashioned for entrapping its prey, is a little world in
itself.

We wandered through a universe of these worlds. As far as
we could see, the damp, flat land was studded with the "hunts-
man's horns" of the tubes and the "sidesaddle flowers" of the
flava blooms. Once, as I looked down at a cluster of trumpets,
a movement beyond caught my eye. In an opening below a
dark decaying log, a scaly head thrust out and drew back like
the quick flicking of a tongue. I stood motionless. The head
appeared again. Every perfect green-tinted scale caught the
sunshine. The lizard, a blue-tailed skink, seemed newly formed
of polished metal. It was close to its curious breeding season
in which the female lays three or four eggs and then solicitously
curls about them, protecting them for weeks, only to ignore
the young completely as soon as they appear from the egg.

Her further attention is unneeded. The baby lizards can care for themselves from birth.

All over the Cape Fear region the soil is deficient in nitrogen. By absorbing the soluble nitrogenous material from the bodies of captured insects, the carnivorous plants of the coastal plain make up for this lack. L. G. Willis, a soil chemist we visited near Wilmington, believes that the insect diet also contributes needed copper. This metal, almost entirely absent in the soil, is present in small quantities in the blood of insects.

The following day, in different places, we saw other traplines running across wide expanses of open land or beside hardpan basins. I remember one stretch where the ground had been burned over late in winter. Wiry grass blades were pushing up through soil that was dark and wet and glistening. Here, for yards on end, the earth was covered with a rich red mat, a carpet formed of the close-packed rosettes of the sundew. Each coglike plant lay flat on the ground. At the end of the stems, the round leaves, about the size of shirt buttons, supported a maze of purple-tinted tentacles. A hundred fifty or more grow on a single leaf. Those at the center were stubby; those at the edges of the leaf were longest. Each ended in an oval swelling. Within this swelling, a gland produces drops of glistening glue. Where the sun struck the droplets, all the leaves sparkled as though covered with dew.

For the gnats and mosquitoes and other winged minutiae we saw drifting above the red rosettes, the droplets represent a deadly dew. If they touched no more than two or three of the maze of tentacles they were caught fast as though on Tanglefoot. The pitcher plants were vegetable pitfalls. Their traps were passive. But the snare of the sundew is combined with action.

As soon as an insect is caught, the tentacles move, almost like the fingers of a closing hand, to carry the victim to the center of the leaf. Other tentacles touch it. Other drops of glue increase the plant's hold upon it. Thus it is enfolded by a curious rolling motion. And all the time the tentacles are pouring out additional fluid. The struggles of the victim rapidly cease. Wrapped in the leaf, surrounded by the mucilage of the sundew, it drowns, usually in less than a quarter of an hour.

Now the leaf of the plant becomes the counterpart of the animal stomach. Digestive juices begin dissolving the insect; the leaf begins absorbing the nutriment. The sundews we saw closing that morning would remain closed for several days. Then when all the nutriment had been obtained from the victim, the tentacles would disengage themselves, fan slowly outward, and the leaf would assume its original position. With droplets of glue glistening in the sun, it would lie in wait for another victim.

The stimulus that sets in motion this chain of actions is apparently both mechanical and chemical. A tentacle will begin to move at a pressure of less than $1/70,000$ of a grain. Darwin found that a sundew would react to $1/20,000,000$ of a grain of phosphate in aqueous solution. To close entirely, the plant needs chemical as well as mechanical stimulus. Thus if you drop water on the leaf or put a small pebble on it, it may begin bending its tentacles but soon returns them to their original position. But substitute a drop of milk for water or a bit of meat for the pebble, and you see the leaf close over it as it would enfold an alighting insect. Thus it demonstrates its amazing ability to differentiate between edible and inedible substances.

At the time he was making his classic experiments with insectivorous plants, Charles Darwin noted an interesting thing about the mucilage of the sundew. It is a powerful antiseptic. It halts almost completely the action of bacteria. In one test, Darwin placed a bit of meat on a sundew and a second piece on moss. Later he examined them both under a microscope. The meat taken from the sundew was free of bacteria while that which had lain on the moss was "swarming with infusoria."

Also antiseptic is the glue of another carnivorous trap. This is the "butter" of the butterwort. Shepherds in the Alps have used it for generations as a healing salve. During the days we wandered among the rooted traps of Cape Fear, the blue spring flowers of the butterworts were rising among the yellow of the sidesaddle flowers and the red of the sundew. Each nodded at the top of a slender stalk which rose from the center of a rosette of pale-green fleshy leaves. The sides of these long and narrow leaves curl inward, forming troughs in which the glue of the trap is secreted. The upper surface of each leaf is shot through with an infinite number of tiny glands, as many as 25,000 to the square centimeter. From these glands comes the thick glue that traps small insects and the digestive juices that dissolve all except the hard chitin shells of the victims. Like the sundew, the butterwort combines adhesion and action. Once a small insect alights and is trapped, the curled sides of the leaf roll slowly inward, squeezing out more glue from the hundreds of thousands of glands on its surface.

In all the plant traps that we encountered, it is the leaf that is modified to capture prey. In the pitchers, the leaf is rolled into a tube with the edges joined; in the sundew, the leaf bears moving, glue-studded tentacles; in the butterwort, the leaf curls inward and its upper surface is equipped with immense numbers of small glands. But the most remarkable leaf of all is found in the plant we had come to Wilmington especially to see, the celebrated Venus's-flytrap. Sundews range around the globe. There are more than a hundred different species, the greatest variety being found in Australia. But in all the world there is only one species of flytrap. And nowhere else on earth is it found except on the Carolina coast.

Before the American Revolution, John Bartram sent living flytraps to England. They caused a sensation among botanists. In 1768, Carl Linnaeus wrote to John Ellis, who had sent him pressed specimens from London: "Though I have doubtless seen and examined no small number of plants, I must confess I never met with so wonderful a phenomenon." Darwin rightly called the flytrap "the most wonderful plant in the world."

Its wonder lies in its leaf. The two halves have been compared to upper eyelids with lashes along the edge. They are hinged at the stem so that they open and close in the manner of the jaws of a steel trap. Normally the two segments lie open. Stubby hairs, usually three on each side, form the trigger of the botanical trap. When a hapless insect brushes against these hairs, the jaws snap shut.

Although we saw pitcher plants by the thousands, sundews in vast numbers, butterworts and their blue spring flowers scattered over miles of flatland, we sought the hinged leaves of the flytrap for hours in vain. Immense numbers have been dug and sold to nurseries and 10-cent stores. Around Wilmington, where the original plants were found, the Venus's-flytrap has become scarce. On the afternoon of our second day, somewhere along the Old Shell Road on the way to Wrightsville Beach, we drew up at a filling station. A farmer was just climbing into a Ford truck. Yes, he told Mrs. Appleberry, he knew where we could find flytraps. One of the few places in the county where they still grew in numbers was along the edge of a "bay" on his farm. We followed his truck. And as we did so, the sky darkened. Hardly had we reached the spot when pelting rain began. It continued hour after hour, all the rest of the day, far into the night—the driving deluge of a long spring rain.

The following morning, under cloudless skies, we returned to the bay. This shallow basin underlaid by hardpan, a kind of swamp without standing water, stretched away into a tangle of low bushes, ferns, and scattered pines. Where natural drainage descended the slight dip at its edge, the flytraps grew. It is in such places, where white soil drains down into dark, that they are most often found. Such plants as hound's-tongue, round-leaved boneset, blazing star, and running blueberry are frequently associated with them. But Venus's-flytrap is never found where ragweed grows. Wire grass sometimes invades flytrap areas, pushing back or eliminating the insectivorous plants. And when bushes grow too tall, reducing the sunlight, the flytraps disappear.

Around us the green rosettes of the extended leaves spread away amid low vegetation. Some were small, hardly three inches across; others were half a foot in diameter. Each suggested a circle of spoons extending outward from a common center. Most of the traps were held open at an angle of 40 or 50 degrees. A few were opened as far as 80 degrees. The shiny upper surface of each hinged leaf was flushed with red. There a vast number of minute tinted glands were massed together. From them pours the fluid that digests the victims of the flytrap.

I squatted beside one trap in which this fluid had completed its work. The leaf had opened again, revealing the husk of a large dark fly. Everything except the legs, the wings, the chitin shell of the insect had been digested. Half a dozen minute ants were investigating the remains of the fly. They found no nourishment in it. The plant had sucked it dry. It had dissolved and absorbed everything edible before the jaws of the trap had opened.

In this case the victim of the flytrap was a fly. In most instances, however, it is likely to be some crawling ground insect, an ant or a beetle. I watched one dark beetle, about three-eighths of an inch long, wander over the jaws of another trap later that day. It may have been attracted by the sweetish fluid exuded on the leaf. It plodded this way and that, stopping often. Minutes passed before it blundered against the trigger hairs of the trap. With a quick movement like the swift closing of a hand, the halves of the leaf came together. The trap was sprung; the beetle was caught.

The speed with which the jaws of the trap snap shut depends upon the temperature. The movement is speeded up by heat, slowed down by chill, just as the activity of the insects is increased by hot days and lessened by cool ones. Under a midsummer sun, a flytrap will close from a wide-open position in a single second. That movement comprises a complex series of events.

When the beetle touched the trigger hairs, minute electrical disturbances resulted. The stimulus ran through the living cells of the upper side of the leaf. These cells are swollen with water under pressure, pressure that holds the trap open against the tension of the spring. Now this force suddenly gives way. The water escapes into spaces between the cells. The spring mechanism, formed of the woody substance in the veins, snaps shut the trap.

As the jaws close, the trigger hairs, hinged at their bases, fold against the surface of the leaf like the retractable landing gear of an airplane. The long spines, extending out from the edges of the jaws, meet and intermesh. At first the two halves of the leaf remain slightly concave like clamshells. They do not press tightly together. The imprisoned insect finds itself in a barred cage. If it is small enough it still can slip between the bars of the interlacing spines. Darwin thought this provision kept the plant from wasting its time on tiny creatures relatively valueless as food.

Studies made by Frank Morton Jones near Wilmington have shown that this is so in practice. He collected fifty Venus's-flytraps containing insects and measured the victims. Only one of the fifty was less than five millimeters—about one-fifth of an inch—long. Only seven were less than six millimeters. The rest were ten millimeters or more, with the largest having a length of thirty millimeters—almost one and one-fifth inches. Grasshoppers and millipeds have been found captured by flytraps. I placed a dark angleworm, which came to the surface of the ground beside me, on one trap. Its writhings touched the triggers and the jaws closed upon it. But it was too long, too slender, too slippery for the plant to hold. Jones concluded that the flytrap victims ranged from those as large as the leaf could imprison down to those about a quarter of an inch long.

Smaller insects are able to creep between the bars of the cage.

Several times I ran a grass blade across the leaf of a plant to watch the action of the trap. A single contact with the trigger hairs is not enough. They have to be touched twice or two have to be touched in quick succession. This also aids the plant. It prevents it from needlessly closing on every fragment of a falling leaf or other inanimate object that touches it. The traps that I sprung with my grass blade would remain closed for from twenty-four to thirty-six hours. Those containing insects often stay shut for a week while the assimilation of the food takes place.

After the first swift movement of the trap closing on its prey, the two halves begin a gradual flattening out, pressing together in a deliberate squeeze that continues from a half to twelve hours. At the same time the red-tinted glands begin pouring out their digestive secretions. The trap becomes a stomach absorbing the edible part of its prey. Formic acid is present in the fluid secreted by the glands. It inhibits the action of bacteria and prevents decay within the plant. If a slender piece of meat is placed in a flytrap, part inside and part out, the protruding portion will decay while the part inside will be entirely free of bacteria. If the rotted portion is placed within a fresh leaf, the odor disappears.

As the days pass and the trapped insect is reduced to nothing more than a hollow chitin shell, pressure begins building up in the surface cells of the leaf. Slowly the spines, interlaced like the fingers of two hands, disengage. The twin jaws of the trap fall gradually apart. The meal is over. The plant is "hungry" again. With trap reset, it awaits the coming of a new victim.

How many times in succession does a single trap capture and digest its prey? In 1923, in an almost-forgotten chest in an attic at another Wilmington—Wilmington, Delaware—that question was discovered in a letter that had crossed the ocean half a century before. Charles Darwin had asked it of his American correspondent, the Delaware botanist, William M. Canby. So far as Canby could discover, a leaf caught insects as many as three times but never more.

Watching these flytraps attracting insects with bait and color, closing over their prey like pouncing animals, digesting them, opening their trap leaves to repeat the performance—watching them with wonder that remained unwearied—we saw them as things apart from the stolid unconsciousness of ordinary plants around them. A special cunning had been wrought into these creations of sap and tissue and chlorophyll. They were geniuses of the plant world.

In all that prehistoric trapline where we wandered among prototypes of pit and Tanglefoot and steel-jawed trap, these plants were the ones we had most wanted to see. One other thing Mrs. Appleberry had promised us. So far it had eluded us. This was the painted bunting, that little avian rainbow, the nonpareil.

On the afternoon of our last day in the Cape Fear region, after we had eaten hamburgers at a roadside restaurant known as "Jesse James'" and were driving slowly down a byway off the Old Shell Road, even this came to us. Mrs. Appleberry had described its song and we all were listening as we rode along. Nellie heard it first. It came from the top of a high pine at our left, a sweet warble that was broken off only to begin again. We scanned the upper branches through our glasses. Flashes of movement appeared and disappeared among the topmost needles. The interrupted strains of the tantalizing song continued. Five minutes went by. Then into a sunlit opening surrounded by shining pine needles darted a bird of breathtaking beauty. As it flitted and turned in its feeding, we saw the soft rose-red of its breast, the indigo blue of its head, the brilliant green of its back. No other bird native to North America is so colorfully beautiful. It is well named the nonpareil.

Thus our stay in the Cape Fear region, amid the strangeness and wonder of botanical traplines, was bounded by the beauty of birds—by the beauty of birdsong at the beginning, by the beauty of bird form and color at the end.

TWENTY-SIX

LAKE OF THE DISMAL SWAMP

─────────

LEAVING behind the insect-trapping plants of Cape Fear we drove northward in a great arc to the east. We skirted Pamlico and Albemarle sounds. Just below the Great Dismal Swamp on the North Carolina–Virginia line we cut directly east toward the Cape Hatteras shore. We came to a long bridge spanning shallow Carrituck Sound. Beyond lay Kitty Hawk, Kill Devil Hill and the wild coastal dunes where the Wright brothers, less than 50 years before, had collected shells and botanized and watched birds during spare time while assembling their machine for the first airplane flight in the history of the world.

Ten years before we had visited Kitty Hawk. In our minds were memories of its lonely beauty, its deserted beach, the bleaching bones of a whale skeleton and the great hills of sand that ran in a chain parallel to the shore. We crossed the bridge. Nowhere else in our travels did we come upon change so sweeping. Instead of a secluded shore we found miles of immense summer resort hotels—the Wilbur Wright, the Kitty Hawk, the Kill Devil Inn, with restaurants, lunchrooms and a Casino dance hall thrown in. The isolated shore that had remained so little changed since the days of Sir Walter Raleigh's lost colony had disappeared in a rush of recent construction. We drove for miles and still were unable to cook our camp supper beyond range of the multitude of blank staring windows that rose at frequent intervals along the shore.

The next morning, leaving this tamed wildness behind us, we drove north from Elizabeth City, following a highway that ran between the Great Dismal Swamp and the sea. Along the way we noticed what we had frequently noticed before: how the poetry of the common people is written on the map. In the mountains, in the hills, along the coast, we had found place-names touched with poetic insight. The namers of old were poets of the pioneers; roadside signs are their monuments. They originated such stirring and memorable names as Cape Fear, Hungry Mother Creek, and the Great Dismal Swamp.

Running along the eastern edge of this swamp we recalled other colorful names we had encountered in our wanderings: Jumpoff Mountain, Bear Swamp Road, Tar River, Sleepy Lagoon, Money Bayou, Singing River. But none seemed more apt than the name bestowed upon that somber fastness that stretched away to the west, forbidding, untamed, mysterious— the Great Dismal Swamp.

Years before, I had penetrated into its fringes. Bill Ed Temple, the famous bear hunter of the North Carolina–Virginia line, had told me of his adventures in the heart of the swamp around Lake Drummond. A canal, dug in George Washington's day, leads in to this aloof body of water. Along this canal we hoped to reach the Lake of the Dismal Swamp.

Not far from the spot where the canal meets the Inland Waterway, somewhere south of Deep Creek, we pulled up at a country store. A local man named William Crockett, we learned, occasionally takes fishermen in to the Lake with an outboard motor. But he was not at home; nobody knew where he was. Our chances of visiting Lake Drummond ebbed. As we talked, a spry little man of about sixty-five, wearing a kind of sea captain's cap and followed by a white dog, appeared down the road. He was William Crockett.

He was related, he told us as he prepared his boat for the trip, to the pioneer scout, Davy Crockett. Not originally a Dismal Swamper, he had come to the region twenty years before. As a boy, he had quit school because he had nosebleeds and a doctor had told him going to sea would be good for the nosebleed. He sailed the sea for years; once he was washed overboard in a storm but was attached to a rope and so was saved. After seafaring, he became a professional fisherman along the coast and later a lumberjack. He couldn't row a boat the way he used to, he explained, because a tree fell on him and hurt his back. In the sunshine, he squinted until he seemed walking around with his eyes shut. Every snag and stub in Lake Drummond, he declared, was as familiar to him as the fingers of his hand.

"Oh, I'm good!" he kept repeating during our trip. "I'm good! I know it and everybody admits it!"

While he was regaling us with reminiscences, he was baling out brown canal water from the bottom of his rowboat. A small boy of about five watched him solemn eyed.

"Have you got a leak in your boat?" he inquired.

"Oh, no," Crockett answered airily. "This is just rain water."

"Then why is it the same color as the water in the canal?"

"He's got me! He's got me!" Crockett chuckled. "He's a smart one! He's a smart one!"

We started down the long brown lane of water toward Lake Drummond. The overhanging banks of the ancient canal were white with clouds of wild cherry blossoms. Hercules-club had already shot six feet into the air. Thick fern tangles ran down to the water's edge and here and there, for a hundred feet at a time, the bank was mantled with a heavy cape of interlacing vines of honeysuckle, wild grape, and woodbine. And beyond stretched the somber, tangled woods of the great swamp. Trees rose high above us; leaned out over the old canal. But the teeming wildlife we had expected was not there. Even in this high tide of the year, the month of May, the swamp seemed only sparsely inhabited. In exaggerated form this impression was recorded in the first published description of the area by William Byrd of Westover. Writing in the early years of the eighteenth century he observed: " 'Tis remarquable that, towards the heart of this horrible desart, no beast or bird approaches, nor so much as an insect or a reptile."

From time to time as we rode down the canal we saw on the surface of the brown water before us long strings of bubbles. A local belief holds that such bubbles are sent up by big turtles walking along the mud of the bottom. In fact, they show the location of masses of decaying vegetation. Once, when Crockett had passed over a line of bubbles, the gases of decomposition became so buoyant that a whole section of the canal bottom tore loose, in the manner of a floating island, and shot to the surface. His first thought when he heard the roar and rush behind him was that a big alligator was bearing down on him from the rear. But there are no alligators in the Great Dismal Swamp or its canals. For this, Crockett is thankful.

"The canal's my bathtub," he said. "I don't mind snakes. But if I saw an alligator I would jump straight up out of the water!"

We passed a stand of cane, the plant of the famous canebrakes of the South. This high, jointed grass suggests a forest of bamboo. Crockett knew it as "pipe-stem reed." Whenever he breaks the stem of his pipe he replaces it with a section of cane. It is hard and hollow and almost as durable as the original stem. Puffing away through such a makeshift stem, the ex-sailor and ex-lumberjack steered us down the canal. Several times, in moments of absent-mindedness, he barely missed running into the bank. Each time, as he veered away and avoided disaster, he assured us anew:

"I'm good! Everybody admits it!"

The water of the canal varied from dark chocolate in the middle to amber-tan where it shallowed away at the edges. Down this 30-foot waterway, cypress from the interior of the swamp formerly moved to market. Six canals, in the early days, were cut into the Great Dismal to connect Lake Drummond with the outside world. Some were excavated by slave labor.

One, leading to the northwest, was named after George Washington, who valued the 4,000 acres he owned in the swamp at $20,000 at the time of his death. The canal we followed, known as the Feeder Ditch, extends straight as a taut cord for three miles to reach the eastern shore of Lake Drummond.

As we advanced, turtles, flat, black, and as large as dinner plates, slid into the water. Once a dripping muskrat scrambled up the bank, fleeing from us paradoxically by land instead of by water. Below cave-ins that left little caverns in the embankments, all walled with twisted roots, whirligig beetles spun. With ripple trails glinting and shimmering in the sun, they seemed miniature comets speeding across a brown sky. From time to time catbirds mewed in the tangles and once we caught a fleeting glimpse of one of those gold-and-blue birds of the Okefenokee, a prothonotary warbler.

When we had climbed into the boat, the white dog had curled up just behind Nellie and me. Crockett had said:

"Poochie likes everybody and everybody likes Poochie."

Halfway down the canal, Poochie woke up. He put his forelegs on the side of the boat, his head on his forepaws, and watched the scenery go by. After a time I became aware of a slow, steady, unobtrusive pressure against my left side. Poochie was pushing his pointed nose like a wedge between me and the gunwale on which I rested my arm. Eventually I discovered that the dog had the choice position at the edge of the seat, resting one foreleg comfortably on the side of the boat while I sat with my elbow on my knee. Then I began a slow, unobtrusive pressure of my own. After a time Poochie was back where he had started. I looked down at him and saw he was looking up at me with something like a twinkle in his eye. We understood each other. We were gentleman dogs.

While Poochie and I were understanding each other, Nellie was watching the flight of a pair of spotted sandpipers. For more than a mile they kept ahead of us down the canal, alighting, rising again, skimming low over the water with alternately beating and rigid, downbent wings, uttering their plaintive calls which, to me, invariably suggest the whetting of a knife. The tide of migration had swept far beyond us now. The sandpipers were probably resident birds.

Each time they fluttered down to a mossy log or bit of mud, they teetered violently as they came to rest. Their numerous common names—teeter, teetertail, teeter snipe, teeter-bob, tiptail, and seesaw—are derived from this habit. It is a peculiarity they share with a number of other species, particularly those which feed along the water. Teetering is a habit that runs through various groups. Water thrushes pump their tails so regularly that they are popularly known as water wagtails. The wagtail of Europe, a member of the pipit clan, is called by countryfolk the "washerwoman" because its tipping, teetering movements suggest a woman scrubbing clothes at a washboard. The dipper or water ouzel of western states, placed by taxonomists somewhere between the nuthatches and the wrens, bobs its body as it moves among the rocks of rushing mountain torrents. Young spotted sandpipers, just out of the egg, downy little balls on slender legs, will teeter like an adult.

Why do birds associated with water so often teeter? Nobody knows exactly. The mystery of the tip-ups has been a subject for debate among bird watchers for generations. Some consider teetering a mere idiosyncrasy, a mannerism such as the tail fanning of the redstart, the tail wagging of the palm warbler, and the tail pumping of the alighting phoebe or sparrow hawk. Others explain the seesaw movements as arising from the fact that sandpipers have long legs, that their center of gravity is high. However, herons, with even longer legs, do not teeter. It has been noticed that when a sandpiper lands among others of its kind, all the birds seesaw rapidly. This has suggested that the movement may be a recognition mark. One naturalist has pointed out that such birds as water thrushes and ouzels may have difficulty making their voices heard above the rush of water among stones and that the teetering may have something to do

with communication between mated birds. An opposite hy·
pothesis has it that the teetering, against a background of mov·
ing water, makes the birds less conspicuous, that by matching
motion with motion they are providing themselves with a kind
of camouflage.

Thus, there is a profusion of hypotheses but no conclusive
answer to the mystery of the teetertails. The little sandpipers
of the Dismal Swamp canal teetered for reasons good and
sufficient for themselves. They teetered instinctively, without
thought, probably for no reason at all of which they were aware.

A quarter of a mile this side of the lake, we came to the
locks that hold back the waters of Drummond. The caretaker's
house here is the only permanent home in the Great Dismal.
As we approached the locks, a monarch butterfly drifted overhead. It was flapping deliberately. Its flight was unhurried. Yet
its course was set to the north and every flap of its wings carried
it in that direction. In all the region of the swamp, it was the
only monarch we saw.

It took us nearly twenty minutes to haul the boat up the
embankment by the locks to the higher level. It was a laborious
business accomplished by means of a hand-operated wheel,
dragging the boat up a narrow-gauge track with a cable that
wound itself with exasperating slowness on a steel drum. But
within five minutes after we had climbed into the boat again
we were heading out into the Lake of the Dismal Swamp.

Five miles long and three miles wide, its waters lay flat, without a ripple, without a swell, smooth and silky and stretching
away to a low blue-tinted horizon that seemed more a mirage
than a reality. On all that expanse, no other human being was
visible. Under a cloudless, windless sky, its miles of shallow
water lay tinted an ethereal blue, a strange and magical color
we had never seen before. For years afterwards we would see
it in moments of memory. We called it the Lake Drummond
blue. Only once later, during our long trip, did we come upon
anything approaching it. That was the tinting of an immense

slick, stretching silky and blue across the northern end of Lake Champlain on a breathless morning in June.

Even as we turned north and rode across its surface, Lake Drummond seemed remote. It seemed still beyond our reach, receding before us. Its ancient isolation was only transiently disturbed by our passing, disturbed hardly longer than it took our ripples to disappear and the sound of our motor to die away.

A local saying is that Lake Drummond has a wooden bottom. Surely it has a wooden rim. For all around the shore great stubs and stumps and fallen cypresses lay just above or under the surface. Long enduring and slow to decay, they have strewn the shore line while the water of the lake has risen and descended with cycles of rainfall and drought.

Crockett cut the outboard motor and we paddled close to one immense cypress rising from the water. Its multitude of weathered roots testified mutely to a full 6-foot drop in the level of the lake in recent times. During the winter of 1930–31 the waters fell away to an unprecedented distance, the shore line in some places receding as much as a thousand feet. During this period of abnormally low water, Crockett familiarized himself with the location of the main snags and stubs along the shore. Below the surface they present a constant menace to small boats, ripping out sterns and bashing in floor boards, particularly during the sudden windstorms that sometimes sweep across the lake. At such times, the shallow sea builds up great swells that carry a boat, caught near the shore, up and up and then crash it down on the stumps and stubs below.

Moving cautiously, we edged inshore, winding about, sliding past huge submerged stumps dimly visible through water brown with leachings. What rocks are to the Maine coast, stumps, left by long-ago lumbering operations, are to the shore of Lake Drummond. One ancient cypress lay prostrate on the shore, fallen away from the water. Its flaring, hollow base, fully five feet thick, pointed toward us like the muzzle of an ancient blunderbuss. In time of storms, Dismal Swampers sometimes hole up in such hollow trees, taking care to rout out snakes beforehand. A few years before our visit, I was told, a hollow tree reached a local sawmill in the dead of winter. Unaware that it was the hibernating place of a large knot of snakes, the workmen pushed it toward the circular saw. As the whirling blade cut down the length of the log, snakes flew in all directions and workmen exploded out into the open air.

Threading his way out from shore again, Crockett started his motor. Within two hundred yards of shore he takes no chances. Oars propel him fast enough. As the Mississippi River pilot must know the sand bars, so the Lake Drummond swamper must know the long-enduring cypress snags. Well away from the dangerous shore line, we increased our speed and the dense tangle of trees and vines beyond the cypress stubs slipped past us. The shore seemed like the coast of a land held by the enemy in wartime, inscrutable and hostile.

Behind its curtain of spring foliage lay the great swamp with its dark juniper water, its deadly pockets of quicksand, its high trees, its areas of peat pockmarked with fireholes, its rank tangles of blackberries with canes 20 feet in length, its treeless tracts of matted vines known as "lights." Over 750 square miles, it spread its spring fertility, a wild lushness that is hardly more tamed today than it was in the time of William Byrd.

As we turned around at the top of our run, Crockett stopped the motor again. He removed the reed pipestem from his mouth and called attention to the fact that Lake Drummond is the setting for Thomas Moore's famous ballad, "The Lake of the Dismal Swamp," written in Norfolk, Virginia, something more than a century before. He asked us if we would like to have him recite it and we said we would. The lake was his stage and the curtain had gone up. With histrionic gusto he finished the poem, repeating a second time: "Where all night long, by a firefly lamp, she paddles her white canoe."

His words echoed back from the shore. They seemed to carry for a prodigious distance across the stillness of the lonely lake. Set in a saucer of land, only 22 feet above sea level, with low surrounding country, Lake Drummond has unusual acoustic properties. Under certain atmospheric conditions it is possible to catch the clash of freightcar couplings in the switchyard at Suffolk, more than ten miles away. I noticed that we could hear a blue jay scream to the west where the shore was three miles distant. A second jay answered on our shore, somewhere to the north of us. Its shrill voice seemed to echo all around us. Yet the exact position of the source of the sound remained a mystery. The calling had a curious flitting quality, now here, now there, now close at hand, now farther away.

We often hear of the ventriloquism of certain birds. In the woods we search the boughs of a tree in vain, sure we will find a singing bird among their leaves, only to discover it perched to right or left in another tree. Thoreau, in his *Journal*, misidentifies some birds because, obviously, he saw one bird and heard another. Ability to determine the direction and distance of the source of a sound is a specialized skill not entirely dependent upon keenness of hearing. Two persons, equally able to hear a birdsong, standing side by side, will often differ widely as to the direction from which they think the sound is coming. Four of my friends, Roger Tory Peterson, John Kieran, George Miksch Sutton and Ludlow Griscom, have the keenest ears I know in their ability to pick the exact spot where a bird is singing.

A few years ago, while leafing through a bound volume of miscellaneous pamphlets at the New York Public Library—a bound volume that probably had not been taken from the shelves for decades—I came upon some interesting facts in connection with judging the distance and direction of sounds. Two American scientists, L. D. Ikenberry and C. E. Shutt, reported the findings of a long series of experiments in the *Kansas*

University Quarterly for January, 1898. They had discovered that the distance of a sharp noise can be estimated more accurately than the distance of a smooth tone. Our distance judgment is most accurate with the right side turned toward the sound. We overestimate the distance of both sharp and smooth noises within 35 feet and tend to underestimate the distance when the source is beyond 35 feet. In the matter of judging the direction from which the sound comes, they found that we are most likely to be right when the sound comes from the side, least likely to be correct when it comes either from the rear or the front.

Returning to the canal a good way out from shore, we became conscious of a multitude of tiny dimples, small shimmering spots, glinting in the sun and starring the blue sheen of the lake. At first I thought they were produced by a scattered host of water bugs. Then we began running through the dimples. In each was a winged insect suggesting a horsefly that had fallen into the water. Crockett stopped the engine and I fished one of the insects into the boat on an oar. It was a golden-banded honeybee.

Far across the surface, toward the middle of the lake, the water was strewn with the insects. Some lay motionless, others were sending out ripples with their vainly vibrating wings. The bees were scattered over at least half a square mile of water. A catastrophe of spring had overtaken a swarm of wild honeymakers.

The day before, Crockett recalled, a strong wind had risen out of the northwest. Issuing from some hollow cypress tree, the insect colony had lifted over the treetops in a whirling, joyous swarm. Before they could find a new home, the wind apparently had caught them, carried them out over the water. Unable to cross the lake and heavily laden with the honey that bees always consume before they swarm, the insects sank lower and lower and in the end were scattered like seed across the water. How many thousands of honeybees, floating and doomed, were strewn over the surface of the lake, we could only guess. It was an almost eerie sight, this final memory of Lake Drummond. In these wild and lonely surroundings, we had come upon the living wreckage of a springtime disaster.

TWENTY-SEVEN

MAY AT MONTICELLO

OUR speedometer touched 11,000 miles on that eighty-sixth day of our trip. We had been running west through Virginia where May had turned locust trees into creamy clouds of white and fire-pink blazed along embankments and lions and tigers bared their teeth on billboards that marked the trail of the earliest circus of spring. Now, in midmorning, we were climbing the wooded mountain road that led to Monticello.

Automobiles with license plates from more than twenty states had already mounted the road ahead of us that morning. They had brought people of varied interests and diverse outlooks to do homage to the many-sided genius of Thomas Jefferson. Most were attracted by the patriot, the statesman, the humanitarian. Some were interested by the architect, the inventor, and we—in addition to all these—by the naturalist. An often-overlooked facet in the life of this extraordinary man is his not inconsiderable contribution as a pioneer naturalist in America.

Thomas Jefferson published the first accurate and extensive list of birds in this country. He kept careful meteorological records for decades. He set down detailed facts about the trees of Virginia. He classified its animals. He recorded the comparative weights of red, gray, and black squirrels. He was the first American to make a scientific report on the fossils of the New World.

In 1787, when Jefferson published his celebrated *Notes on Virginia*, he listed all the birds known in the area. The total was fewer than 130 species. Today, according to Dr. J. J. Murray, of Lexington—editor of *The Raven*, official organ of The Virginia Society of Ornithology—the state list includes 400 species and subspecies—344 of the former and 56 of the latter. In all the United States east of the Rockies the number of full species is well under 450. So Virginia's 344 indicates the richness of bird life in that state. Driving across it, we noted down the different kinds of birds we saw as we rode along. By the time we came to Monticello our list had reached 85.

And at Monticello, birds were all around us—wood thrushes, towhees, brown thrashers, ovenbirds, yellowthroats, ruby-crowned kinglets, catbirds. We saw—to use the terminology of the Jefferson list—the lettuce bird or the goldfinch; the Virginia nightingale or the cardinal; the fieldfare of Carolina or the robin. We did not see, and no one will ever see again, two of the species on the list. Both of them—the passenger pigeon and the Carolina paroquet—have in the intervening years become extinct. But we saw two other birds not on the list and unknown in America when it was made. These were the comparatively recent introductions, the English sparrow and the starling. Jefferson, however, was one of the few Americans of his day who would have recognized them. In all probability he had seen them abroad while representing his country in Europe.

On that May morning one hundred twenty springs had passed since Jefferson died on his mountaintop overlooking the valley where he was born. One hundred sixty years had gone by since he published his *Notes on Virginia*. Yet the natural history of Monticello remained virtually unchanged. Bluebirds sang on the fence posts. Phoebes flitted in and out of the open doors of the old stables. A robin had built its nest at the top of one of the white columns of the west portico. And brown thrashers ran across the grass beneath an ancient linden tree that once provided shade for the third President of the United States.

Off to the east, beyond the mountainside where spring-clad trees stretched in a tumbling sea down the slope toward the Piedmont, a trio of turkey buzzards swung slowly, curving on the wind, hanging on the updrafts, drifting far out over the valley above tiny fields snipped from the plush of wooded hillsides, then sliding back to go riding low above Monticello. And all that morning the brilliant blue sky was filled with the metallic crackling of the chimney swifts.

Beside Jefferson's grave, we watched a chipping sparrow tilting its rusty cap this way and that as it fed on dandelion seeds. Fluttering into the air, it would alight on a bending stem and ride it to the ground. Occasionally, as it plucked the seeds, it would lift its head for a quick survey, with dandelion fluff projecting like a scraggly white mustache on either side of its bill. Before swallowing each seed, it clipped off the parachute, which floated to the ground. At the end, beneath the denuded stem the accumulated fluff looked like a little windrow of foam clinging to the grass. How many thousand dandelion seeds never take root because of the feeding of a single sparrow!

The birds of Monticello provide one of the outstanding memories of a naturalist's visit. The trees provide another. Here, rooted where Thomas Jefferson had planted them in the eighteenth century, stood ancient tulips, lindens, copper beeches, sugar maples, European larches. Here were noble trees, patriarchs that brought to mind Sir Thomas Browne's observation of long ago: "Generations pass while some trees stand and old families last not three oaks."

In beginning one of his Socratic dialogues, Plato wrote: "Scene: Under a plane tree . . ."

Under a tree . . . That phrase recurs frequently in the history of human thought. Thinkers as diverse and as far removed as Gautama beneath his Bo tree in the Far East and Ralph Waldo Emerson under a New England pine have been associated with trees. "He spake of trees, from the cedar tree that is in Lebanon even unto the hyssop that springeth out of the wall." So the Book of Kings in the Bible describes King Solomon, whose wisdom was proverbial in his time.

Around us, on this May morning, rose trees that had been associated with the thoughts of Jefferson. He had walked beneath their boughs, rested in their shade, seen them against blue sky and red sunset, watched them in wind and rain. They were part of his life when the author of the Declaration of Independence was evolving and strengthening his own eloquent philosophy of justice and human rights.

Now they were clothed in a new installment of green. For the leaves, life was new. For the trees, the events of spring represented merely an old, old sequence. One hundred twenty, one hundred fifty times, or more, a fresh mantle of leaves had taken the place of those which had fallen in autumn. Their green varied from tree to tree, almost from branch to branch. And beyond, along the mountainside, the shadings of spring were manifold. At no other time of year, except in autumn, is there greater variety of color in a woodland than in spring. A thousand and one subtle shadings of green, lost in summer, characterize the new foliage. Autumn colors are flaunting; they catch the eye. Spring tintings are delicate and often overlooked.

Every hour, under that brilliant morning sun, each square yard of outstretched leaves was manufacturing something like one fiftieth of an ounce of sugar. The broad ribbon leaves of an acre of growing corn will produce, in a single summer day, as much as two hundred pounds of sugar which is converted into the material of the plant. Leading to all the leaf factories of the trees around us was the running transportation system of the sap. Spring had increased its volume, had stimulated its flow. Coursing through the channels of trunk and branch and twig, it moved often under surprising pressures. In one laboratory experiment, scientists found that even the lowly tomato plant can produce pressures ranging up to about one hundred pounds to the square inch—sufficient to carry sap to the topmost twig of a California sequoia. Each tree at Monticello, beech, linden, maple, tulip, was being nourished by its own particular kind of sap. As in human blood groups, the fluid within tree trunks is specialized. Oak sap, for example, will not nourish a birch tree nor maple sap a beech.

From the tops of all the trees that Jefferson had planted, lightning rods project upward. This wise precaution protects them from thunderbolts in their exposed position on the mountaintop. In other ways, good sense has prevailed in keeping the house and grounds unchanged. The gardens have been laid out from sketches Jefferson made. The same fine and simple flowers he planted in the different beds—columbine, Virginia bluebells, phlox drummondi, tulips, and stock—grow there still. On this spring day—hundreds of butterfly generations after Jefferson's desire, expressed in the words: "All my wishes end where I hope my days will end, at Monticello," had come true—tiger swallowtails drifted among the garden flowers. And all along the edge of the restored fishpool, honeybees were alighting to drink the brick-red water.

We spent a long time within that noble house whose designing and building might be called Jefferson's lifelong avocation. He began it in his twenties; he was in his sixties when it was done. Everywhere we delighted in evidences of his brilliantly original mind. In turn, we became interested in his revolving study table, his "Petite Format" library, his clock that marked the days as well as the hours, his octagonal filing table with its pie-piece drawers. We had just emerged and were standing near the spot where Jefferson used to set up his telescope to watch the progress being made in building the University of Virginia, at Charlottesville in the valley below, when all the small birds feeding in the open dashed pell-mell into the bushes.

A swift gray shape skimmed past us. It was a Cooper's hawk scudding low among the trees. As it went by, from the bushes around us there arose a confused babel of bird voices. Instead of remaining silent in the presence of the hawk, all the hidden birds joined in a twittering crescendo. We were in the midst of that curious phenomenon sometimes referred to as the "confusion chorus."

The psychology of the bird of prey directs it toward an individual which it pursues. By flocking together in the air, small birds are able to divide the attention of the hawk, to distract it by many shapes in motion. As long as they keep together, and the hawk is unable to cut one individual from the flying mass, all escape. The confusion chorus appears to be a kind of flocking by sound. The calls, coming from all sides at the same time, apparently disconcert the bird of prey. At any rate, the Cooper's hawk swept on without pausing, reached the edge of the mountainside, and slid down out of sight. The twittering chorus ceased. The little birds, mostly chipping sparrows and English sparrows, flitted out of the bushes into the open. Their fright was over. The appearance of danger had set off a sequence of instinctive acts. Now that the danger was past there remained no visible remnant of haunting fear. Monticello in May was once more a place of sunshine and of peace.

In the Forest of Fountainebleau, which Jefferson often visited while American minister to the court of France, the green woodpecker is known by the apt name of the "awakener of the woods." An American bird deserving the same title is the familiar flicker, the "yucker" of Jefferson's bird list. Directly above our heads, as we were starting down the road on leaving, one of these woodpeckers burst into its strident, rolling cry. It filled all the space between the trees and was flung far out over the valley. Then, with that disconcerting suddenness that ends a flicker's call, the sound ceased. This was the last bird voice we heard at Monticello.

A hundred miles by road to the south and west, down the Blue Ridge Mountains, we came to Virginia's famed Natural Bridge, once owned by Thomas Jefferson. George Washington first surveyed it in 1750. Jefferson first called the attention of the world to it in his *Notes on Virginia*. In 1774, just two years before the American Revolution, he acquired it from King George III, of England.

The sum he paid, ironically, was almost exactly the amount we were charged for admission. Commercial interests have fenced in this natural wonder—which ages of running water and not commercial interests produced—and have turned the spot—intimately associated with great men of the nation's founding—into a moneymaking enterprise. Like Niagara Falls, the Grand Canyon, and the geysers of the Yellowstone, all such scenic marvels of the land are part of the country's heritage. The natural wonders of the nation should belong to the nation. They should be part of the park system, open for the enjoyment of all and not closed for the enrichment of a few.

Depressed by this commercialization of natural beauty, we wandered along the paths, past the oldest and largest arborvitae tree in the world—a 1,600-year-old patriarch with a trunk 56 inches in diameter—and under the great stone arch, higher than Niagara Falls, where rough-winged swallows shuttled back and forth and Louisiana water thrushes ran among the rocks, hunting for food in the shallow stream. Nellie compared the short call-note of the water thrush to the striking together of two pebbles and we fell to listing in our minds the birds we knew whose voices suggested sounds in their surroundings—from the liquid, gurgling notes of the redwing in the swamp to the call like tinkling icicles made by the tree sparrow that comes down from the Far North in winter. Thus beguiled, by and by we began to feel better.

That evening, outside a little Virginia town, the day ended with a pleasant adventure. Dusk was far advanced when a small boy came trudging down the dusty road outside our cabin. Bird voices seemed to accompany him, surrounding him and moving with him as he advanced. Whistling to himself, he was imitating robins, cardinals, orioles, bobwhites, meadowlarks. Like Thomas Jefferson, this country boy was more alert, more observant, more richly alive than most of those around him. We envied him this springtime of his interest in wild singers. "The birds of the naturalist," John Burroughs had written half a century before, "can never interest us like the thrush the farm-boy heard singing in the cedars at twilight as he drove the cows to pasture or like that swallow that flew gleefully in the air above him as he picked stones from the early May meadows."

We never saw the passer-by except as a small dark shape moving through the dusk. But we have often remembered that whistling boy. I fell asleep wondering about him—who he was, what he was like, what adventures life had in store for him—and wishing him well.

TWENTY-EIGHT

THE PINE BARRENS

B Y now we could close our eyes and see streaming toward us concrete roads, asphalt roads, gravel roads, shell roads, dirt roads; thousands of miles of roads; some red, some black, some gray; mountain roads, back-country roads, superhighways; roads thick with dust and roads drenched with rain and roads streaked with sunshine and shadow. During the days that followed Monticello we added memories of other roads. We wandered into West Virginia and across the Ohio River and back to the Skyline Drive and the run north to Washington.

The first day of June came and passed. Wind patterns now ran across fields of wheat and, from time to time, we were enveloped in that most nostalgic of outdoor perfumes, the scent of new-mown hay. From the mountaintops of the Skyline Drive we looked over vistas of apple orchards in the Shenandoah Valley—the white of blossoms gone and in its place the green of tiny fruit swelling on the stems. The famed Japanese cherry trees of the Tidal Basin, in Washington, had long since passed their blooming time and in Rock Creek Park the trees were clouded with the full green of summer foliage. After a memorable lunch with two friends, both distinguished writers on natural history—Rachel L. Carson and Louis J. Halle, Jr.—we drove northward between miles of gaudy billboards out into the Maryland countryside. That night we stopped where we had ended the first day of our trip, at Havre de Grace, at the upper end of Chesapeake Bay.

Then the woods had been bare and, in the distance, smoky blue. Now they were massed with green. Then solitary crows had flapped across barren fields. Now the singing of birds accompanied us along the way and the lushness of June lay over the fields. Climbing roses splashed their crimson against the gray clapboards of farmhouses, killdeers circled over lines of green spears lengthening in cornfields, and strawberry pickers were busy just as they had been busy so far to the south and so many days before, at Wachula, Florida. Spring, to most people, means *early* spring. It is the first swallow, the first violet, the first-born that attracts attention. But spring is a season three months long. And these latter weeks, for us, were as filled with interest as the first.

The next morning, in a quick swing to the north and east, we touched four different states, Maryland, Pennsylvania, Delaware, and New Jersey. Cherries were reddening along the Mason and Dixon Line of Maryland's northern boundary. Snow fences lay rolled up beside the highway in Pennsylvania. And in New Jersey we ran between great flat fields of onions, tomatoes, potatoes, and asparagus. We headed east across the state, over Two-Penny Run and Killtime Brook. The fertile farms faded away. The rich dark soil grew sterile and sandy and gray. Around us, upwards of a million acres of scraggly pines and cedar swamps and acid bogs stretched away as far as we could see. We were in the pine barrens of New Jersey—a place of special attraction for me. Sometimes I have wondered what a psychologist would make of my affection for minor melodies, little creatures, swamps and tarns and barrens and dunes, the spurned and disregarded acres of the earth. Wastelands, to me, oftentimes seem the least of all wasted.

Less than seventy-five miles south of New York City, less than thirty miles straight east from Philadelphia, the barrens form a last stronghold of wildness in a long-settled region. Originally a flattened hill of alluvial deposits beneath the

Miocene sea, it lifted in a low island behind the receding water. Later seas flooded around it but it was never submerged again. Ages of leaching followed, dissolving and carrying away essential elements and leaving the remaining sand arid and sterile. The earliest explorers to push across the barrens traveled through an almost continuous forest of pitch pine with stands of southern white cedar rising from the dark waters of swamps. Bog iron from these pine-barren swamps was forged into weapons for America's first two wars and formed the cylinder of the engine on John Fitch's pioneer steamboat.

John James Audubon traveled several times across the Jersey barrens by wagon to study the birds of Great Egg Harbor on the coast. One of these trips he describes in the third volume of his *Ornithological Biography*. Alexander Wilson, Constantine Rafinesque, Thomas Nuttall, and other early naturalists were familiar with the area. William Bartram made pioneer plant-collecting expeditions into the "pines," sending to England many of his discoveries. One of the plates, "Gentian of the Desert," appearing in Edwards's *Gleanings of Natural History*, published in London in 1758, was made from a drawing by Bartram of one of the rare natives of the pine barrens, *Gentiana porphyrio*.

In the years since Bartram and Audubon, the barrens have apparently changed remarkably little. In many places you can walk a dozen miles without seeing either a house or a human being. The concrete ribbon of a superhighway cuts across the barrens carrying a stream of speeding cars between Philadelphia and Atlantic City. But cars rarely stop and only a few hundred yards off the highway conditions almost primeval surround you. The "Pineys" who dwell in the barrens have a picturesque vocabulary of their own. Whirligig beetles are "coffee beans." Radiating pitcher plants are "clock dials." Pine snakes—at one time such serpents were supplied from the barrens to carnival performers all over the country—are "wompers." And king snakes are "swamp wompers." Pioneer communities in the barrens received such odd names as Chicken Bone, Double Trouble, Mt. Misery, Loveladies, Longacoming, and Ong's Hat. There is a Hurricane Brook and a Stop-the-Jade Run. In wandering over this untamed land we passed Hambone Ridge and Apple Pie Hill and Boggly Wallow.

And everywhere we went we came upon sights that reminded us of other places widely scattered along our route. Carpenter bees flying near tunnels in a rustic bridge and sphagnum frogs in the swamps brought to mind the Okefenokee. In a haze of blue, toadflax bloomed all across an open space, recalling the sandy flats of Southern Pines in North Carolina. A bluebird alighted on the rough bark of a pitch pine, bracing itself woodpecker-wise with its tail just as another bluebird had done on the trunk of a royal palm beside the Tamiami Trail. Here in the sunshine sand myrtle was in bloom—the same flowers I had seen whipping in the gale at the top of Mt. LeConte in the Great Smokies. The sheep laurel we saw under the pitch pines we had recently seen at the top of the Blue Ridge Mountains in Virginia. It blooms in both places at about the same time. And above dark swamp water the brilliant, burnished spikes of the goldenclub caught the eye as they had done in the Louisiana marshes, ahead of the charging mudboat, 1,200 miles and 70 days away.

Barrens and dunes and tundras and tarns—spring often comes with especial beauty to these austere places of the earth. Along winding wood roads, where our footfalls were muffled in the fine sand and over our heads the breeze in the pine needles sang one of the oldest songs on earth, we came upon a flower of rare, strange beauty. Emerging from a fountain of slender, arching leaves, a central stalk rose three feet in the air to be crowned by a high-piled mass of floral foam. Snow white the flowers gleamed against their background of fallen needles and rough-barked pines. We encountered them scattered widely over the sandy portions of the barrens. The plant is an odd member of the lily family, the turkeybeard, *Xerophyllum asphodeloides.* It was first described and named by Thomas Nuttall, whose scientific activity ranged over the two realms of botany and ornithology.

If we had been a few weeks earlier, we would have found two other flowers of spring we had enjoyed on previous visits to the barrens—the swamp pink, *Helonias bullata*, with its cloud of delicate lilac blooms, and the pyxie of the pine barrens, the matted, mosslike flowering plant on which André Michaux, in 1803, bestowed the name *Pyxidanthera barbulata.* What hepatica and bloodroot are to the rich floor of the woodland, pyxie moss is to the barrens. It leads the parade of the spring flowers. One year, on the 31st of March, when the barrens were still dun and wintry, I came upon a dense mass of pyxie moss, a foot or more in diameter, across which a host of tiny, waxy-white flowers were scattered like snowflakes.

Not far from Apple Pie Hill, in an area of stunted trees formerly called the Grouse Plain—where, in early days, immense numbers of heath hens were killed by gunners—we came upon half a dozen mats of *Pyxidanthera.* Flowers were gone. But the massed, lance-shaped leaves were shiny and green. Some were only a third of an inch long. One mat, nearly eighteen inches across, was hardly more than half an inch high. Although pyxie so closely resembles moss, at first glance, it is a true flowering plant with centrally located roots and branches that lie flat on the sand, massing closely together.

Later in the year, during the terrific heat of summer days in the pine barrens, the leaves lose their green. They take on a reddish cast. By autumn they often are the color of bronze. The acid, inhospitable soil of the barrens, soil that repels most other vegetation, provides, paradoxically enough, the only environment in which *Pyxidanthera* can survive. Its entire range is limited to small areas on the Atlantic coast. Only in pine barrens between New Jersey and South Carolina—only here in all the world—does this flower of spring appear.

Once, as we were leaning on a bridge watching the spinning

"coffee beans" on the dark water below, a man wearing a sailor's hat appeared out of the bushes carrying a gallon vinegar jug full of crystal-clear spring water. This first human being we had encountered in the barrens proved to be the celebrated "Rattle-snake Asa" Pitman. For years Pitman has hunted serpents for carnivals and zoos. Nowadays, he told us, his catch includes only four or five rattlers a year, taken most often in the vicinity of Mt. Misery.

A little later, on a side road near Ong's Hat, two "mossers" waved as they clattered past in a ramshackle Ford. The rear seat was piled high with sphagnum moss. It had been raked from the swamp water by means of long-handled implements that looked like potato hooks. The men had spent the morning—with dragonflies patrolling past them over goldenclub and pipewort in bloom—along the edge of a cedar swamp. On this spring day, no workshop in the world seemed more attractive than the one in which they had labored.

As we stood looking out over the water in brilliant sunshine, a Fowler's toad lifted the metallic bray of its love song above the other noises of the swamp. This is the common toad of the barrens. North of Trenton, the American toad predominates in New Jersey; south of Trenton, in the region of the pine bar-rens, it is the Fowler's toad that is most numerous.

Least numerous but most famous of all the batrachians that fill the pine barrens dusk with their calling in the spring is the Anderson's tree frog. So rare is it that during the first forty-two years after its discovery in 1864 only six specimens were seen. Hardly more than twice the length of a thumbnail, about an inch and a half long, it is bright green above with lavender stripes running along the sides and with considerable bright yellow below. At such places in the barrens as Hoot Owl Farm, near Oliphant's Mill, the surprisingly loud "quonk!" of the males carries far through the late-spring nights. This brilliant little frog lives in only a few places besides the Jersey barrens, almost always in cedar swamps.

Everywhere along the sandy side roads and trails we walked with an unending vanguard of gray tiger beetles. They took off before us, skimmed along for a dozen yards, landed on their fleet, slender legs, and turned to face us. Sand gray, the color of their background, they disappeared as soon as they stood still. The heat of the June day was stimulating all the insect life of the barrens. Velvet ants, brilliant red wingless wasps, ran on a zigzag course over the hot sand, skirting the pits left by the hoofs of deer, crossing little anthills no larger than a silver dollar, struggling over brown windrows of fallen pine needles. Robber flies, with tapering abdomens the color of cigarette ash, clung to leaves or darted in pursuit of their aerial prey. But the insect of the barrens that day was the gray tiger beetle.

Just south of Lakehurst, at the northern edge of the pine barrens, an unusual number of these insects seemed congregated along the right of way of the Central Railroad of New Jersey. They took off continually before us as we walked along the ties. Unlike the steep climb of a grasshopper's upward spring and flight, the take-off of a tiger beetle is low and straight ahead. It flies fast and close to the ground. At one point along the track we witnessed a remarkable instance of the inability of the beetle to vary its habitual method of taking to the air. Alarmed by our approach, one of the gray insects shot off the ground and crashed head on into the side of a steel rail. It was flung back sprawling on a tie. It scrambled to its feet and tried again. Again it smacked against the steel of the rail. Six times, like an insect battering ram, the tiger beetle flew full tilt into the metal before it lifted itself high enough to clear the obstruction.

Another unusual experience among the insects of the pine barrens took place during another spring in early May. I was traveling through the area with three friends from the New Jersey State Bureau of Entomology, Frank A. Soraci, Robert J. Sim, and William M. Boyd. Not far from New Lisbon we stopped to walk beside a dark, winding stream. Whenever we stood still, black flies swarmed about our heads. They whirled around us. They darted before our eyes. But they made no attempt to bite us. Only the female black fly dines on blood. These apparently were males arriving before the females and congregating about warm-blooded animals for a dipteron rendezvous. We, in their plans, were merely bait.

With its sparse vegetation, its open sand, its shallow sphagnum bogs and swamps, the pine barrens respond readily to the heat of the spring sun. The area warms up more rapidly than does a dense woodland or a protected pasture. Such factors affect local climates and the progress of spring. During our long trip we saw the season seesaw. We saw spring precocious here, backward there, often in consequence of factors that were obscure.

Southwest of the barrens, for example, the region around Salem, New Jersey, experiences each year a noticeably early spring. The same flowers bloom there before they do at Cape May, 50 miles farther south. Certain butterflies appear at Salem before they are seen anywhere else around. In contrast, 60 miles to the north of the barrens, Flanders is known as the "icebox of New Jersey." Here, in winter, the mercury almost invariably stands lower than in surrounding communities. Spring is laggard. And even in mid-August the thermometer sometimes drops to only a few degrees above freezing.

With the sinking of the sun the sand of the pine barrens cools off rapidly. All that day we had seen turkey buzzards riding with hardly a wingbeat, back and forth, mile after mile, buoyed up by powerful thermal currents rising from the sun-heated sand. Now, as the day drew to a close, the soaring birds gradually sank lower. They suggested hot-air balloons cooling and losing their buoyancy. The vultures now flapped more and rocked but little in turbulent air.

On that day, in cedar swamps over which the soaring buzzards passed, another winged creature undoubtedly flitted above the dark water—a small jewel of a butterfly at that time wholly unknown to the lists of science. Two years later it was discovered near Lakehurst by three amateur collectors—Sidney A. Hessel, of Woodmere, Long Island, and George W. Rawson and J. Benjamin Ziegler, of Summit, New Jersey. The first new butterfly discovered in the northeastern United States in forty years, it was named in honor of Hessel *Mitoura hesseli.*

With a spread of slightly less than an inch, this pine barrens butterfly carries its beauty on the underside of its wings. The upper surfaces are dark brownish-black. But underneath the wings have an iridescent greenish hue that is the product not of pigment but of the structure of the scales that act as prisms, breaking up the spectrum and reflecting only rays of certain wave lengths. The green of the Hessel's hairstreak thus is produced as is the celebrated blue of the South American morpho. But the iridescent greenish hue of the underwings is only part of their beauty. They are speckled with chocolate brown and decorated with spots and irregular lines of white. This pattern makes the little butterfly inconspicuous when it is clinging among white cedar twigs. The larva, green with irregular lighter stripings, is even better camouflaged. It is almost impossible to discover when it is feeding among the branch tips of the cedar.

The adult butterflies have a rather placid disposition. The year the hairstreak was first described, Sidney Hessel brought a living adult for me to photograph. It proved remarkably tame. As I worked, it calmly moved about, feeding among shadbush flowers—one of its two main sources of spring nectar in the barrens. The other source is the sand myrtle. Later in summer it feeds most often at the sweet pepper bush, *Clethra alnifolia.*

For a hundred years amateurs, professionals, museum men, collectors for biological supply houses, have journeyed to the pine barrens of New Jersey with their nets and killing bottles. One entomologist even built a "collecting cabin" in the barrens where he attracted lepidoptera by sugaring and by lights. So close to Philadelphia, so close to New York, so long a collecting ground of butterfly hunters, the barrens still had retained the secret of Hessel's hairstreak down to present times—as undoubtedly today it retains other secrets yet to be discovered.

It was after sunset when we left the somber, untamed expanse of the pine barrens. It was dusk when, not many miles away, we were settled down for the night. From a woodland back of our cabin, in the dusk and in the dark, came an ancient song of spring, the tirelessly repeated call of a whippoorwill. Listening there in the soft June night we remembered how Henry Thoreau at Walden had longed to hear whippoorwills in his dreams and how, to him, this final month of spring was the "whippoorwill's moon."

TWENTY-NINE

CITY SELBORNE

THE skyscrapers of Manhattan appeared like a low mirage beyond the Jersey Meadows. We skimmed upward onto the 3½-mile bridge of the Pulaski Skyway. Smoking factories and great parking fields filled with cars slipped past below us. All seasons were the same to their asphalt and brick. But the marshy lowlands west of the Hudson were now green from end to end where, when last we saw them, they were dead, yellow, mottled with patches of dingy snow.

At the end of the Skyway we dipped into the open mouth of the Holland Tunnel, sped beneath the Hudson through a man-made burrow lined with gleaming tile, and popped up into the maelstrom of midmorning traffic in Manhattan. Among the crisscrossing canyons and the great piles of setback buildings that rose like eroding buttes in this badlands of concrete and steel and glass and brick, spring had opened office windows. Men stood on the sidewalks in shirt sleeves. In Greenwich Village flower stands were out. And along avenues a thin line of unconquered trees, struggling to survive amid the motor fumes, had put forth new leaves. Our long, meandering course had returned us close to our starting point.

Working our way uptown, from traffic snarl to traffic snarl, we paused at the Bank for Savings, on Fourth Avenue, to replenish our dwindling funds and to see a good friend, Rowland R. McElvare, Executive Vice-President, the only banker in the world who is also an authority on heliothid moths. Then we

drove north again. We skirted the great green rectangle, walled
in with high apartment buildings, that forms Central Park—
a city oasis where more than two hundred different species of
birds have been recorded. We paralleled the Hudson, up which
long since the shad had run. We passed the park on Riverside
Drive, where, in the year 1946, I saw with amazement a wild
woodchuck sitting under a bush near Columbia University
feeding beside its burrow with traffic streaming above and below it and lofty apartment houses rising behind it.

Well up in the Bronx, we turned aside again—at Van Cortlandt Park. Its 1,132 acres, where American and British soldiers
once faced each other during the Revolutionary War, has been
a haunt of big-city naturalists for generations. John James
Audubon spent his last years not many miles away. E. P. Bicknell, for whom the Bicknell's thrush was named, used to wander
there. A number of youthful bird watchers, destined for scientific distinction, cut their ornithological teeth in Van Cortlandt Park. The first nesting record for the king rail in the
state of New York came from a small cattail swamp bordered
by a railroad and across from a public golf course at the edge of
this city park. One year, when breeding-bird censuses were
taken in thirty-eight different areas scattered across the country, the highest count in the whole United States came from
this same city cattail swamp. In its hundred acres the census
takers counted 840 pairs, 1,680 adult birds.

As Nellie and I approached the marshy pond at the head
of this swamp, we surprised a black-crowned night heron fishing at its edge. The bird gazed back at us with ruby eyes for
fully half a minute before it flapped away with measured wing-
beats, rising over the cattails with redwings in pursuit. A
painted turtle slipped into the muddy water and, in a glinting
flutter of wings, a metallic-blue dragonfly suspended itself for a
moment in the sunshine before us, vibrantly alive, a glittering
creature worlds away from the faded pinned specimen of the
insect box that is a mere reminder of beauty that has vanished,

a tarnished relic of something once surpassingly lovely.

We followed the path along the western edge of the swamp. Bushes closed around us. The surf sound of traffic on the parkway diminished. A catbird mewed close beside us. Then both the noise of traffic and the calling of the bird were swallowed up in the roaring clatter of a passenger train charging down the track of the Berkshire Division of the New York Central Railroad beyond the cattails. As the din receded, we emerged into an open space. At this same spot along the path, I recalled, the erudite John Kieran once had an amusing encounter with beginner's luck.

He met a lady, one spring morning, coming down the trail with bird glasses in one hand and Roger Peterson's field guide in the other. Birds were all new to her, she explained, and the sparrows were bothering her.

"How do you tell one sparrow from another?"

Kieran was beginning to explain about the rusty cap on the chipping sparrow, the snowy patch on the whitethroat, and the dark spot on the streaked breast of the song sparrow when the woman interrupted:

"What sparrow is that?"

She pointed to a bird on the ground a few yards away down the path.

"Lady," John Kieran told her, "take a long look at that bird. It is a white-crowned sparrow, the rarest one around. I haven't seen one here in the spring in years."

And if John Kieran has not seen a bird in Van Cortlandt Park, the chances are it has not been there. He has been going over the same area on almost daily walks since 1912. He was born nearby. Engineers on the railroad recognize him and wave as they go past. Twenty years ago, as he skirted the swamp weekends, he used to meet several boys plowing through the mud, clapping their hands to scare up rails and bitterns. They were members of a remarkable group, the Bronx County Bird

Club. One of the boys was Roger Tory Peterson, another Joseph J. Hickey, a third Allan D. Cruickshank.

During almost forty years, while a sportswriter on *The New York Times*, a columnist on *The New York Sun*, a mainstay of radio's famous "Information Please" and a kind of one-man institution of learning, John Kieran has studied the natural history of Van Cortlandt Park. He has roamed it the way Gilbert White roamed Wolmer forest and the beech woods of the Hanger at Selborne—with unflagging interest in all the splendid commonplaces of nature. This Selborne spirit is not confined to the country; it is not limited to any land or race. It found expression with Gilbert White in the quiet of an English countryside, with John Kieran in a traffic-encircled park in one of the largest metropolises on earth. This stretch of green, an island in a sea of buildings and thoroughfares, has been his Selborne within the city.

Izaak Walton, in setting down *The Compleat Angler*, re-called pleasant hours of "such dayes and times as I have laid aside business and gone a-fishing with honest Nat and R. Roe." So, as we walked about this city park that spring morning, I remembered with delight "such dayes and times" as I have gone afield with honest J. Kieran, Fred Nagler, the artist, and the astronomer, that modest man of wide attainments, the late Dr. Clyde Fisher. Together we had stalked horned larks above those twin subterranean rivers, the old and new Croton aque-ducts that flow under the park in bringing water from the Catskills. We had seen bobolinks fly over us near the site where Jacobus Van Cortlandt, once mayor of New York, built his gristmill about 1700—a building that remained standing for more than two centuries, until it was struck by lightning and destroyed in 1910. We had surprised wood ducks in the swamp and seen ant lions digging their pits in the dust under an oak tree and had come upon solitary sandpipers beside the little pond. And going farther afield, we had seen snowy owls among the dunes at Jones Beach and seventeen-year cicadas emerging amid the Half Hollow Hills of Long Island. Those were long-remembered days with good companions.

For a number of years Van Cortlandt Park has been the scene of John Kieran's own weekly "Information, Please." Many an eminent scientist has gone along the old, familiar, two-mile circuit, across the parade ground, down the railroad, along the swamp, through a hole in the fence, past the pond and up the slope where the glaciers that once covered 5,000,-000 square miles of North America have left their grooves on granite rocks, and so along the parkway to Kieran's house not far from the Hudson River. They all enjoyed themselves as they added to that amazing store of exact information which is filed away behind the guileless countenance of their host.

In *Footnotes on Nature*, a book of substance and charm, John Kieran has given a characteristically charitable account of that ill-starred day when I first appeared in the guise of a visiting expert. The sad truth is that he probably got less information out of me than Admetus got work out of Henry Thoreau and, as readers of Robert Louis Stevenson's essay will recall, "Admetus never got less work out of any servant since the world began." On this particular day caterpillars, no two alike, seemed holding a convention in Van Cortlandt Park. Now caterpillars are not like kittens that are cats from birth or fledglings that are birds from the beginning. Each time a caterpillar sheds its skin and arrives at a new stage in its development it is just as likely as not to assume a different form. Thus the same caterpillar may look like half a dozen different caterpillars while it is reaching maturity. Moreover, there are nearly ten thousand insects in America that begin as caterpillars. Multiply that number by the average number of instars, or stages in development, and the result is as overwhelming as the varied array of immature moths and butterflies that were presented for identification to a wholly inadequate expert that day.

Perhaps to cheer me up in my low estate, Kieran recalled an

experience of his own. He had agreed to talk on the common
birds of the Van Cortlandt Park region before a group in the
Riverdale section where he lives. To illustrate the talk, he obtained hand-colored slides from the National Audubon Society.
Just as he was going on the platform, the projectionist said:

"I notice the name of the bird is given at the bottom of the
slide. Do you want me to call it out each time I show a new
bird?"

"No, no," John assured him, "that won't be necessary.
These are common, everyday birds. I will recognize them as
soon as they appear on the screen."

His introduction over, he called for the first slide. It flashed
on the screen, an immense bird, fully eight feet high, with great
patches of browns and yellows. Kieran stared at it. There was
a long silence. Finally he said:

"That's a bird I never saw in my life. It must be an exotic
species that got in by mistake. What does the slide say?"

The projectionist looked and called out:

"House wren."

In his enthusiasm for birds, John Kieran has been known to
lie on his back in poison ivy the better to see a rare species.
But his walks are never confined to bird watching. All in nature
interests him. At one point, there may be a pause to examine
a patch of coltsfoot which he has been keeping track of for
years; at another, a halt to slip a bit of dog biscuit under a
fence to a puppy friend of his and, a little later, a stop to survey
the *Enchenopa binotata* tree hoppers that each autumn lay
their eggs under ribbons of froth on the twigs of a wafer ash.

One winter day, when John and Fred Nagler had come out
on Long Island to join me in watching ducks at the Tobay
Beach Sanctuary, our trip, for a time, seemed headed on a
beeline for jail.

We had made arrangements to meet at a small pond between Baldwin and Freeport on the south shore of the island.
A number of mallards, a few pintails, and half a dozen shovelers

swam toward the farther shore of the pond as we came out on the edge. For five minutes or so we watched the birds through our glasses. We were turning away when a police car tore down Merrick Road and cut in behind us. A second radio patrol car came racing down Sunrise Highway with siren on. It wheeled into the road skirting the pond and charged down on us. We were cornered.

Across the pond, in line with the swimming ducks, was a red-brick building. During the war it had been a plant where the U.S. Navy manufactured flares. Now it had been relegated to the task of printing booklets of instruction. Some local patriot, seeing us looking through glasses in that direction, had called the police to capture the foreign spies. The dialogue that ensued when the first officer reached us might well have been a skit on a vaudeville stage.

"What are you doing?"

"Looking at ducks."

"What's your name?"

"Teale."

By the light in his eye I could tell he had heard about teal ducks. The light said: A wise guy, eh?

I have friends who are named Crow, Crane, Raven and Rook. Fortunately, they were not along that day.

"Let's see your driver's license."

Somewhat mollified when he saw my name really was Teale, he turned to John.

"What's your name?"

"Kieran."

"Aren't you on television?"

"Yes, I am."

Now everything would be all right. He had recognized John.

"Well, I like you," he said. "I think your program, Kiernan's Alley, is *very* funny."

"Oh, that's another man. That isn't my program."

"Is his name Kiernan?" a second policeman called from the other car.

"No, it's Kieran."

"Well, I'm glad to hear that."

"Why?"

"I don't like Kiernans."

"Why?"

"I married one!"

On another occasion, when I was out with Roger Tory Peterson during the early days of World War II, the quiet of a Long Island field trip was similarly shattered by the siren of a radio car. Roger had just set up his camera to photograph the nest of a European goldfinch in a vacant field near Seaford. He had hardly hidden himself behind a bramble patch, ready to snap the shutter by remote control, when the faraway wail of a siren grew in volume. A patrol car bore down on us in response to a telephone call. It reported some very suspicious activity in a vacant field.

In thinking it over, it occurs to me that I could not find three more congenial cellmates in the world than John Kieran, Fred Nagler, and Roger Peterson. I can't imagine anybody else I would rather go to jail with! We would have the whole outdoors to talk about. A good stiff term in durance vile with such companions would be almost as good as a college education.

By the time Nellie and I left Van Cortlandt Park that June day and started north once more it was well past noon. For a considerable way we still rode on city streets. Fitted together into a straight line, the thoroughfares of Gotham would stretch for 5,000 miles—clear to California and beyond almost halfway to Hawaii. The parade of houses, seemingly without end, brought to mind a saying of our friend, William T. Davis, the Staten Island naturalist:

"Only a few human beings should grow to the square mile. They commonly are planted too close."

But eventually the houses thinned and we were in open country. We rode northward on the Sawmill River Parkway, crossed the Hudson on the Bear Mountain Bridge, and swung north again on the western side of the river. We passed over a small stream with the shuddery name of Murderer's Creek. We stopped on the Storm King Highway to watch a bald eagle soar by. We rode mile after mile through a pleasant riverbank country of orchards and vineyards and stone walls. Roadworkers were cutting grass beside the highway, the long, luxurious grass of spring. We stopped for the night a few miles south of the Mid-Hudson Bridge.

About sunset we drove on to West Park, the home of John Burroughs, to see his son, Julian. A mile and a half back in the hills, in 1895, Burroughs had built his famous Slabsides. And here at West Park, overlooking the Hudson, twenty years earlier, he had constructed a home of his own design, Riverby, the house that gave the title to his tenth book and the building of which is related in the chapter "Roof-Tree" in *Signs and Seasons*. Local stone, gray and weathered, went into the masonry while timbers and boards came from special trees the naturalist selected in the woods and helped fell and saw.

We never did see Julian Burroughs that evening. Along the way, fire engines passed us at high speed. As we neared Riverby, people were running down the road. Fire hoses already wound like great serpents beside the highway and down a slope, where dense, dark smoke poured into the sky and rolled out over the river. After surviving unscathed for almost three-quarters of a century, John Burroughs' Riverby was burning to the ground.

Afterwards we thought how strange a thing was the coincidence of our arrival. We had been journeying for four months. We had traveled 14,000 miles. Our plans had altered constantly. Anywhere along the course, a delay here, a speeding up there, would have changed the hour and day of our coming to West Park. Yet our long journey through time and space had brought us to Riverby at the precise hour of its tragic end.

THIRTY

WIND FOREST

ALL along Cape Cod, sea and shore, dune and moor, bog and pond and open headland streamed and writhed before us in the gust-driven rain of a great spring storm. The wind of a nor'easter was pummeling the lower vegetation, cuffing the locust trees, belaboring creeks and inlets, lashing the waves into the seethe of towering surf. Nowhere since Mt. LeConte, in the Great Smokies, had we met so violent a storm.

Across almost the length of Massachusetts we had ridden in sunshine. The white of wild strawberry blooms, the pink of roses, the blue of flags were with us all the way. This was a land of graceful elms and of sugar maples, with their massed foliage rising above the brows of hills like cumulus clouds, green thunderheads. Pansies and snowball bushes and lilacs bloomed in dooryards and, in country gardens, rhubarb lifted the mass of its cream-white flowers. Observing how rhubarb was just beginning to bloom in the Berkshires, was in full flower at a lower elevation, we recalled the mountains and valleys of the Blue Ridges and that day when we had gone in and out of spring. Our first bobolinks rose with jingling songs from a meadow beyond a stone wall east of Ware. In quaint early natural histories, groups of creatures are given such picturesque designations as a waddling of ducks, a pride of lions, a spring of teals, an exalting of larks, and a charm of goldfinches. If there is a gaggle of geese and a clamor of rooks, why not a jingle of bobolinks? Or a flutter of terns?

By the time we had crossed the Cape Cod Canal and had run a gantlet of Jolly Whaler tea rooms, Slick Chick hamburger stands, Blue Moon dance halls, and Puss-in-Boots diners, the storm was almost upon us. Lilacs tossed beside gateways formed of whale ribs. Gusts struck the surface of fresh-water ponds and ran like thousands of water striders across them. And the perfume of the blooming locust trees was whirled away on the rising wind.

Before we reached Orleans, at the elbow of the cape, we were creeping through a deluge with headlights on. Men at filling stations were clad in gleaming yellow slickers. Ripped by the gusts, falling in clouds and sheets of varying density, the downpour seemed to shimmer like an aurora in the sky. Unmindful of the storm, robins ran over the cut grass beside the highway. Wet days are harvest days for these worm hunters. As happy as a robin in the rain!

Twilight of a sort had already descended on the storm-lashed cape by 3:00 P.M. Battened down in a snug cabin at Orleans, we rode out the gale. It continued all that night and nearly all the next day. During lulls in the drumming gunfire of the raindrops we could hear a phoebe in the storm outside our cabin. With its nest nearby, it was calling "Phoebe! Phoebe! Phoebe!" until it seemed likely to wear out its little throat. I timed the bird. During the space of a minute it called on the average of once every two seconds.

Tiring of inactivity during the second day of the tempest, we drove up the cape, once as far as Provincetown, another time toward the ocean near Wellfleet on the Cahoon's Hollow road. At its end the vague mass of an immense promontory lifted above us, sheeted in falling rain, with the white smother of the surf at its foot. The next day the rain had passed and the headland was printed sharply against the blue of a clearing sky. The wind still worried the blufftop, with long gusts driving a sandblast of flying quartz down its side. But its force was ebbing. By midafternoon the wind was dead.

We climbed the side of the promontory, passing through a maze of circles traced on the sand by the swinging blades of the beach grass. Sand covers the headland; but the promontory is no more a hill of sand than Cape Cod is a magnified sand bar. A glacial moraine that can be traced back through Long Island and into the continent as far west as Michigan constitutes the backbone of the cape. It is the sturdy gravel of this glacial deposit that forms the high rampart of the Cahoon's Hollow headland.

Thoreau remarked—and who can write of Cape Cod without recalling some words of his?—that to stand on the outer beach is like standing on the deck of a ship 30 miles at sea. Here, on this lofty headland, we were in the crow's-nest of the vessel. We looked down from the lip of the sheer descent on the seaward side to the storm-scoured beach, more than 140 feet below, where shattering waves were endlessly weaving patterns of lace with their foam on the sand. We looked out over the immense panorama of empty sea that spread away with its infinitely varied tintings of blue and purple and green. Somewhere under this water was the Lost Atlantis of the cape, Nauset Island, long since washed away, the land Leif Ericson is supposed to have touched six full centuries before the Pilgrims came to Provincetown.

Behind us, all across the crest of the promontory, the low vegetation seemed cowering, lying low, fearful of lifting its head. The scythe of the wind had just passed by. Wherever we walked over the summit of this sea bluff, life was in miniature. Everything was stunted. We seemed on a hilltop in Lilliput.

Here were knee-high shrub oaks, ankle-high bayberries, goldenrods that hardly rose to our shoetops. I measured one beach plum, complete with miniature sprays of white blossoms. It was five inches high. A twisted pitch pine, supporting ten cones on its tough little twigs, measured 28 inches from top to bottom. A patriarch among the oaks, with its upper branches dead and silvered with age, had a height of 26 inches. Striding along the horizon line of the lofty promontory, we were like giants in seven-league boots. We stepped over trees. We traversed in a few strides whole forests of Lilliput oaks.

Thoreau, who had walked across this headland nearly a century before, spoke of the little oaks as appearing dwarfed "almost into lichens which a deer might eat up in a morning." I cut through the trunk of one oak with my pocketknife. Although its diameter was hardly half an inch, the fibers were like wires. I whittled for more than ten minutes before I chewed my way through to the other side. Later I sawed and polished a section and counted the annual rings. The tree was twenty-one years old. Its height was 15 inches. During more than two decades, its average annual growth had been less than three-quarters of an inch.

Once when I was striding across a thick tangle of these Tom Thumb trees, the ground dropped out from under me. I sprawled forward on the wiry mass of the interlacing oaks. They supported me as though their twigs were made of metal. I had stumbled into a hollow about three feet deep and three or four paces across. The oaks filled the hollow like drifted snow. They stretched in a smooth expanse, their tops level with those of the other trees, revealing no evidence of a depression or the fact that the trees there—slightly more protected from the wind—had a greater height.

Wherever the stunted trees were massed together in dense groves or miniature woodlands, their tops seemed sheared smooth, mowed off, trimmed level by the wind. These diminutive woods of the blufftop are wind forests. They are created largely by gusts and gales and coastal winds. According to the United States government's *Atlas of American Agriculture*, the average velocity of the wind during the year at Cape Cod is fourteen miles an hour. This is one of the highest average velocities in the country. The fact that the oaks in the little hollows grow higher but their tops rise no farther than the level of the other trees around them testifies to the importance of the wind in determining the size which they attain.

The mechanical action of the wind, the abrasive granules of the flying sand, the salt of the spray, all these affect the trees. The moving air also sucks moisture from the headland, which is normally deficient in both fertility and moisture. Underfed, underwatered, subjected to the wearing action of the wind, open to the full fury of the gale in their exposed position, the trees remain pygmies as long as they live.

In such locations, R. F. Daubenmire points out in his *Plants and Environment*, the wind sucks moisture from the vegetation as well as the soil. It constantly bends the leaves, causing alternate contraction and expansion of the intercellular spaces. This forces out saturated air and draws in drier air, thus desiccating the plant. The very cells of the tiny trees are stunted. They become fixed at subnormal sizes. As a result, each part of the tree is produced on a diminutive scale.

This, in general, is what happens. There are, however, a number of botanical riddles in connection with the production of wind forests, problems so close to home that scientists have largely passed them by. Surprisingly little study has been given to these midget trees of the headlands.

"We could get money for expeditions to Zanzibar or Borneo," one botanist told me by way of explanation, "but if we suggested going to Cape Cod, everybody thought we just wanted a vacation."

During our days on the cape we wandered widely. We visited Race Point and Highland Light and Great Hollow and First Encounter Beach. We passed men working in cranberry beds and recalled that three out of every four cranberries eaten in America come from the bogs of Massachusetts. We drove past weathered locust trees splotched with brilliant yellow lichen; watched gray tiger beetles run along Nauset Beach on legs that seemed plated with gold; passed across rolling moors that spread away in a golden sea where waves and mounds of poverty grass, *Hudsonia*, were covered with tiny flowers of spring. But always we were drawn back to the great hill at Cahoon's Hollow and the Lilliput woods at its top.

We saw the headland first through veils of falling rain. We saw it later in the full glare of the sun. And once I walked among the little trees in the quiet of a moonlit night when the sea spread out in mellow light below and the faint rumor of the waves reached the hilltop and the air was fragrant with the perfume of sweet ferns crushed beneath my feet.

Past dusty miller and blooming beach peas, richly, royally purple, we repeatedly made the ascent to the top. At one place the wind had undercut the beach grass on a sandbank and revealed, in a vertical profile, that the roots of the grass plumbed straight downward for a distance of three feet and two inches. Near the top we passed through a zone of poverty grass and then we were among the wind-swept vegetation that crowned the headland. There we had a sea bird's view of the sea.

Less than a hundred paces carried us from one end to the other of the blufftop. At each step the vegetation had a tough, wiry, springy feel beneath our feet. Even the bearberry vines and the sweet ferns seemed partly made of metal. To all these stubborn, humble, enduring plants the season had brought its changes. Flowers in miniature—the elf-sized bells of the stunted huckleberry bushes, the half-finger-length sprays of the dwarfed beach plums—hung only a few inches above the ground. And all across this land of little trees and pygmy vegetation, new leaves clothed every growing thing, from tiny goldenrod to weed-sized oak.

As we pushed among the trees we saw another sign of the season. Swellings were appearing on the tender new twigs of the oaks. The midget gall wasp, *Callirhytis futilis*, had been busy in the spring sunshine. Each swelling marked the spot where an egg had been inserted in the tissues. The immature wasp would remain within the gall, protected, until it emerged as an adult. In the treetops of the little oaks, all over the wind forest, we saw old galls, each with a small round exit hole.

A large number were on dead twigs. They were hard and weathered to a silvery gray, the veterans of many a gale.

Each time we visited the headland, during those June days, dozens of small depressions in the sand held blundering, top-heavy May beetles lying on their backs clawing the air. One morning, following my tracks of the previous afternoon across an open stretch of sand, I found six beetles upside down where they had tumbled into the depressions left by my heels. At another spot I came upon a May beetle that had been able to claw itself around and around while upside down. It had worn a kind of blunt, shallow ant lion's pit in the sand. The heavy, reddish-brown beetles were appearing from the earth during the night; mornings we came upon their round emergence holes in the sand. Apparently many of the insects never succeeded in righting themselves once they tumbled upside down. Their clawed feet were unable to find anything to grasp in the shifting, almost fluid, sand. On one walk across the blufftop we counted nearly twenty of the insects lying, with their feet in the air, lifeless.

This catastrophe for the beetles proved a harvest for the headland ants. Minute red ants swarmed over the dead insects. Dark ants, about a quarter of an inch long, probably *Formica cinerea*, struggled to drag beetle fragments across the sand to their nests. The greatest activity occurred among the mounds of low *Hudsonia* that extended in a wide archipelago of rounded islands, gray-green and gold, down the open sand below the wind forest of the crest.

During the better part of one cloudless morning I sat in the sand beside one of these mounds of beach heath watching the work of a colony of the larger headland ants. The entrance to their nest was at the downhill edge of the mound and their territory seemed to extend for about twenty feet down the slope across an area of open sand strewn with a few sparse clumps of beach grass and two or three small mounds of *Hudsonia*. The workers never went above the mound, which was about three feet long and a foot and a half across. Another similar colony had its nest on the uphill side. The workers from this colony appeared to forage only up the slope. Most of the hunting ground of both colonies was a bare desert of sand. The surface of this Sahara was shifting, unstable; yet across and back, in all directions, these insect Bedouins found their way.

And the booty they discovered in this unlikely area was surprisingly varied. Over a period of about two hours I noted down the loads brought home to the one nest by the foraging workers. Some of the entries in this record are given below:

10:10 A.M. Two ants appear dragging a dead ant of their own species. Its abdomen is deflated and flat.

10:14 A.M. One ant appears with a dead pillbug in its jaws. It holds it by one end and the pillbug curves back over its head like a half-moon. Just before it reaches the entrance to the nest, a gust bowls it over. Tumbling down a slope, first the ant, then the pillbug on top, the insect and its burden roll to the bottom of a small depression. There the ant regains its feet and continues to the nest.

10:22 A.M. An ant brings in a small green aphid.

10:31 A.M. A grayish spider is the burden of another worker.

10:39 A.M. Two ants appear dragging the body of a small brown caterpillar. One ant is at each end. They pull the caterpillar sidewise up the sand. At one point, the middle of their burden catches on a tiny clod as it drags along. For almost a minute the two ants tug and struggle until, by unequal pulling, they seesaw the caterpillar free.

10:44 A.M. An ant arrives with a small red ant, dead, in its jaws.

10:50 A.M. A worker comes in with a lump of something soft and translucent. Is it partially dried honeydew produced by aphides?

10:59 A.M. One of the legs of a May beetle is brought home in the jaws of a hurrying worker. The insect carries its burden on a beeline across the sand to the entrance of the nest.

11:02 A.M. A single ant comes up the slope easily carrying what seems a tremendous load, the front section of the chitin face of a May beetle.

11:13 A.M. Another dead pillbug arrives.

11:15 A.M. An ant brings in a small green caterpillar with a black head.

11:22 A.M. A worker arrives with the wing of a small wasp. It carries it jauntily as though it were as light as a feather.

11:31 A.M. This time it is the leg of a fly that is brought in.

11:45 A.M. Laboring straight up the slope, three ants appear dragging a formidable burden, a black, square-bodied beetle fully half an inch long. Time and again they reach the top of some little rise only to have the soft sand give way beneath their feet. They slip and roll back and begin again. As they near the nest, half a dozen other ants join them. But nine ants seem to make less progress than three. They stumble over each other. They pull in opposite directions. The black beetle moves like a pushball, with the tide of battle going first one way, then the other. Fully twenty minutes of furious labor goes into getting the beetle across the last foot of sand.

11:53 A.M. A worker comes in with a small greenish bug in its jaws.

12:06 P.M. The shard of a reddish beetle is brought in by a worker.

12:11 P.M. Another May beetle leg arrives.

12:20 P.M. Two workers labor up the sand dragging a greenish caterpillar seven-eighths of an inch long.

In order to identify these varied burdens, I had to intercept the workers at the entrance to the nest. To the colony that morning, the world must have been a place bewitched. Worker after worker, laboring to bring home its hard-won booty, would almost attain the goal only to have the prize snatched away. This was a Black Friday in the economy of the anthill. However, in the end, like a good king in a fairy tale, I dumped all the accumulated plunder back on the threshold of the nest when I was leaving.

During the time I sat beside the *Hudsonia* checking on the economy of the headland ants, other insects labored on the hilltop. Dark bumblebees were garnering the yellow pollen of the poverty grass. Weak brownish moths fluttered from island to island across the archipelago of the *Hudsonia* clumps. Two tiger beetles, almost indistinguishable from the sand until they moved, raced in fits and starts, one in pursuit of the other. Crane flies drifted by like oversized mosquitoes and parasitic wasps, hunting their prey, flew up and down, in and out, among the leaves of the Lilliput oaks.

Over the wind forest, over the *Hudsonia* islands, over the sheer drop of the bluff to the beach, tree swallows shuttled back and forth hour after hour on a hunt for aerial insects. Recently owners of bogs all along the Massachusetts coast have been putting up birdhouses for tree swallows. These white-bellied birds have proved invaluable as a natural-control on insects that injure cranberry vines.

Back of the headland, where it dipped into a tangle of twisted pitch pine trees, we heard at intervals a wild, ecstatic little birdsong. In the distance it faintly resembled the jingling of a bobolink. It was the flight song of a yellowthroat. A number of American birds, such as the pipit, the horned lark, the mourning warbler, the yellow-breasted chat, the woodcock, the ovenbird, and even the upland plover, make flight songs. This is a characteristic of species that nest on or near the ground. In the spring they mount into the air and pour forth the melody of their song. Foremost among such aerial singers is the far-famed English skylark.

The most obvious birds of the Lilliput forest, during the days we were there, were a pair of song sparrows. They fluttered from twig to twig—treetop birds two feet from the ground. Somewhere in the wiry tangle they had their nest. Wherever we went the male bird followed us with his uneasy "chip!" or "timp!" Fluttering to a favorite perch among the dead branches of a diminutive oak, a hundred times a day it would burst into its song with its musically buzzing climax, a song that someone had translated into: "Hip, Hip, Hurray, Boys! Spring is Here!"

Shortly before we left the headland for the last time I experienced a curious adventure in perspective. Lying at the edge of the pygmy forest, with the song sparrow, worried, alert, hopping from treetop to treetop nearby, I let my eyes explore deeper and deeper among the twisted trunks and intertwining branches. I had looked thus, completely within a world of distorted proportions, for a long time when suddenly I became aware that the little trees were little no longer. They had expanded. In my mind I seemed walking in a woods of wind-twisted trees of normal size.

Then, just as my eyes lifted along the level of the treetops, a brown thrasher, with set wings, came sweeping low over the tangle from the dip behind the headland. Seen with my distorted perspective, the bird appeared immense, almost a creature of fabulous proportions sailing above a forest. For an instant I was torn in different directions by a world of two perspectives. Then the wind forest fell back to its normal size. The brown thrasher assumed its natural form. I arose to descend the hill. The dwarfed woodland was dwarfed once more.

THIRTY-ONE

THE CRANE FIELDS

IT probably is a great compliment to the writings of Henry Thoreau that both Nellie and I, growing up a thousand miles from New England, should experience the sensation of coming home whenever we cross the line into Massachusetts. Driving northward up the state from Cape Cod to Concord, that June day, we were reversing a journey Thoreau had made exactly ninety years before. At 8:30 in the morning on June 12, 1857, he had started south on his last visit to the sand roads, the open beach, and the headlands of Cape Cod.

The Concord he left in the spring and the Concord we reached in the spring are amazingly alike. Nine decades have brought changes to the town but no revolution. And out in the country and along the three rivers—the Sudbury, the Assabet, and the Concord—scenes and wild activity that attracted Thoreau remain to attract others of like mind three generations later.

Almost all that afternoon, in humid heat, we drifted or paddled on the rivers. They reach a wilder Concord than the highways. A black-crowned night heron, an American bittern, a green heron flapped up from the marshy river edges and flew downstream ahead of us. Turtles tumbled into the water from fallen trees. And the husks of dragonfly nymphs, brown and glistening, clung to the stems and leaves of the pickerelweeds. For a long time below the town we skirted wet, lowland levels. These heron-haunted tracts were known to the early English

settlers of the region as The Crane Fields. Now a federal wildlife refuge, they are so little altered by the years that The Crane
Fields might stand as a symbol of enduring Concord nature.

In many ways the most altered spot associated with Thoreau
is Walden Pond, the small body of water he made known the
world around. Throngs from Boston and elsewhere—ten thousand or more on a summer Sunday—come to swim in the lake
and picnic on the shore. Behind them they leave fearful and
wonderful evidence of America's high standard of living. With
Walter Harding, Secretary of the Thoreau Society, and his
wife, one July morning in 1949, I made a circuit of Deep
Cove, the indentation in the Walden shore line close to the
site of Thoreau's cabin. As we walked along, I jotted down
all the things we encountered at its edge. Published in the
Thoreau Society Bulletin for July, 1949, the list includes:

One hundred and sixteen beer cans, 21 milk bottles, 7 Coca-
Cola bottles, the remains of 14 campfires, a shoe box, eggshells,
soap, half-eaten sandwiches, Dixie cups, cracker boxes, soda
straws, cigarette packages, comic books, tabloid newspapers,
playing cards, broken glass, paper napkins, mustard bottles,
firecrackers, banana peels, orange skins, a baby-food jar, a piece
of pink ribbon, the thumb of a leather glove, a flashlight battery, and a dollar bill. Since 1950, conditions at Walden have
changed. Bathing is not permitted in the cove and the litter
has largely disappeared from its shore.

Nellie and I arrived at Walden Pond in the morning, in the
middle of the week, after the fever of the previous Sunday's in-
vasion had subsided. Sunshine and peace lay over Deep Cove.
Three fat tadpoles sunned themselves in the shallows. A spotted sandpiper fed at the water's edge. And behind us on the
hillside that leads to the cairn marking the site of Thoreau's
hut, the droning song of an early cicada rose and fell. It began
with a sizzle like a partially opened pop bottle, increased to a
snore, ascended to a high-pitched bandsaw buzz that filled
the hot woods and drowned out the "Teacher! Teacher!

Teacher!" of an ovenbird and even cut through the grind and whine of a Diesel engine hauling freight cars on the Fitchburg line that skirts the western end of the pond. Then it descended through snore to sizzle and silence again.

During one of these pauses in its strident song we heard a rattling on the bark of a pitch pine tree and saw a gray squirrel scrambling upward with a slice of buttered toast in its mouth. Changed conditions have brought new habits to wild creatures at Walden. Here, where trash baskets overflow with picnic remains, squirrels and chipmunks dine on fare unknown to their kind in Thoreau's day. The purple grackles, on summer mornings, come in flocks to feed on fragments dropped by picnickers of the day before. I have seen as many as a hundred grackles on the bathing beach and the shores nearby. Their grating clamor carries far down the pond, on windless days almost to Deep Cove.

"One attraction in coming to the woods to live," Thoreau wrote in *Walden*, "was that I should have leisure and opportunity to see the spring come in." It still comes in with the age-old beauty of wildflowers and the age-old song of woodland birds. And, in the main, spring at Walden antedates the crowds. Not far from the bathing beach, near Emerson's Cliff, that day we found pink lady-slipper in bloom. The white flowers of wild strawberries, the tiny bell-blooms of the huckleberries, the yellow-cinquefoil, and the flower-carpets of the false lily-of-the-valley, these are part of the Walden Woods in spring.

Oak apples, those spherical homes of larval gall insects, had already swelled until many were an inch in diameter. The tinier homes of another insect hermit, the white masses of froth sheltering young froghoppers, gleamed on the stems of plants and even on the needles of the pitch pines. Still other solitary insects, flat, dust-colored ant lions, lay hidden at the bottom of pits sheltered beneath the roots of an undercut oak beside the Indian Path.

Some of these pits were unlike any I had ever seen before. Within the tree, carpenter ants were excavating galleries. Two piles of discarded "sawdust," one four inches high, lay beneath small openings in the tree. An ant would appear at an opening with a bit of wood in its jaws, lean far out, drop the fragment, and then return for another load. Twenty-five bits of wood were thus dropped in the course of one minute. Where this material had spread out over the sand and gravel beneath the tree, several of the ant lions had excavated their pits, digging the traps in sawdust instead of sand. Thus a by-product of the labor of the ants were the pits in which some of them would lose their lives.

Beside the Indian Path on the opposite shore of Walden, we came upon a legal notice tacked to a tree. It was headed "Fishing Restricted" and began: "All fishing prohibited between November 1 and April 14." I was just reading the impressive signature, "The Commonwealth of Massachusetts," when a white-faced hornet alighted on the cardboard. At once we heard a small, steady, rasping sound. The insect, unawed by the Commonwealth of Massachusetts, was chewing up the sign, gouging out bits of its surface. All over the cardboard, little pits and roughened places testified to the repeated visits of the hornets. Here, in the spring sunshine, the wasps were mining paper for their paper nests.

A foretaste of summer heat lay over the woods and over the pond—where long lines and swirls of greenish pollen from the pitch pines floated on the surface. As we walked through the woods, in and out of openings, up rises and down into little ravines, the temperature seemed changing constantly. My pocket thermometer proved this impression was correct. It also bore witness to the truth of Thoreau's observation, set down in his *Journal,* that the difference in temperature of various localities is greater than is generally supposed.

Taken only a few feet or even inches apart, the temperature may show surprising variations. On the sunny side of a telegraph pole beside the Fitchburg Railroad, where it enters Deep Cut beyond Walden Pond, for example, the mercury rose to 108 degrees F. Only eight inches away, on the shady side of the pole, it dropped 25 degrees. With the thermometer face downward on black cinders beside the right-of-way, the mercury stood at 100 degrees. On light-colored sand, just six inches away, the reading was 98 degrees. Under the same sunshine, the heat-absorbing, darker material accounted for two additional degrees in temperature.

On another morning, when the temperature in the deep shadow of an oak at the edge of the Walden Woods was only 67 degrees, the reading in the less-dense shade of a white pine nearby was a full ten degrees higher, 77 degrees, and in the speckled light and shade beneath a sweet fern it was seven degrees higher still, 84 degrees. In the shadow of the highway bridge over Deep Cut, that same morning, the thermometer recorded 74 degrees. A foot beyond the shadow, on a railroad tie in the sun, it was 115 degrees.

Almost as much as the rivers, The Crane Fields, the Walden Woods, and Walden Pond itself, the Fitchburg Railroad played a prominent role in Thoreau's study of nature. Its right-of-way was, he noted in his *Journal*, "perhaps our pleasantest and wildest road." The tracks had reached Concord in 1844, the year before he went to Walden. They provided the shortest path between his father's house and the pond when he was felling pines to form his cabin. He never tired of recording events along its right-of-way. So often was he encountered walking the tracks that trainmen hailed him as a fellow employee of the railroad.

While the wandering footpath follows the lay of the land, the railroad charges straight ahead. The path that led Thoreau through the woods from Walden to Fairhaven Bay skirts the lowland stretch of Well Meadow. It winds along the contour line just above the marshy tract, following a comparatively level course where footing is solid. Indians probably used the path before Thoreau and deer may have laid it down before the Indians. It leads the traveler from place to place with the least effort; its course was determined by the logic of gravity.

But the railroad right-of-way levels its own course. It cuts through hills and stretches built-up roadbeds across depressions. It lays bare nature and carries the walker, frequently, through the least-tamed part of the country. A highway passes by the front door where yards are clipped, where company is received and the world watches its manners. A railroad right-of-way passes by back yards. It sees the world at ease, making no effort to put its best foot forward. It is one of those unfashionable byways where, as Thoreau expressed it, man meets man instead of polished shoe meeting polished shoe. Both the naturalist and the philosopher find much of special interest along a right-of-way.

Some years ago, when government soil men were trying to study the profile of prairie soil as it had been in pioneer days, the only place they could find it unchanged was along the tracks of a transcontinental railroad. Untouched by civilization, unchanged except by fire, such ribbons of land crisscross states and extend from coast to coast. They are natural sanctuaries. Here, where no plow has ever cut, vanishing species of wildflowers still bloom. In one instance, a botanist listed all the plants found in a pasture and on the adjoining railroad right-of-way. More than forty species growing beside the tracks had been extirpated beyond the boundary fence. Only twenty miles from New York City, a friend of mine discovered a rare fern, virtually unknown elsewhere in the region, growing at the foot of an embankment on the Long Island Railroad.

One young botanist, a generation ago, made a valuable collection of plants by spending his summer vacations along railroads. Riding on local trains through the South, he would get off at a country station and walk—with his suitcase and plant press on his shoulder—ten or fifteen miles to the next station, botanizing as he went. There he would board another local train and repeat the performance farther on. Now, however, plants that represent conditions as they were before the tractor, even before the oxen, are threatened by chemical discoveries. Some railroad officials have been experimenting with killing sprays, shot from moving cars, to keep the right-of-way "clean of weeds." If this should become general practice, the long sanctuary provided wildflowers by railroads would be no more.

The distance between Walden Pond and the "Texas House," where the Thoreau family lived in 1845, is slightly more than a mile along the railroad. We followed it on one of those June days—through Deep Cut, under the highway bridge, along the elevated roadbed with fields stretching away at a lower level on either hand, into the outskirts of the town. Late spring and all the life of late spring were around us. Sulphur butterflies, monarchs, and tiger swallowtails fluttered or drifted across the tracks from field to field. Where decades of fine, fallen cinders formed dark patches on the right-of-way, the sand of tiny ant-hills formed staring white disks on a black background. Gray tiger beetles sprinted across the sand and cinders beside the rails. They chose, by preference, the hottest sections of the track. Mad dogs and Englishmen—and tiger beetles—go out in the midday sun.

Twenty-four wires now run along the poles beside the Fitchburg line. Thoreau's famous "telegraph harp" has more strings today than it had when he listened to it a century ago. On these wires bluebirds alighted, their soft-voiced warbles blending with the song of a veery somewhere back in the Walden Woods. We talked of all the varied species of birds we had seen perching on roadside wires during our trip. We had come to know many as far as we could see them by their manner of clinging to their support—the bluebirds sitting almost bolt upright, the grackles leaning far forward as though to balance their tails.

One bird we heard singing beside the right-of-way that morning was an individualist, like Thoreau. It sang a different song, a song of its own. We saw it flitting, in flashes of black and robin-red, in and out of the bushes at the edge of the timber. It was a male towhee. While other ground robins gave voice to their familiar song—variously recorded as "Time for Teeeeeee!" "Drink Your Teeeeeee!" and "Acorn Treeeeeee!"— this bird seemed unable to stop, once it got started. It kept on in a "Time for Tee-hee-hee-hee-hee-hee!" Its song continued in a kind of limp or stutter at the end. We could recognize it as far as we could hear it down the track.

Other variations, less obvious, probably mark the songs of nearly all birds. Their voices are as varied as the voices of human beings. It is only the coarseness of our hearing, the wavering of our attention, the scantiness of our acquaintance-ship that lead us to assume that all meadowlarks whistle alike or all bluebirds warble the same. A friend of mine spent every spare minute of his boyhood with his pet pigeons. He grew to know them so well that he could recognize ten different birds by slight variations in their cooing. That specialist in American bird songs, Aretas A. Saunders, studied records of 884 song sparrows and found that no two sang exactly alike. There were variations in duration, in accent, in pitch, and in quality. More-over, the same bird does not always sing in the same way. The song sparrow is found from coast to coast. It is one of the commonest and best-known songsters in the country. Yet Saunders is of the opinion that no two of all the innumerable males sing identical songs.

One song sparrow sang over and over again from the top of Deep Cut. There is health and robustness in the voice of this brown, streaked little bird. His is a functional song. Here is no dreamer, no poet, no lovesick swain, no nightingale. Here is nothing soft or sad or melancholy. His is a sturdy, practical, New England song. It rang in our ears as we watched a squad-ron of half a dozen dark dragonflies patrolling the tracks, dart-ing, up, down, to the side, in their gnat-catching. I had turned from the dragonflies and had my glasses on the sparrow when a grinding roar grew in volume and the pride of the Fitchburg division of the Boston and Maine Railroad, a Diesel-powered streamliner, hurled itself into the cut. Its noise drowned out every other sound. Yet by the movement of the bird's throat I could see it finish its song. For it, passing trains were an old story, a familiar feature of the day. It was like the frogs of a New York marsh that leap into the water at a footfall but keep on croaking when freight trains, thundering across a wooden trestle, set all their marsh to quaking.

High up among the sweet ferns and baby birches on one side of the cut we saw a tongue of sand that had cascaded downward for three feet or so from the mouth of a woodchuck hole. Thoreau spoke of railroad cuts providing cliffs for swallows; they also provide mountainsides for woodchucks. We saw five holes in hardly a quarter of a mile in passing through Deep Cut. I scrambled up to one. The sand was without tracks. The hole was apparently deserted.

But smaller forms of life were active there. A black carpenter ant was struggling across the sand, its uncertain footing slipping from under its clawing feet. It carried something yellow in its jaws. I caught it between thumb and forefinger and looked at its burden through a pocket magnifying glass. It was the tiniest of baby grasshoppers, a yellow-brown midget locust, hardly $\frac{1}{16}$ inch long. That day was a day of baby grasshoppers. I saw them at several places along the track. Some seemed so small they must have hatched from the egg that very morning. Yet even the tiniest hurled themselves through the air in surprising leaps.

We had left Deep Cut behind and flat farmlands were spreading away on either side of the track when we stopped to watch a different kind of broad-jump champion. This was a small, yellowish, jumping spider that stood out against the black of its cinder background. Although it was only about $\frac{1}{8}$ inch long, it leaped three inches—twenty-four times its own length—four times in succession when I touched it with the tip of a pencil.

One day in 1851, when Henry Thoreau was walking along this same stretch of track, he came upon a plant he had never seen in Concord before, blue-flowered chicory. That evening he recorded his discovery in his *Journal* and added a query: Might not this and other plants have been distributed along the Fitchburg Railroad, the seeds—mixed with grain or dirt—being blown from the passing freight cars? His surmise was correct. In this manner plant colonies have spread far inland from the coast.

More than one thousand species of plants, including such familiar weeds as Queen Anne's Lace and black-eyed Susans, have come to America on ships. When the Swedish traveler Peter Kalm visited this country in 1750 he found many of the common weeds of Europe already established in New York and New Jersey. Some years ago, when Dr. Henry Svenson, botanist of the American Museum of Natural History, visited the Galapagos Islands, off the western coast of South America, he was surprised to find there a native of the Bahamas, "burnt weed," a small relative of the poinsettia. How had it leaped entirely across the continent of South America? Apparently it had come on whaling ships which, in the early days, were in the habit of stopping in the Bahamas for water and later among the Galapagos Islands for the meat of giant tortoises. Another botanical riddle in South America has a somewhat similar solution. European plants were found in two widely separated areas on the east and west coasts. The explanation lay in the habit of early colonists sailing to Australia with their sheep. They stopped to let the animals graze before rounding Cape Horn, then stopped again to pasture them on the west coast before starting the long voyage over the Pacific. In early times, vessels coming to America to carry cotton to England arrived laden with soil as ballast. This introduced alien plants into the United States, species that made their first appearance long ago around the southern ports of Charleston and Savannah.

From the coast, railroads have provided the circulation system that has carried these newcomers inland. Near the tip of Cape Charles, in Virginia, the vicinity of a railroad switchyard is a place of special interest to botanists. Here empty freight cars from north and south are cleaned. Dirt from distant places is heaped together; seeds that have been carried over the rails sprout; northern and southern plants intermingle in strange confusion. After original stands of foreign plants have sprung up along railroad right-of-ways, the trains continue, year after year, carrying seeds farther along the course. On a late-summer day I once saw an express train rushing through northern Indiana surrounded by a whirling cloud of thistledown. Mile after mile down the track, the cyclone of air it produced sent fresh swirls of parachuted seeds scudding behind the train along the right-of-way. In this manner the synthetic gales of passing trains advance seeds across the country.

Thus from seeds transported by rail and from seeds whirled along the track behind speeding trains, many of the plants now long familiar to the region had come to Concord. On the day we walked along the right-of-way, crunching on cinders or tightroping along the rails or taking odd-length steps to walk on the ties, only a few plants were in bloom. The white of blackberry tangles, the purple of vetch, the blue of spiderwort, these we saw. But the flowers of early spring were gone and green predominated.

From Deep Cut to the edge of Concord, the Fitchburg line runs most of the way on a roadbed considerably higher than the surrounding farmland. It forms a kind of catwalk above the fields. For a long time, as we returned on this railway in the spring, we stood watching an old man cultivating corn in a field below us. The smell of fallen engine grease was strong in the hot air. A passenger train rushed past, tumbling tattered papers behind it, filling the air with a fine rain of cinders, and leaving the bitter taste of coal smoke on our lips. Without looking up, the old man kept on, up one row, down another, past a scare-crow with felt hat awry and shirt sadly deteriorated by the weather. How many times had he walked over this same ground! How well he knew each inch of his land! How impossible, we said to ourselves, is the goal: to know the spring as a farmer knows his fields!

Late that afternoon we headed north again, almost for the last time. Our odyssey with a season was nearing its end. Upper New England would occupy its final days. Driving northward to Manchester, New Hampshire, before cutting across into Vermont, we covered the distance of Thoreau's week on the Concord and Merrimack rivers before the setting of the sun.

THIRTY-TWO

GREEN BOUNDARY

―――――――――

"TIME is ever precious to the student of nature."

Many times during our long trip we recalled these words of John James Audubon. They returned to us now with special emphasis as we drove north along the western border of Vermont. We were in the one hundred twentieth day of our trip. Only one week and one day remained of the season we had followed so long. We were living the last chapters of a book that we were reluctant to close.

North of Cape Cod spring speeds up. Like the migrating bird that increases its daily flying distance as it nears its nesting ground, the spring accelerates its advance as it sweeps into the north. And every hour of sunshine is precious across the upper reaches of the map. Plants live shorter lives and faster lives along the northern limits of their range. The same species of plants mature more quickly in Newfoundland than in New England.

The growing season, as measured from the last frost of spring to the first frost of autumn, falls from about two hundred days in the vicinity of New York City to about one hundred fifty days along the St. Lawrence and to as few as seventy-five days in upper Saskatchewan. But these days are long days with maximum sunshine. At the time of the summer solstice, the end of spring, when more sunshine falls on the region of the Arctic Circle than on the equator, far-northern plants achieve phenomenal growth. Fifteen-pound cabbages, twelve-pound turnips, seven-pound cauliflowers are produced by the swift growth of a few weeks. At the delta of the Mackenzie River, 250 miles north of the Arctic Circle, potatoes planted on June 14 are often belt high and have tubers as large as hen's eggs four weeks later. Their growth is forced by days with more than twenty hours of sunshine in them.

The working day of all the plants and trees around us was lengthening as we drove northward among the great green hills of Vermont. It was lengthening all over New England, all over America, all over the Northern Hemisphere—as it had lengthened, day by day, ever since spring began. Every twenty-four hours it would be increased by added minutes of sunshine until the last day of the season, the twenty-first of June. Then the tide would turn with the longest day of the year.

In Vermont this accelerated growth of late spring was being recorded mainly in green. Spring is many-colored in the Carolinas. It is primarily one color—with infinitely varied shadings—in northern New England. We encountered scattered patches of brilliant hawkweed and robin's plantain and several times we saw the massed blue of wild flags following some moist depression down a pasture slope. But in the main we traveled through a world that was green. These were the Green Mountains. And this was the green spring.

Ferns ran in banks and waves along the ditches. They flooded away as far as we could see across the woodland floor. They fringed the cracks of rock ledges and they crowded close to granite boulders that were scattered like sleeping cattle across pasture hillsides. Here was the fernland of the East.

Here also was the heart of New England. People ended sentences on a rising inflection, a kind of vocal question mark that revealed an aversion to reckless speech and a cautious "it's-a-sheep-on-this-side" attitude of mind. People talked more about the weather and had more weather to talk about than anywhere else on our trip. Here we dined on salmon chowder and date pie and chicken shortcake. Sheds and barns and houses began to be joined together. And that night we slept in a tourist cabin equipped with lightning rods.

All the way to Lake Champlain, the next day, we passed brimming brooks and flooded lowland meadows. The fluff of willow catkins dappled the surface of streams, and on pasture walls along ferny byways wild grapevines held clusters of new-formed fruit no larger than birdshot. We passed stone chimneys that stood as monuments to houses long burned, and apple trees and lilacs that marked the site of clearings since overgrown. Mountain weather alternately bathed us in brilliant sunshine and drenched us in pelting rain. Once a whole family of scarecrows loomed up on a hillside garden plot as we rounded a turn—a father, a mother, and three children represented by castoff garments flapping on their pole skeletons. Kingbirds, each a tyrant of his little field, perched on telephone wires beneath which dandelions were going to seed. In one level valley dandelions extended away in tens of thousands of white globes. For more than a mile we ran through drifting silvery fluff.

We were in a land of pastures and dairies and big barns. We were in a land of bobolink meadows. Near the lower end of Lake Champlain we passed the most memorable cows of our trip, a herd of Jerseys lying in a lush pasture, yellow with buttercups. With eyes closed they chewed their cuds, the sun warm on their backs after rain, a perfect symbol of the peace and plenty of spring. They reminded us that of all farm animals the life of the cow is one of the best. It is not overworked like draft animals. It is well fed because it is to its owner's advantage to see that it has ample food. It is allowed to go its own way most of the time. It is not killed for meat, at least not until its life has been lived. And here in the spring, amid the green rolling hills of upper Vermont, cow life seemed at its best. In the calm light of sunset the luxuriant growth of some pastures looked so tender, so juicy, so delicious a shade of green that I, myself, longed to be a grass eater.

Somewhere during our wanderings of the next few days we came upon a reddish mountain of sawdust that had been left in a clearing by lumbering operations several years before. Rains had packed the material into a solid mass with an almost perpendicular face twenty or twenty-five feet high. Two-thirds of the way up half a dozen holes penetrated this vertical wall. Swallows had excavated their nesting chambers in the sawdust as they normally do in banks of sand or clay.

Never before had we encountered such a nesting site. Arthur Cleveland Bent, in his *Life Histories of North American Fly-catchers, Larks, Swallows and Their Allies,* published in 1942, lists only two similar observations. One was reported from Otsego Lake, Michigan; the other from Franconia, New Hampshire. Both, oddly enough, were made in the same year—1902.

Around the sawdust pile we saw no swallows. The holes apparently were deserted. Both bank and rough-winged swallows tunnel into sand and clay; which had tunneled into sawdust? The round holes bunched together identified their makers as bank swallows. The rough-wings are solitary nesters and the entrances to rough-wing tunnels tend to be more elliptical than round.

Such clues and hints and signs are all around us in the out-of-doors. Reading them aright is the great game of the naturalist. A nesting kingfisher, for example, can be recognized by the way it carries a fish in its bill. The bird always swallows a fish headfirst. But when it is carrying its catch to the nest it holds the fish reversed, head out, so that it will slip easily down the throat of a fledgling. Again, the yellow of a brown thrasher's eye gives a clue to the age of the bird. As a brown thrasher grows older its eye becomes lighter. Up until a few years ago no one could tell the sex of a baby ring-necked pheasant except by dissection. Then a scientist at the Loyalsock Game Farm, in Pennsylvania, noticed that he could separate the males from the females as soon as they emerged from the egg by differences in the color of their eyes. Similarly, William

T. Davis, the Staten Island naturalist, was able to look at a luna moth and tell whether it had emerged from the cocoon before or after the first of June. He had noticed that those emerging before June had a reddish tinge running along the rear edge of the hind wings.

Near Windy Top Farm, on a high slope overlooking Lake Champlain, we asked an elderly Vermonter what was the first sign of spring he noticed in the north country. He stood for a long time rasping a calloused thumb along the stubble of his jaw.

"Crows come back," he said succinctly.

Now, except for stragglers, all the birds were back that were coming back. Barn swallows, home from Brazil, skimmed over the northern pastures. Yellow warblers, home from Yucatán, darted along the roadside. Bobolinks, home from Argentina, sang on the fences. The great spring migration was over. The tide that had ceased running north would reverse its flow a few months hence and would carry with it millions of migrants now mere maturing germs of life in nests in fields and bushes and woods all along the border.

As we drew nearer the green boundary of Vermont and Canada, and zigzagged eastward across the state, the woods grew darker, evergreens increased, the forests were edged with carpets of bunchberry starred with white blossoms. White-throats sang all along the way. And from the dim interior of the woods we heard the voice of the hermit thrush at evening.

Our course at one place carried us close to Jericho, Vermont, the birthplace of Wilson A. Bentley, the Snowflake Man. Working under primitive conditions with crude equipment in the farmhouse where he was born, Bentley spent his life recording the beauty of snowflakes in photographs. In time this self-taught village scientist became recognized as one of the world's leading authorities on ice crystals.

At the opposite side of the state, along the Connecticut River below St. Johnsbury, we skirted another Vermont village known to science because of the activity of a second self-taught naturalist, Wendell P. Smith. Although, because of childhood illness, he never attended school a day in his life, he has been elected to learned societies, has contributed to leading scientific publications, and for twenty years has been assistant state ornithologist of Vermont. All his discoveries have been made on his own hill-country farm. Most of his life has been devoted to studying the natural history of a hundred acres.

For years Smith has added facts to his Hibernation Calendar, noting the last appearance of animals in fall and their first appearance in spring. Each winter he carefully places twigs and leaves over the woodchuck and chipmunk and skunk holes on his acres. Then during the early spring he makes the rounds on his daily walks, jotting down the dates when the sticks are pushed aside by the emerging animals. His statistics, amassed in this way and published in the *Journal of Mammalogy*, have provided valuable source material for students of hibernation.

When we visited his ridgetop farm later, he led us to the scene of one of his most interesting studies, a rocky pine and hemlock woods comprising about fifty acres. Spring after spring he had combed this woods on a census of nesting birds. Up to 1938 the maximum count had been 84 pairs of breeding birds. Then in the fall of that year a great hurricane swept along the Atlantic coast and far up the Connecticut Valley. Instruments in the region of Wells River, only 60 miles from the Canadian line, measured the velocity of the wind at between 85 and 90 miles an hour. Strange birds—a gannet, a Leach's petrel, a greater shearwater, a yellow-billed tropic bird—were carried inland up the valley. When the gale died down Smith fought his way through devastation in his woods. Of the 105 pine and hemlock trees a foot or more in diameter only two or three remained standing. The whole character of the hilltop had been altered. Openings were formed. Bushes sprang up. New conditions brought new nesting birds.

The count went up year by year. In the spring of 1948 it

reached its peak—182 pairs of nesting birds. Then the tide turned. As we walked about over the wooded hill with its outcropping ledges of rock we saw young evergreens rising from between the fallen trunks. Natural reforestation was taking place. The area was filling in, returning to its former character. Soon after the hurricane mourning warblers appeared. They seemed attracted by the wild raspberry bushes that had sprung up in the openings. Now the raspberry bushes were crowded out and the mourning warblers had left. By 1950 Smith reported his count had dropped from 182 to 175. He expects it to continue to decrease until it is back to its original figure as the woods regains its pine-and-hemlock forest character. These records made within sight of the house where he has spent most of his life have given ornithologists one of their most dramatic pictures of the rise and fall of the bird population of an area under rapidly changing conditions.

East of this hilltop woods, where a ravine cuts steeply downward toward the river, we walked beneath a clump of large white pines. Somewhere above us amid the dense interlacing branches a pair of great horned owls had nested that spring. I picked up one of the pellets that had been disgorged by either a young or an old owl and dropped it at a stab of pain. The barbed end of a porcupine quill had jabbed into my forefinger. Gingerly I picked up the pellet again. It was riddled with small quills embedded in coarse brown hair. A second pellet nearby also contained quills. The largest were an inch and a half long; most were half an inch long or less. All were black-tipped, barbed, and needle sharp. Later on, at home, I painstakingly separated the tightly massed hair and quills. A count revealed that the two pellets contained a total of 1,402 porcupine quills.

Nowhere in ornithological literature have I encountered an instance of owl pellets containing porcupine quills. There have been cases in which great horned owls have been found dead with quills in their throats. In such instances the bird had apparently attacked a large porcupine, receiving the quills in its open mouth. But in this case more than fourteen hundred quills had been swallowed, had remained in the stomach, and had been disgorged again. Dr. T. Donald Carter, of the Department of Mammals of the American Museum of Natural History, identified the hair and quills as those of a young Canada porcupine, *Erethizon dorsatum dorsatum*.

At time of birth, the quills on such porcupines are soft. Could the owl have dined on such a soft-quilled porcupine? The chances are slight as the quills harden in a matter of hours and are hard before the young animal begins moving about where an owl would see it. Did the digestive juices of the owl's stomach soften the quills? I do not think so. All the quills were straight and hard and showed no distortion, as would have been the case if the pellets had been compressed while the quills were in a plastic state. Moreover, as the stomach juices do not soften the bones of swallowed animals, they are not likely to have softened the immeasurably harder quills. Nobody knows the fate of the bird that bolted down this hazardous meal. But, at least, Smith had come upon no dead great horned owl in his daily walks about the farm.

North of St. Johnsbury, as we neared Lake Memphremagog and the Quebec line, the country grew more grandly wild. Dark cedars and feathery larches, white birch trees and balsam firs dotted or mantled a green land of hills and ravines. Here we seemed driving through a second no man's land of the seasons. In southern Florida spring and winter had been intermingled and indistinguishable. In this north country at the top of the United States, an area predominantly green, summer and spring seemed already one.

A winding road—on a clear June morning after rain—carried us to a hilltop somewhere east of Memphremagog. We stopped at the rocky edge of a pasture. A little rill gurgled past us, its banks strewn with bluets. The sight of these demure flowers recalled the bluets beside the sandy road on Bull's Island and the bluets on Silers Bald. Goldfinches passed in their rocking-horse flight. We had seen our first goldfinches in a cypress swamp below the Tamiami Trail with the smell of smoke growing stronger in the air. We had seen them over the Suwannee, at the edge of the Okefenokee Swamp, above Newfound Gap. We had seen them all along our trip just as we had seen yellow swallowtails and fresh strawberries and violets. Memories of such recurring sights would knit the days of our trip together.

Beyond the hilltop lay Canada. It too was green—the bright green of pastureland, the darker green of spruce and balsam. Across the fields and hills and woods below us ran an invisible line, the political watershed between two countries. On different sides of the line the thoughts and resources of people flowed to different centers, their lives revolved about different hubs. But to the spring the line was nonexistent; it had swept across it unchecked as it rushed into the north.

For a time we debated whether to follow it across this green boundary into Canada. Instead we decided on a quick giant's swing over into Maine, along the Androscoggin River, back among the celebrated Shelburne birches and south through Pinkham Notch into the heart of the White Mountains. This hillside overlooking Canada, this green height with its goldfinches and bluets, was the point farthest north on the map touched by our long drifting journey with the spring. But our travels with the season were not finished.

As spring goes on and on, it also goes up and up. Altitude corresponds to longitude in its northward sweep. Instead of moving across the map we would move up the mountains. Instead of following spring into Canada we would follow it into the sky. By retreating 50 miles south of the border we would advance—as spring advances—the equivalent of 500 miles north of it. An ascent above timberline on Mt. Washington would coincide with the advance of spring as far north as Hudson Bay.

THIRTY-THREE

TIMBERLINE

W E were cloud climbers as well as mountain climbers on the next to the last day of spring. As we worked our way up the steep trail to Hermit Lake, that lonely little tarn near timberline on Mt. Washington, we ascended through successive layers of dank rain-mist. The warm saturated air was rich with the smell of forest mold. Six times, going up and coming down, we walked through showers.

In our haste to get started under the ill-humored sky, we skipped breakfast. As we began climbing we munched on two ham sandwiches, saving a lump of maple sugar for emergency rations later. There was no uncertainty about the Tuckerman Ravine trail we followed. It did not dip or level off; it kept on up and up. Much of the way we labored along a kind of roadway that nature had paved with irregular granite cobblestones. Half a mile up this trail we overtook two women from Ohio who had made even less preparation for the climb than we had. They were turning back after ascending that far along the rocky path in high-heeled, open-toed shoes. In a Sunday supplement they had read about spring skiing in Tuckerman Ravine and had set out to see it during an hour's stopover!

Paralleling our ascent, the white water of Cutler River tumbled down the mountainside toward the east. It roared or murmured as the windings of our trail carried us nearer or farther from its rocky bed. In the midst of the crash and smother of its cascading water tiny larvae were clinging by suckers at the ends of their tails to the downstream side of boulders. Their massed bodies clustered so thickly on some stones that they resembled moss. These immature insects were the larvae of that scourge of the north woods, the black fly.

All were busy sweeping microscopic bits of food from the water into their mouths with fan-shaped brushes. Some tossed at the end of silken threads to feed in the swifter current or let themselves down from rock to rock. Others were wrapped in golden-brown pupal cases fringed along the top with tracheal gills that provided oxygen for the transforming insects within. Still others were ready for the great adventure of riding a bubble of air upward through tumbling water to the surface.

This air is stored beneath the pupal skin. When the winged adult black fly, about $\frac{1}{10}$ inch long, is ready to emerge, the skin splits suddenly. Soaring upward encased in a bubble the fly pops forth into the aerial world in which it spends the rest of its life. In mountain streams of the North its emergence is an annual drama of spring.

All during the lower part of our climb these humpbacked insects whirled about us in a cloud, a cloud that moved along with us up the trail. They darted into our ears. They flew up our noses. We saw the trees through a maze of gyrating motes. But they were motes with red-hot pokers. They kept us slapping in spite of insect repellent. Their thirst for blood always seems greatest before a rain.

But as we ascended the black flies decreased. Finally we left the tormentors almost entirely behind. We ascended through zones of insects as well as through zones of birds and plants and trees as we made our two-mile climb that day. In Pinkham Notch, at the beginning of the trail, we passed bird or pin cherries with blossoms gone and fruit already swelling on the twigs. Ascending the mountain we passed other pin cherries, first with blossoms just fallen, then with flower clusters in full bloom. Similarly, as our climb carried us backward through the season, we saw the waxy white of bunchberry blossoms become tinged with pale green that grew progressively darker until the petallike bracts were as green as the leaves around them.

Beeches lifted their silvery trunks beside the trail at first. Then they fell away and we climbed through evergreens. The smell of balsam replaced the odor of the forest mold. Twigs became speckled or bearded with the gray of usnea lichen. In the still, heavy air the silence of the woods increased as we climbed. The constant murmuring of droplets of collected moisture falling from leaf to leaf among the deciduous trees of the lower slope had been left behind. The living carpet of the moss extended in ever-deeper plush across the rocks and fallen trees of the mountainside. Slow as was our climb, it was equivalent to shooting northward, jet propelled, across whole zones of life.

Botanists have calculated that, as far as changes in vegetation are concerned, an ascent of 1,000 feet up a mountain is equal to a northward journey of 600 miles. Our climb of about 2,000 feet to Hermit Lake carried us, botanically, to northern Labrador. An ascent to the treeless rocks at the top of Mt. Washington is—so far as plants are concerned—a trek into the north beyond the timberline, across the Great Barrens, above the Arctic Circle.

Twice as we climbed toward the low ceiling of the sky it descended to meet us, enveloped us in gray winter light, then passed on down the mountainside. Looking back we could see the tops of lower mountains rising through the fields of fog. Looking up we could see still other clouds coming down the slope toward us. All the stones underfoot, all the moss gardens and lichen gardens beside the trail, all the leaves of the wood oxalis, all the boughs of the firs and spruces glistened with moisture. Fine curtains of rain drifted through the air, coming and going in the uncertain mountain weather.

In spite of the rain, in spite of the lowering skies, we felt elated. We sat beside the trail on a granite rock sprinkled with mica and ate part of the maple sugar. A little later, on a particularly steep section of the climb, a college boy with a pack on his back overtook us. He eased his load onto a flat rock while we talked. Then he shouldered it again and started up the trail in high gear. Looking after him was like watching a man climbing a ladder from below.

Near the end of our long ascent we jumped from rock to rock to cross Cutler River close to its source. Somewhere beyond, just before we reached Tuckerman Ravine, a side path led us off to the right, past a deserted log shelter, among stunted spruces and balsam firs. Through wet hushed woods we finished our climb to Hermit Lake.

We saw it first through mist and mistlike rain, a brooding little tarn, about half an acre in extent, walled around with evergreens. Long shreds of fog clung to the shore-line trees. Somewhere in the misty woods behind us a red-breasted nuthatch blew its tiny, tinny horn. We had stood there hardly five minutes before the changeable mountain weather made another sudden shift. The drizzle ceased. The vapors parted, broke up, moved away down the mountainside. In the clearing air we saw the towering cliff of Lion Head lifting its brown bare rock high above us.

Long scars down the mountainside marked the paths of rockslips of the past. The upper half of the largest was filled with hard-packed snow. From the lower end of this glacier-in-miniature streams of water poured in bright streaks down the face of the rock. In such snow-springs above timberline mountain streams are born. On the back wall of Tuckerman Ravine—that vast, crescent-shaped, glacier-carved bowl high on Mt. Washington—the lifeblood of the melting snow runs in innumerable rivulets down the almost vertical rock to form the famous "Stream of a Thousand Falls." Watching the swift descent of the new-born brooks on Lion Head, I recalled the line from James Thomson's *The Seasons* about the mountain that "pours a sweep of rivers from its side." A little leather-bound copy of Thomson's grand old classic of the outdoors had traveled with us on our trip. I had picked it up just before the start in a secondhand bookshop on 33rd Street, in New York. We had read it little by little, at odd moments—under palms and beside the sea and along woodland trails. We were finishing it here, where our trip was ending, in the White Mountains of New Hampshire.

A single crow flapped silently across the tarn and disappeared into the evergreens beyond. Under the brightening sky other birds of the timberline were becoming active. Slate-colored juncos, trilling their bell-songs, flitted among the trees and the moldering, mossy stumps. They reminded us of those other juncos far to the south, high on Mt. LeConte and Clingmans Dome. Another singer, unseen among the trees, also transported us to those southern mountaintops. I was examining the new spring cones—purplish, almost like berries—on a stunted evergreen no higher than my waist, when the hollow of the lake and the wet woods around it were filled with the long, sweet, unwinding monologue of a winter wren—the "musical axle" song we had first heard in the Great Smokies.

Alone among the birds that live on the slopes of Mt. Washington, the slate-colored junco sometimes nests above timberline, constructing its little cup of grass and bark and roots on the ground among the boulders of the high rock barrens of the mountaintop. Another bird that nests close to timberline, even among the twisted, prostrate spruces of the heights, is the Bicknell's thrush. By field marks alone, this subspecies is almost indistinguishable from the gray-cheeked thrush. Yet during the spring breeding season the two birds can be told apart infallibly by their positions on the map. Only the Bicknell's thrush nests in the New England mountains. The gray-cheek, *Hylocichla minima*, breeds beyond the borders of the United States, nesting mostly below treeline in northern Canada. Although the Bicknell's thrush is not a vertical migrant like the Carolina junco, it rises up mountainsides at the end of its northward spring flight in order to reach surroundings similar to those which its close relative travels far north to find.

During our slow descent of the rocky trail later that day we saw the bunchberry blossoms change from green to white again. We watched the spruce and balsam fir lose their dominance and beech and yellow birch appear once more. We descended through clouds and climbed downward amid curtains of fine rain. We discovered black flies waiting for us along the lower stretches of the trail. On our descent we also found ourselves moving through successive zones of singing birds. From the juncos and winter wrens and white-throated sparrows of the dark upper forest, we passed through a realm of thrushes, with olive-backed and hermit thrushes predominating, and came to the redstarts and myrtle warblers of the lower hardwoods. These ill-defined bands of avian life on a mountainside are most apparent in spring, during the season of song.

Among the varied bird voices along the trail we caught a lisping, sibilant, one-pitch little song, a mystery strain we had never heard before. It was in the woods around Hermit Lake. It was in the twilight of the mist. It was all along the upper reaches of the trail. But the singer evaded us. Time and again we heard the modest little song, swelling in the middle and diminishing toward the end, coming down to us from the tops of the evergreens. Finally Nellie spotted the singer. It was a male blackpoll warbler. Previously we had seen this bird only on migration, never on its high nesting and singing ground among the mountains.

Somewhere I have read that at the end of the day the average man is ¾ inch, and the average woman ½ inch, shorter than at the beginning. On this day of mountain climbing, when we reached the bottom of the trail on weary feet we felt as though we had been jolted down and shortened far beyond the average. But once more we had seen spring recede and advance in two great waves as we climbed and descended the mountain. At Hermit Lake we had found the counterpart of a far-northern spring—a tardier, shorter, speedier season. Some hours later, riding the famous cog railway up the other side of Mt. Washington, we went even higher, to the bare summit of the peak.

As we drove down a long woods road on the way from Fabyan to the base station of the railroad, a Cooper's hawk skimmed from among the trees and sailed down the road ahead of us. In hot pursuit darted a pugnacious midget, a warbler made brave and reckless by its nest nearby. Not long before we had come upon another warbler, an ovenbird, chasing a robin across the road with all the fire and dash of a kingbird. And just before we reached the start of the cog railway, we saw a second Cooper's hawk being pursued by nearly a dozen robins, redwings, and grackles. Whenever the hawk landed, the birds, calling and darting about, landed near it. When it took wing they were after it again. The bravery of nesting time is a feature of the spring. It is then that the courage of songbirds is at its peak.

Sitting in the little one-coach train, with the blunderbuss smokestack of its tilted engine belching dry cinders behind us, we ground and puffed and labored upward. We were lifted one foot for every three we advanced. We were carried through a 15-degree drop in temperature, the mercury descending one degree for every 300 feet gain in altitude. In an hour's time, we were transported the equivalent of thirty days' advance in the northward sweep of spring.

The top of Mt. Washington is 6,284 feet above sea level; about 4,500 feet above the start of the cog railway. Although it is only 150 miles from Boston, the rock-strewn summit has the climate of the arctic barrens. The wind velocity there has reached 231 miles an hour, the highest mark ever officially recorded anywhere in the world. Fog blankets the peak more than 50 per cent of the year. During every month of the twelve it snows at the top of Mt. Washington. The highest summer temperature recorded there is 73 degrees. Rising higher than any other land in the Northeast, its rocky summit has a day forty minutes longer than that along the coast. In 1605, fifteen years before the Pilgrims came to Plymouth Rock, the lofty bulk of Mt. Washington was sighted from the sea.

Nearing timberline we watched the spruces and birches shrink and flatten and hug the ground. We saw them pressing close to the rocky soil in mats of twisted twigs or huddling together like sheep in a storm or cowering between rocks, rising barely an inch above the protecting ramparts of granite. A white birch with reddish bark and willows only a few inches high grow close to timberline on Mt. Washington. Wind and cold and rarefied air play their part in dwarfing the prostrate trees. One long-dead spruce had been polished by the wind until its trunk and limbs were as smooth as ivory and as shining as silver in the brilliance of the mountain sunlight. Among the diminutive living trees, all, even the smallest, had responded to the tardy coming of spring. We saw each flattened evergreen decorated with new-formed cones, soft and glistening with pitch.

As the trees grew smaller, the immense prospect of the mountain scene widened around us. A dwarfed world of lakes and forests and lesser mountains extended to the horizon, extended west to Lake Champlain, extended north to the green boundary of Canada. Just beyond a titanic ravine on the mountainside we saw a whole forest of dead, wind-polished trees. Flattened by some great wind in the past, the trunks all lay in the same direction like a swath of hay after the swing of a scythe.

Across the mountaintop ran a giant's jumble of gray rocks splotched with green lichens. When we first swept our eyes over this expanse from the vantage point of Summit House, it seemed as dead and sterile as the moon. But when we looked closer, stooping to examine the little patches of thin soil accumulated between the rocks of the fell-fields, we found gray-green mosses and lacy lichens and low-lying alpine plants already in bloom. Spring had climbed the mountain before us. By the tenth of June these flowers that bloom above the clouds have begun to open their petals.

Writing in *Appalachia* some years ago, Stuart K. Harris noted the plants he found in alpine gardens within ten minutes' walk of the Lakes-of-the-Clouds hut above timberline on Mt. Washington. His list included rhodora, spring beauty, Labrador tea, alpine azalia, crowberry, mountain heath, bog bilberry, and the evergreen moss plant with needlelike leaves —*Cassiope hypnoides*. One of the alpine plants he found on the mountaintop, *Diapensia lapponica*, is a close relative of the little pyxie moss we had seen in the sandy pine barrens of New Jersey. Like *Pyxidanthera*, it grows close to the ground in dark mosslike mats against which the white flowers stand out conspicuously.

A tribute to the beauty of such mountaintop flowers in the spring is contained in the name of the trail we saw wandering from north to south across the rock barrens of the summit. It is known as the Alpine Garden Trail. At frequent intervals along its course mounds of boulders mark the way as an aid to hikers caught in sudden fogs or blizzards on the mountain. As we were gazing down on this line of cairns from the highest rocks of the summit we became aware of a spot of bright yellow dancing toward us over the gray expanse of stones. It was a tiger swallowtail butterfly, a colorful insect we had seen all along the way from the Far South to New England. Over our heads, over the streamlined Summit House, on into the west it fluttered. We wondered what alpine blooms had fed it as it journeyed across the treeless roof of the New England mountains.

The cairn-marked path below us forms one section of the long Appalachian Trail. How many times had we crossed the track of this trail during our zigzag northward trek! Now we were looking at it for a final time. We were parting company with it as we were parting company with the season. This rocky summit represented the farthest limit of our journey with the spring—through space. One day more and we would reach the end of our journey with the spring—through time.

THIRTY-FOUR

THE LONGEST DAY

D URING all the days of our travels—in the Everglades, along the delta marshes, on a barrier island, in the Great Smokies, among the pine barrens and the Lilliput forests of Cape Cod and the green hills of the border—we had wondered vaguely about this final twenty-four hours of spring. What would the day be like? Where would we be? What would we be doing? In what surroundings, bright or gloomy, would we come to the end of our travels with a season?

Now we knew the answers. This was the final day, the summit of the spring.

We awoke before four o'clock. Already a clear sky was brightening above the birchtops outside our cabin window in Crawford Notch. By four, robins were singing and the wooded steeps above us echoed with the calling of an ovenbird. Then came the pure sweet stráin of the whitethroat, most moving of all the voices of this north-country choir. Long before five even the bottom of the deep ravine, where dusk comes swiftly and dawn is retarded, was filled with daylight. With this sunrise the tide of light reached its annual flood to begin the long slow rollback to the low ebb of December.

During that day—between the earliest sunrise and the latest sunset of the spring—we roamed amid the beauty and grandeur of the mountains. They formed a fitting climax for our travels with the spring. Where else except in America would that journey have carried us through such variedly impressive scenery, such altering forms of plant and animal life, such diverse events of natural history interest?

I remember we stopped for a long time that afternoon to watch the dance of the Mayflies above Echo Lake and Profile Lake below the Great Stone Face. All through Franconia Notch, over the two lakes and the Pemigewasset River, these pale-yellow ephemera drifted through the air, luminous in every open space lighted by the lengthening rays of late afternoon. Half a hundred hung in a small cloud above one spot on the shore of Echo Lake. Spotlighted by long fingers of sunshine coming through the treetops, they bobbed and turned and fluttered in a shining throng that extended from about two to six feet above the ground. Here hour after hour they engaged in a curious mating performance such as we had never witnessed before.

Every few minutes one of the dancers would leave the throng and climb steeply into the air. At a height of eight or ten feet it would turn downward and plunge in an almost vertical descent through the May fly cloud. A foot or so from the ground it would level off and curve upward again. During each swift descent, as the diving insect passed through the bobbing dancers, three or four would dart in pursuit. Apparently the plunging May fly was the female, those that joined in the pursuit the males. All through the sunset and on into the twilight this love dance of the ephemera continued.

A mile to the north, where Lafayette Brook tumbles down a rocky ravine on a plunging descent toward Gale River, we heard the last bird chorus of the spring. All up the mountain steeps hermit thrushes and whitethroats and wood thrushes and veeries and olive-backed thrushes sang in the sunset. From time to time a small dark form fluttered into the air above the trees of the ravine. Clear and sweet, a warbling, twittering jumble of notes came down to us. We were hearing the flight song of the ovenbird—the mysterious, never-identified "night warbler" of Thoreau's *Journal*.

In this choir whitethroats predominated. We grew to recognize different singers by variations in pitch and quality. One would begin with a long, exquisite violin note and others up the ravine, some higher pitched, others lower pitched, would repeat the sad sweet overtones of their melody. It is a song of the New World, a song of hope and confidence; it is a song of the Old World, a song of wisdom and sadness. It seems to put to music the bravery of the spirit, the courage of the frail.

In an often-quoted admonition, Mark Twain advised famous men to think up their last words beforehand rather than to depend on the inspiration of the moment. If we had planned beforehand the ending of spring's longest day, nothing we could have imagined would have excelled the glory of that final sunset. From the high aerie of the bridge spanning Lafayette Brook we watched it spread across the sky over the darkening mountains that, range on range, rolled away into the west. As the warmth of the sunlight ebbed and the air grew chill in the valleys below us, rivers of mist rose above rivers of water. The winding course of every stream was marked by vapor in the air above it. Gazing down, we could trace the progress of invisible watercourses meandering through the forest below. Contour lines had been traced on the air by mist.

During one time of strange and eerie beauty, all the curls and billows of the mist glowed red, rising like slow tongues and sheets of fire above the treetops tinged by the flames of the western sky. Nowhere else on our trip except over the lonely barrier beach at Bull's Island had we encountered so memorable a sunset as this final fading of the daylight in these final hours of spring. It was the sunset of the day, the sunset of the season, the sunset of our trip with the spring.

Unseen in the brilliance of midday, a new moon—a faint greenish-silver parenthesis mark in the sky—had moved across the zenith. Now, as the colors faded in the west and the long slow twilight of the summer solstice began, it increased in brightness. Below it in the deep dusk of the valley toward Franconia, pinpoints of electric lights at farms and villages glittered in the gathering night. Here in this wild and beautiful spot amid the mountains, the dark woods, the rising mist, the new moon hanging above the silhouettes of the peaks, we waited, in spite of the night chill, until the last sunlight of the spring had ebbed from the sky.

Miles to the south, in a cabin by the Pemigewasset, later that night we built a blazing fire of birch logs in the fireplace. We sat for a long time in the warmth of this flickering hearth-fire talking of our journey with a season, of our incomparable good fortune, of the adventures we had shared together. Never in our lives would there be another spring like this. It was late when we stepped out to look at the sky. From horizon to horizon the heavens were clear, filled with the glinting of the stars. And almost as we looked, in the night, under the stars, spring was gone. It was summer when we awoke.

Everywhere in the Northern Hemisphere spring had come and gone. The season had swept far to the north; it had climbed mountains; it had passed into the sky. Like a sound, spring spreads and spreads until it is swallowed up in space. Like the wind, it moves across the map invisible; we see it only in its effects. It appears like the tracks of the breeze on a field of wheat, like shadows of wind-blown clouds, like tossing branches that reveal the presence of the invisible, the passing of the unseen. So spring had spread from Georgia to North Carolina, from Virginia to Canada, leaving consequences beyond number in its wake. We longed for a thousand springs on the road instead of this one. For spring is like life. You never grasp it entire; you touch it here, there; you know it only in parts and fragments. Reflecting thus as we started south on that first morning of summer—on the day of the summer solstice, the longest day of the year—we were well aware that it is only on the calendar that spring comes to so sudden a termination. In reality its end is a gradual change. Season merges with season in a slow transition into another life.

Driving home to a house where all the calendars marked February and where piles of mail recorded four months on their postmarks, we crossed the Whitestone Bridge onto Long Island. And then—so near the irrevocable end of our journey—we turned aside, we wandered about, we made delays. We followed the Jones Beach parkway to its end, we visited the Massapequa cedars, we stopped at a pond where wild ducks sunned themselves on a grassy bank, we drove nearly a hundred miles before we swung into our driveway. Even then I let the engine idle, loath to cut the switch. Reluctantly I turned the key. The sudden stopping of the motor put a period to our long adventure with the spring.

INDEX

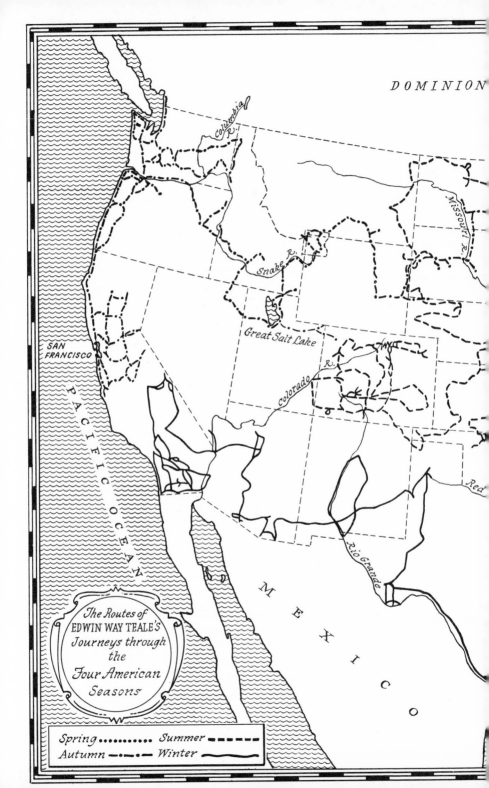

DOMINION

PACIFIC OCEAN

SAN
FRANCISCO

Great Salt Lake

Columbia R.

Snake R.

Missouri R.

Colorado R.

Red

Rio Grande

MEXICO

The Routes of
EDWIN WAY TEALE'S
Journeys through
the
Four American
Seasons

Spring .... Summer — — — —
Autumn —·—·— Winter ~~~~~

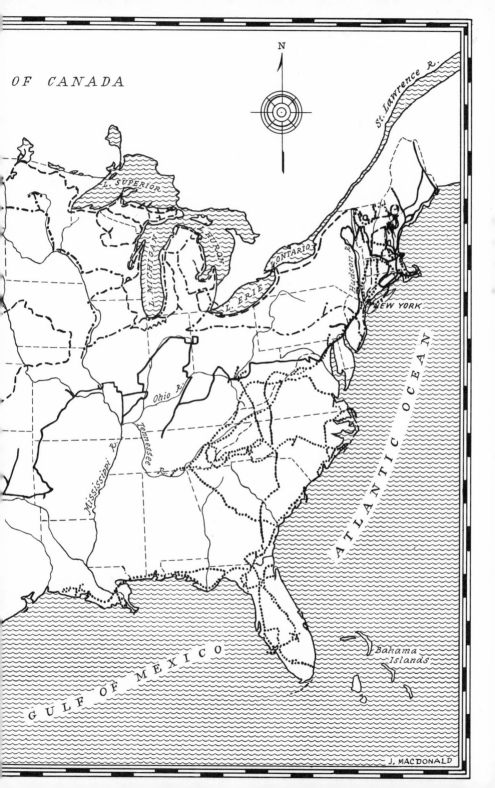